CW00553623

Medieval Stereotypes and Modern Antisemitism

Medieval Stereotypes and Modern Antisemitism

Robert Chazan

UNIVERSITY OF CALIFORNIA PRESS

Berkeley / Los Angeles / London

University of California Press
Berkeley and Los Angeles, California

University of California Press
London, England

Copyright © 1997 by The Regents of the University of California

Library of Congress Cataloging-in-Publication Data
Chazan, Robert.
   Medieval stereotypes and modern antisemitism / Robert Chazan.
     p.   cm.
   Includes bibliographical references and index.
   ISBN 0–520–20394–1 (cloth : alk. paper)
   1. Jews—History—70–1789.   2. Antisemitism—History.   3. Judaism—
Controversial literature—History and criticism.   4. Jews—Public
opinion.   5. Christianity and antisemitism.   6. Stereotype
(Psychology)
DS124.C43   1997
909'.04924—dc20   96–29259
                                                                CIP

Printed in the United States of America
1   2   3   4   5   6   7   8   9

The paper used in this publication meets the minimum requirements of American National Standard for Information Sciences—Permanence of Paper for Printed Library
Materials, ANSI Z39.48-1984 ⊗

To Saralea

Contents

Introduction

Throughout the twentieth century intense religious, ethnic, and racial hatred and strife have shaped world history. Such hatred lay at the core of World War I, was central to the horrors of World War II, and, despite the high hopes of the postwar period, has by no means abated. Researchers from a variety of disciplines have attempted to analyze the roots of these societal animosities in an effort to understand them and to reduce their destructive impact.

Because anti-Jewish sentiment has been enduring and pervasive, it has attracted much of the concern with intergroup prejudice. Particularly in the wake of the genocidal Nazi assault on European Jewry, attention has focused on the recurrent pattern of anti-Jewish animosity and violence. What are the roots of this apparently endless hostility? How might the cycle of hatred and persecution be broken? Indeed, can this cycle be broken?

Earlier optimism has largely dissipated. Emerging from the limitations imposed by premodern theocratic societies, nineteenth-century Jews— along with many sympathetic non-Jewish observers as well— were convinced that historic anti-Jewish animosity and violence resulted from the medieval nexus between church and state and that modern dissolution of this link presaged an era of diminishing anti-Jewish animus. These nineteenth- and early twentieth-century hopes were dashed by the Nazi atrocities, stimulating a quest for fuller comprehension of the constantly shifting but seemingly ubiquitous antipathy toward Jews.

Not surprisingly, no consensus has yet emerged in this quest for understanding. Some have chosen to emphasize continuities, highlighting what they see as unaltered anti-Jewish thinking and behavior, traceable from antiquity to the present. Others, while acknowledging historic factors in the evolution of modern Jew-hatred, focus on the rapid change and dislocation that characterize the nineteenth- and twentieth-century Western experience; these analysts emphasize the innovative social, political, economic, and intellectual circumstances that gave rise to modern antisemitism and its dissociation from prior anti-Jewish hostility. This disagreement reflects, inter alia, differing views of historical progression—a sense of relatively consistent human history versus a sense of disruption and alteration in human affairs; it also reflects divergent methodological tendencies—an emphasis on the impact of ideas as socially efficacious versus a focus on the economic and political structures underlying major social movements.

As study of nineteenth- and twentieth-century antisemitism and its antecedents has deepened, however, it has become increasingly clear that this modern phenomenon has synchronic and diachronic dimensions and must be understood in terms of both contemporary societal patternings and prior ideational legacy. Modern antisemitism can only be grasped within the context of nineteenth- and twentieth-century sociopolitical realities, with full awareness of new intellectual developments as well. At the same time, to treat antisemitism solely within the context of the nineteenth and twentieth centuries means the loss of considerable insight. European societies adversely affected by the tumultuous developments of this challenging epoch were guided in their reaction to change and disruption by a set of received perceptions and stereotypes. Failure to attend properly to these potent traditional views can only impede the fullest understanding of what is both a new and an old phenomenon.

Whatever the changing economic, political, and social constellations that occasioned modern antisemitism, the upheavals attendant on modernization focused disequilibrium and its discontents disproportionately on the small minority community of European Jews. This somewhat strange focus can only be understood against the backdrop of prior European anti-Jewish thinking. Those committed to laying bare this ideational legacy have regularly highlighted the role of traditional Christian thinking in providing explosive negative stereotypes that directed intense societal animosity against Europe's relatively small Jewish minority. While the work of such investigators, perhaps preeminently Jules Isaac, has produced useful results, both theoretically and practically, their findings have been flawed in one major way: the assumption of a relatively fixed Christian stance toward Judaism and the Jews over the ages. Isaac himself, for example, focused on the classical period of Christian history, identifying early and fundamental anti-Jewish motifs and assuming their transmission through the centuries.

Negative Christian perceptions of Judaism and the Jews, however, have by no means remained static. The pre-nineteenth-century ideational legacy that exerted such significant impact on recent anti-semitism was itself the product of earlier combinations of evolving circumstances and preexistent perceptions. The central concern of this study is to examine a major stage in the evolution of Western anti-Jewish views and to track the emergence of stereotypes that had a profoundly negative impact on the course of subsequent Jewish and world history. My argument is that an earlier period of significant change and dislocation in the West—the dynamic and creative twelfth century—saw the interaction of new societal circumstances and a prior ideational legacy. This interaction produced an innovative view of Jews fated to influence anti-Jewish perceptions down into our own century. The vibrance and importance of this creative epoch assured for the new stereotypes a dominant role in subsequent Western thinking about Jews and their faith.

During the closing decades of the tenth century, a new set of Jewish communities began to develop in the heart of northern Europe. This new Jewry, which the Jewish world subsequently came to call Ashkenazic, grew strikingly during the eleventh and twelfth centuries, spreading from its original base in northern France and the Rhineland westward across the English Channel and eastward through the German lands and into Poland. In effect, a rapidly evolving area of the West attracted a new Jewry, and, stimulated by the complex dynamics of its own development and by the somewhat unusual features of its immigrant Jewry, this area spawned innovative stereotypes of Jews and their characteristics. Because northern Europe and its creativity played such a central role in the subsequent development of Western culture, its idiosyncratic views of an idiosyncratic Jewry came to dominate the Christian perception of Jews to which the modern West, particularly

European societies, fell heir. There is much irony in all this: A young Christian majority and its young Jewish minority generated new and damaging views of Judaism and Jews; this innovative imagery continued to exert significant influence on Western thinking, even after the root assumptions of medieval civilization had been shattered and replaced.

While the central focus of this study is the twelfth-century evolution of innovative anti-Jewish stereotypes and their impact on subsequent Western thought, the inquiry will have implications in yet a second direction. One of the unresolved puzzles of medieval Jewish history has been the shifting fortunes of early (tenth through fourteenth centuries) Ashkenazic Jewry. Immigrant Jews were attracted into the developing areas of northern Europe from the late tenth century. Despite serious impediments, this young Jewry grew and spread. At some point in the late twelfth or early thirteenth century, however, rapid growth and development came to a close and decline set in. This point of transition has not been sharply identified and, more important, the dynamics of change have not been fully explored. The present study will advance a thesis as to the shifting fortunes of early Ashkenazic Jewry as it moved from healthy growth to precipitous decline.

Our investigation of twelfth-century anti-Jewish motifs will have one last useful ramification. Twentieth-century medievalists have identified the twelfth century as an important stage in the movement of Europe toward its eventual position of centrality in Western civilization. This sense is reflected in widespread agreement on a "twelfth-century renaissance," a period of intellectual and spiritual vitality that set the stage for the subsequent efflorescence of European thought. Of late, admiration for twelfth-century change has been balanced by growing awareness of its underside. A number of contemporary medievalists have highlighted the persecutory patterns that emerged during the twelfth century, directed at diverse societal outgroups. The most encompassing theorizing about this new persecutory pattern has been advanced by the English medievalist R. I. Moore. The title of his major work, *The Formation of a Persecuting Society*, indicates sharply the thrust of Moore's analysis. Among the outgroups regularly cited by Moore and others, the Jews of the twelfth century figure prominently. Thus, careful study of the development of new anti-Jewish perceptions should help refine our grasp of the broader tendency toward rejection of outgroups by twelfth-century European society.

In fact, study of the twelfth-century Jewish outgroup offers a specific advantage worthy of note. Moore and others indicate that a major impediment to studying twelfth-century rejection of outgroups is lack of materials from the minorities themselves. Heretics, lepers, and homosexuals have left us almost no data of their own, necessitating reconstruction of their experience and their rejection from the records of the persecuting majority, indeed a very limited segment of the persecuting majority. The Jews alone of the major twelfth-century outgroups have left us their own written materials, sources that enable us to correct for inevitable biases in the records of the majority. The combination of external and internal sources for twelfth-century Jewry thus puts researchers in an unusually advantageous position to conduct their analyses.

This study will carefully track the emergence of damaging new stereotypes of Jews in twelfth-century western Christendom. Better understanding of these innovative images will illuminate the broader tendencies toward the rejection of outgroups which is such a striking feature of the twelfth-century West. This analysis will, in addition, clarify the dynamics of growth and decline in the young Jewry that developed across medieval northern Europe and that subsequently came to dominate much of later Jewish history. Most important, I shall argue that these new stereotypes embedded themselves in Western consciousness and played a substantial role in the evolution of subsequent anti-Jewish thinking, eventually influencing nineteenth- and twentieth-century antisemitism. Anti-Jewish perceptions generated during a vibrant period in Western history have proven remarkably enduring, devastating to the Jewish minority of the West over the ages and, in moral terms, to the majority as well.

1

An Immigrant Jewry: Protection, Persecution, Perception

The northern reaches of Europe lay outside the broad swath of southern European Jewish settlements that extend back into antiquity. Well prior to Roman domination of the Mediterranean basin, Jews, starting from their point of origin in the Near East, moved westward along the northern and southern shores of the Mediterranean Sea. This westward movement was much enhanced by eventual Roman control of the entire Mediterranean littoral. By the beginning of the common era Jewish settlements extended all along the shores of the Mediterranean, attaining its most westerly reaches.

The disparity between the lands of southern Europe and northern Europe made it most unlikely that Jews settled along the Mediterranean would have been attracted in significant numbers into the backward areas of the north. The differences in climate and physical conditions alone would have served as a significant deterrent to Jewish immigration. Jews migrating northward would have encountered, in addition to a new and strange physical environment, a society lagging far behind their Mediterranean ambience in economic development and lifestyle. Jews traveled into northern Europe during the centuries preceding the turn of the millennium and occasionally founded small Jewish enclaves. No permanent and significant Jewish communities, however, were established.[1]

What changed matters, beginning in the late tenth century, was the vitalization of northern Europe.[2] As this backward area emerged

1

from its torpor, new opportunities were created and some Jews responded to these opportunities by making their way northward. The interest of adventuresome Jews was often matched by the desire of aggressive rulers to attract such useful immigrants to their domains. Indeed, the sponsors of Jewish immigration were often the most far-sighted and successful of the new magnates of the north.[3]

Thus, a crucial characteristic of early Ashkenazic Jewry was its newness as an immigrant community.[4] This newness influenced its limited size, its restricted economic outlets, and the broadly hostile views widespread among the Christian majority. Failure to recognize this newness and its impact on northern Europe's Jewish minority and Christian majority can only result in considerable misreading of the innovative anti-Jewish stereotypes spawned in the exciting young civilization of the north.[5]

Protection and Persecution

Most crucial for successful Jewish settlement in the reaches of northern Europe was physical security. Two factors lead us to suspect minimal Jewish security in northern Europe of the late tenth, eleventh, and early twelfth centuries: the general lawlessness of the area and the broad reputation of premodern Ashkenazic Jewry as a community regularly subject to physical assault.

Ubiquitous violence in the rapidly developing areas of northern Europe is widely attested in the sources and is regularly emphasized in modern historical research.[6] This violence reflects the vitality of the period and the primitive level of governance in the region. Because movement, change, and growth were coupled with limited capacity on the part of the authorities to harness the tensions that regularly accompany rapid transitions, aggression was endemic at every level of society. At the lower levels the strong preyed upon the weak; at the higher levels the unbridled rapacity of the most capable barons and lords resulted in the crystallization of larger and more effective principalities. Those who possessed and dealt in the kinds of goods that invited depredation were particularly susceptible to violence. Urban traders constituted an especially inviting target; when such urban traders were, in addition, newcomers, non-Christians, and in fact Jews, the temptation to assault and robbery was even greater.

While the prevalence of violence in tandem with the reputation of premodern Ashkenaz as the locus of considerable anti-Jewish persecution would lead us to suppose general Jewish insecurity, a close look at the evidence suggests that such was not in fact the case. Let us examine Jewish security/insecurity by looking first at persecution perpetrated by the authorities of northern Europe and then turning our attention to outbreaks of popular violence.

Evidence survives for but one significant outbreak of government-instigated persecution of Jews in the early period of Jewish settlement: the dimly illumined disruptions that took place at the end of the first decade of the eleventh century.[7] Five sources depict these events, three from the Christian side and two from the Jewish camp.[8] The picture that emerges from these disparate sources is hardly full and satisfying. Broadly speaking, it seems that early manifestations of heretical activity, passingly documented for Reims and Orléans, occasioned some governmental persecution of Jews, taking the forms of compulsory preaching in one locale (Limoges), occasional expulsion (Mainz), and sporadic physical violence inflicted by a few barons of northern France (King Robert of France and Duke Richard of Normandy are specified). Our fullest source for this set of events—the Hebrew narrative account—suggests, however, that the Jewish communities of northern Europe were quickly successful in negotiating an end to persecution. Whether this report can be fully trusted or not, these events occasioned no lasting damage to the rapidly developing Jewish communities of northern Europe.

The most extended and harmful anti-Jewish violence in our period, that which accompanied the early stages of the First Crusade in 1096, shows no serious evidence of aggression perpetrated by the established authorities of northern Europe, either by those who did not participate in the expedition (the major governmental figures in northern Europe) or by those who took part. The extensive Hebrew reports speak of only one major baronial leader of the crusade who exploited Jewish fears in order to squeeze funds from endangered Jews.[9] Thus, even the turmoil associated with crusading occasioned no shift in the protective stance of the authorities and no exploitation of the volatile circumstances in the direction of anti-Jewish violence. Governmentally instigated persecution of the Jews, whether motivated by simple cupidity or more serious concerns on the part of the authorities, does not seem to have been a feature of this earliest stage in the history of Ashkenazic Jewry and does not seem to have taken any serious toll on Jewish life.

Popular anti-Jewish violence was somewhat more widespread during the late tenth, the eleventh, and the early twelfth century. The limited materials available for the early eleventh-century persecution indicate that the fleeting governmental anti-Jewish initiatives were accompanied by outbreaks of popular assault as well. The Hebrew narrative, Adhémar of Chabannes, and Raoul Glaber all make reference to popular attacks on the Jews. Indeed, two of these three sources indicate Jewish awareness of this popular antipathy and reveal early manifestations of the Jewish willingness for martyrdom that is the hallmark of the much more serious assaults of 1096.[10]

The great outburst of anti-Jewish aggression during this first stage in early Ashkenazic history, roughly from the late tenth through the mid-twelfth century, took place in 1096, in association with the popular northern European crusading expeditions. I have elsewhere analyzed this outburst in considerable detail.[11] Let me recapitulate my major findings. The outbreak was occasioned by idiosyncratic interpretation (or misinterpretation) of the crusading message within the popular German crusading bands coupled with latent hostility on the part of factions in the Rhineland towns.

Pre-1096 burgher hostility appears in the interesting sources that depict the founding of the Speyer Jewish community in 1084. The Latin charter that served to set the conditions of settlement for the Jews migrating to Speyer stipulates the building of a wall around the Jewish neighborhood so that these new Jewish settlers "not be easily disrupted by the insolence of the mob."[12] The Hebrew account of the establishment of the Speyer community describes a fire that devastated the Jewish neighborhood of Mainz, leaving Jews fearful of burgher wrath. Jewish anxiety was enhanced by the slaying of a Worms Jew in Mainz in order to rob him of what was incorrectly perceived to be a valuable object of gold or silver.[13] This latent burgher animosity burst into full-scale violence under the extreme conditions of 1096. What permitted the overt and violent expression of long-standing hostility was the chaos generated by the crusade. The recruitment and passage of ill-disciplined armed bands dismantled the normal constraints governing the social life of the area.

The second contributory element to this violence against Jews was an interpretation (or misinterpretation) of the crusading message which deflected anti-Muslim animosity into more wide-ranging hostility toward all enemies of the Lord and his chosen Christian followers and vengeance on all who had allegedly brought harm to Christians and Christendom. This broader message of hatred and vengeance fastened itself readily on the Jews. Given the traditional ecclesiastical teaching of Jewish enmity toward Christendom and purported Jewish culpability for the crucifixion of Jesus, the anti-Jewish inferences are hardly surprising. The combination of crusading rationale for anti-Jewish assaults, long-standing burgher animosity toward the Rhineland Jews, and disappearance of the normal governmental constraints against aggression resulted in frightful attacks on the major Jewish communities of the Rhineland.

When we examine the dimensions of this violence, we find that, as lamentable as it was and as disastrously as it affected three of the major centers of early Ashkenazic Jewish life, the assaults were in fact quite limited in scope and duration. Major attacks devastated the Rhineland Jewish communities of Worms, Mainz, and Cologne. The Jewish population in all three towns was in effect destroyed, with the numbers provided by the subsequent Jewish narratives suggesting approximately eight hundred Jewish casualties in Worms and approximately eleven hundred in Mainz.[14] While no numbers are provided for Cologne, the impression of almost complete destruction of the community and the sense that its pre-1096 population was probably similar to that of Worms and Mainz makes a total of some three thousand Jewish victims of the attacks a reasonable estimate. There is no solid evidence that these three assaults constitute a symptom of more wide-ranging aggression. To the contrary, the lengthy Hebrew 1096 narrative was clearly committed to amassing the broadest and fullest possible evidence of Christian bestiality and Jewish suffering and heroism. The failure of this narrative to report further devastating assaults makes it likely that the heavy losses were confined to these three major localities.[15] To be sure, in other places popular crusading bands rationalized anti-Jewish aggression and in other towns burgher hostility flared up. But by and large the duly empowered authorities maintained law and order and afforded requisite protection to Jews living under their jurisdiction.[16] The net result was a terrible but limited calamity, one that represents the exception and not the rule for Jewish life in northern Europe from the late tenth through the mid-twelfth century.

This conclusion about the limited impact of the First Crusade on European Jewry is reinforced by the evidence of the Second Crusade. Again the same ingredients for anti-Jewish attacks were present: distortion of the crusading message and latent burgher hostility. There was, however, one overwhelming difference between 1096 and 1146— awareness of the potential for explosive violence and determination on the part of the ecclesiastical leadership, the secular authorities, and the Jews themselves to avert anything like the bloodshed that had accompanied the First Crusade. This shared determination resulted in steps to obviate aggression, and these measures were highly successful.[17] Although we possess a Hebrew account of the Second Crusade replete with all the rhetoric and imagery of the Hebrew First Crusade narratives, in fact the anti-Jewish violence of 1146 involved only minimal losses and reveals a maximum of effective measures to preclude anti-Jewish outbreaks.[18]

While the primary stimulus to Jewish immigration into northern Europe had been economic opportunity, an acceptable level of security had to be established for these vulnerable immigrants. The authorities of this developing area were for the most part able and willing to provide requisite security.

Early Anti-Jewish Stereotypes

The focus of our concern is neither the violence suffered by the earliest Jewish settlers in northern Europe nor governmental suppression of the potential for anti-Jewish outbreaks. I wish rather to investigate the perceptions that underlay popular resistance to Jewish settlement.[19] From the beginning of their sojourn in northern Europe, the Jewish immigrants and their descendants faced considerable popular antipathy. Identifying inchoate and inarticulate majority perceptions of the early Ashkenazic Jews is no easy task, but such identification is crucial for the purposes of this study. Precise reconstruction of majority perceptions of Jews during the late tenth through the twelfth century is impossible. The sources that would enable us to fashion a precise reconstruction are simply not available. In particular, we must note the lack of personal memoir material that would illuminate the thinking of broad sectors of northern European society. The best we can do is establish loose approximations of majority views of Jews during this period through examination of significant forms of majority behavior toward the Jewish minority, medieval depictions of the motivations for such behavior, and recurring imagery in those literary sources that have survived.

This analysis will involve no effort to distinguish views in diverse economic and social classes. The data simply do not permit such discrimination. In particular, rigid differentiation between ecclesiastical and secular attitudes in this period is untenable. The church pervaded every nook and cranny of society; churchmen were vitally involved in the general life of society and shared broadly held perspectives of the period.[20] Thus, the best we can hope to achieve is delineation of diverse images of Jews, without attempting to associate these views with particular elements in society.

Using behaviors and their explanations as an index to widely held perceptions of the Jews carries with it a number of dangers. Most problematic is the tendency of medieval (and modern) sources to focus on the disrupted and disruptive rather than the normal and integrated. Reading the sources that have survived, one is tempted to see Jewish life as a series of crises, lived out in an atmosphere of unremitting tension and anxiety. But we can safely assume that the Jews of late tenth-, eleventh-, and early twelfth-century northern Europe did not live in a state of unremitting tension and anxiety. Had that in fact been the case, immigration, through which early Ashkenazic Jewry grew and developed, would hardly have taken place. Even the bloodshed associated with the First Crusade led to no significant movement of Jews out of the area and in fact had no discernible impact on continued Jewish immigration. Those urban centers that were the scenes of major loss of Jewish life—Worms, Mainz, and Cologne—were quickly repopulated by new Jewish settlers. Immigrants are most unlikely to settle in areas where they find their lives and property in constant jeopardy and where they sense unabating hostility. The unrelenting Jewish movement into northern Europe reflects a sense that, occasional dangers notwithstanding, the area had much to offer and that majority antipathy, while real, hardly constituted an overwhelming obstacle.

Surviving source materials on occasion reflect normal human relationships and positive Christian perceptions of Jews. Christians worked comfortably in Jewish homes, engaged in business dealings with Jews, and established economic partnerships with Jewish colleagues. At points of minor and major crisis, Christians rallied to the aid of their Jewish neighbors.[21] Perhaps the most striking examples of such normal human relationships and positive perceptions come from the turbulent spring months of 1096. The sources indicate explicitly that in a number of instances Christians came spontaneously to the aid of Jewish inhabitants of the German towns. Let me cite two instances, using evidence derived from post-1096 Jewish sources that can hardly be suspected of unduly sympathetic depiction of Christian behavior and thinking.

The first incident occurred early in the buildup of tension in the major Rhineland city of Mainz. An alleged wonder-working woman and her goose provoked taunting of the Jews of Mainz. The taunting escalated into the threat of violence. At this tense juncture, with a mixed group of crusaders and burghers poised on the verge of assault, "some of the burghers came and would not allow them [to do so]. At that time they stood . . . and killed along the Rhine River, until they killed one of the crusaders."[22] To be sure, many details of this incident are murky. Clearly, however, a group of Christian townsmen rallied to the aid of endangered Jewish neighbors. While we are not privy to the perceptions that stimulated this behavior, these actions surely reflect positive views of the endangered Jews of Mainz.

Perhaps more striking yet is the behavior of Archbishop Ruthard of Mainz. His actions are also known to us from a Jewish report, an account that is highly unfavorable to the archbishop. Nonetheless, even in this negative account the genuine liking of the archbishop for one of the leading Jews of his city is not masked. To recapitulate the outlines of the story: Archbishop Ruthard promised to protect his Jews, gathered them in his fortified palace, but abandoned them in the face of the crusaders led by Count Emicho. Left on their own, the Jews of Mainz were quickly overcome by the crusading forces and either were killed by their attackers or took their own lives. Only a small band of armed Jews led by Kalonymous ben Meshullam held out, hidden in an out-of-the-way room in the archbishop's palace. At this juncture we might anticipate total abandonment of these Jews by the archbishop. Yet in fact Archbishop Ruthard sent one of his men with an armed entourage to extricate these Jews from their perilous refuge. The depiction of the succeeding events is revealing: "The minister [of the archbishop] placed them in boats and ferried them across the Rhine river and brought them at night to the place where the archbishop was, in the village of Rüdesheim. The archbishop was exceedingly happy over

R. Kalonymous, that he was still alive, and intended to save him and the men that were with him."[23] In the end Archbishop Ruthard failed to save even these Jews, for which he was excoriated by the Jewish chronicler. Yet despite the sad outcome of the archbishop's efforts, the antipathetic Jewish narrator acknowledged the genuine affection of the archbishop for the Jew Kalonymous.

One last piece of evidence from the 1096 tragedy is most instructive because it is so generalized. While the typical Jewish response in the face of the crusading threat was to find safety through the established authorities, many Jews were caught in circumstances that moved them to seek refuge with Christian neighbors. We can only conclude that, despite the negative outcomes depicted in the Hebrew sources, the Jews who sought such refuge must surely have anticipated that their neighbors were genuinely committed to saving them.[24] Such anticipation on the part of the Jews bespeaks prior friendly relationships and positive Christian perceptions of these Jews. It is unthinkable that Jews caught in these trying circumstances would entrust themselves capriciously to neighbors of whose intentions and attitudes they were uncertain. This recurring pattern clearly reflects the existence of normal, indeed warm human relations between Jews and their neighbors based on some sort of positive Christian view of Jews.

Unfortunately, we are in no position to assess in any depth the imagery that governed these normal and positive human relations. Our sources never speak of the perceptions that undergirded such relationships, and there is no way to penetrate this silence. We can only speculate as to common and positive views that individual Christians held of individual Jews whom they had come to know and respect, just as Jewish behavior reflects common and positive images (similarly unavailable to us) of Christian neighbors.

More widespread than depiction of positive relations is the focus on death and destruction in our sources. Northern Europe of the late tenth through mid-twelfth century was an area of rapid development exhibiting the kind of change that generally breeds lawlessness and violence. Indeed, one gauge of the maturation of northern European society is the movement toward greater order, in particular the emergence of governments capable of policing the territories that fell under their jurisdiction. Prior to the development of such effective governance, roads were generally unsafe, brigands roamed everywhere, theft and bloodshed were everyday occurrences. In some measure Jews suffered along with everyone else in these primitive circumstances. In many ways, however, the Jews were in an especially precarious situation as a result of their economic activities. Traders were a particularly attractive target for the lawless, and in many instances what Jews suffered was inflicted on them not qua Jews but rather qua urban traders.

While Jews were on occasion the victims of general insecurity, we can clearly see that some of the violence suffered by early Ashkenazic Jews was the result of their Jewishness and was occasioned by broadly held negative stereotypes of Jews and Jewish behavior. A number of the anti-Jewish images current in tenth-, eleventh-, and twelfth-century northern Europe reflect the realities of early Ashkenazic life. This was an immigrant community, and immigrants are rarely appreciated by their neighbors and competitors. Some of the most farsighted of the new rulers of northern Europe strongly encouraged Jewish immigration. This governmental support should not be taken, however, as indicative of broad approbation for the new arrivals. Among large segments of the northern European population, immigrating Jews must have aroused the hostilities that are the normal lot of recent settlers. While the imagery of Jews as immigrants was almost certainly widespread, it is rarely reflected in the sources. We might hypothesize that more compelling anti-Jewish stereotypes obliterated the rather mundane negative image of Jews as newcomers.

A second anti-Jewish perception was likewise grounded in the realities of majority Christian and minority Jewish existence in northern Europe: the image of Jews as religious dissidents. This stereotype does find occasional expression in the sources. Let me note an instance of this perception stemming from the early eleventh-century persecution of Jewish communities in northern France and Germany. The lengthiest surviving source, an anonymous Hebrew narrative, has the following to report about the initiation of the anti-Jewish campaign:

The gentiles murmured and plotted, intending to wipe out, to kill, and to destroy all the Jews in the land. The king and queen then took counsel with his officers and barons within the boundaries of the kingdom. They said to him: "There is one people spread throughout all the provinces, which does not obey us. Its laws and teachings are different from those of all peoples. Now let us go and obliterate them, so that the name of Israel be no longer remembered, for they are a snare before us. Let us announce throughout all your land that whoever does not accede to us and does not heed our words will die." The king and his officers were in perfect accord and agreed on this plan. On a certain day, the king sent for the Jews who dwelled in his land, and they came before him. He then said to them: "Behold I have sent for you, so that you might reveal your views and not hide anything from me. I took counsel with my officers and servants. My desire is for one unified people. You will be powerful and respected. Turn to our teaching because it is more correct than yours. If you refuse, I shall put you to death by the sword. Now take counsel and answer on this matter."[25]

The tone of this account is clearly folkloric, heavily influenced by the traditional tale of persecution found in the biblical book of Esther. So too much should not be made of it.[26] It does nonetheless seem likely—indeed inescapable—that awareness of the Jews as a religiously different group should have been widespread throughout northern Europe. Given the brute fact that this area, unlike, for example, the Iberian and Italian peninsulas, showed little religious diversity, the special and anomalous status of the Jews as the sole legitimate dissenting group had to permeate Christian consciousness.

Differing from the majority religious faith was in and of itself a negative attribute of the Jews migrating into northern Europe. Since Christians were so decidedly in the majority and Jews constituted such a tiny minority, members of the majority were hardly likely to see the Jews as simply different; they were much more likely to perceive the Jews as wrongly different. Given the origins of Christianity within the Jewish community of first-century Palestine and its resultant claims to the legacy of biblical Israel, Christian tradition suggested that Jews represented not a neutrally dissenting community but in fact a religiously misguided group that had misunderstood its own divinely revealed heritage. This view was obviously quite negative, projecting the Jews as living in error that they should have readily been able to understand and rectify.

The economic circumstances of the early Ashkenazic Jews and their firm alliance with the political authorities created two further sources of irritation. The first involved resentment of Jewish commercial activity, partially on the part of rural folk suspicious of all business dealings and more significantly on the part of Christian traders who had to be resentful of the alleged need for Jewish business acumen and of the advantages proffered the Jewish immigrants. In 1084 Bishop Rudiger of Speyer invited Jews to settle in his town, explaining that their presence would enhance the glory of that town considerably.[27] One can only surmise how the Christian businesspeople of Speyer felt about this denigration of their abilities and about a purported need for interlopers. Further, the special privileges accorded the Jewish newcomers to the town of Speyer surely exacerbated this irritation.[28] Normal feelings of competition, heightened by the sense of the Jews as immigrants and non-Christians, played a role in the negative imagery attached to these early Ashkenazic Jews.

Anger over Jewish business competition fostered by the ruling class led to yet another negative image that was realistically grounded, this time in the Jewish alliance with the political authorities. This alliance was an indispensable prerequisite to Jewish settlement in northern Europe. Immigrating into a generally dangerous and specifically hostile environment, the Jews had to depend on both general and specific guarantees of protection and support. While indispensable from the Jewish perspective, the close relationship between the Jews and their lords aroused animosity in a number of sectors of northern European society. Generally, any elements opposed to a given ruler would inevitably see the Jews in a negative light. The most specific and intense resentment of the alliance of the Jews with the authorities was evoked among the municipal elites anxious to expand their control over life in the burgeoning cities of northern Europe. Much progress had been achieved by burghers in increasing their powers in the budding municipalities. The direct political relationship between the Jewish immigrants and their lords made these Jews in effect baronial allies planted in the midst of the towns. The two most direct expressions of this relationship and the two most serious infringements on burgher rights were Jewish independence from the municipal court system and their exemption from municipal taxation. In both these respects the Jews were answerable directly to baronial authority, an arrangement as useful to the Jews as it was distasteful to their Christian burgher neighbors.

To be sure, we find few sources that directly reveal these two sources of resentment, the economic and the political. The Jewish chroniclers of the anti-Jewish violence of 1096, however, emphasize the role that burghers played in this violence. Burgher anger surely fed off the already noted stereotypes of Jews as newcomers and dissidents and the imagery of the Jews as hostile, to be addressed shortly. At the same time, these sources of animus were certainly augmented by burgher resentment of Jewish business competition and anger over Jewish impingement on the rights and liberties the towns were beginning to extract from the authorities. On both levels, the Jews constituted a source of considerable annoyance and antipathy that exploded into violence on the part of some Rhineland burghers when the arrival of the popular crusaders and the breakdown of law and order enhanced anti-Jewish sentiment and obliterated the normal constraints against acting out such hostility.

While resentment surfaced over the Jews as immigrants, dissidents, businesspeople and business competitors, and allies of the barony, these reality-based sources of antipathy were outweighed by traditional imagery that predated Jewish arrival in northern Europe. Clearly, the dominant anti-Jewish stereotype in northern Europe—as elsewhere—derived from the New Testament depiction of the Jews as hostile toward Jesus and his followers, their animosity culminating in the breathtaking act of killing the Messiah promised them. While Christian spokesmen sporadically diminished Jewish culpability, for example, by emphasizing that Jesus was after all fated to suffer and die, medieval Christendom in general chose to focus on the imagery of the Jews as deicides.[29]

Like their Jewish contemporaries, medieval Christians tended to assume a continuity of attitudes and behavior, thus regularly viewing their Jewish neighbors of the tenth or eleventh or twelfth centuries as imbued with precisely the same characteristics that led their ancestors to press Pontius Pilate for the crucifixion of Jesus. Indeed, the Matthew account of the condemnation of Jesus portrays the Jews of Jerusalem calling for his death in the face of Pilate's equivocation. When the Roman insisted on his innocence—"My hands are clean of this man's blood"—Matthew has the assembled Jews accepting responsibility throughout the ages: "His blood be on us and on our children." Medieval Christians tended to see their Jewish neighbors as precisely those children of the Jerusalem Jews. Recently, Elaine Pagels has argued that the Gospel portrayal of the Jews involved a demonization of these opponents, a projection of Jewish (and other) opposition onto a cosmic canvas, again assuring for future Christian readers a sense of Jewish hostility that knew no bounds of time and place.[30] In the Middle Ages, as in all periods, real human contact could efface such imagery, and we have already seen that on many occasions it did. Nonetheless, the overwhelmingly deleterious impact of the New Testament imagery cannot be gainsaid.

The stereotype of Jews as enemies is widely attested in sources from our period. The most significant expression of this theme came in the popular crusading attacks of 1096. Throughout both Christian and Jewish accounts, Christian perception of Jews as eternally hostile to

Christianity is omnipresent. From the Christian side, we might note Albert of Aachen's depiction of the popular crusading bands that attacked the Rhineland Jewish communities. According to Albert, these crusaders asserted "it to be the beginning of their expedition and of their duty against the enemies of the Christian faith." [31] More graphic in presenting the Jews as historic enemies is Guibert of Nogent's version of the rationale with which the popular crusading bands assaulted Jews: "We wish to attack the enemies of God in the East, after traveling great distances. However, before our eyes are the Jews, and no people is more hostile to God than they are. Such an arrangement is absurd." [32]

The Jewish chroniclers of the Rhineland assaults, who are far fuller in their depiction of the catastrophe, present the same portrait of crusader animosity toward Jews, who are perceived as enemies, indeed Christianity's profoundest enemies. [33] These Jewish writers emphasize repeatedly the image of the Jew as the enemy on whom vengeance must be taken. Their general introductory depictions of the early development of the First Crusade and of the related anti-Jewish violence highlight this theme. The older and better organized of the two major Hebrew narratives presents the following rationale for the crusaders' attack on Jews: "Behold we travel to a distant land to do battle with the kings of that land. We take our souls in our hand in order to kill and to subjugate all those kingdoms that do not believe in the Crucified. How much more so [should we kill and subjugate] the Jews, who killed and crucified him." [34] The same rationale appears in the longer of the two original Hebrew narratives:

Behold we journey a long way to seek the idolatrous shrine and to take vengeance upon the Muslims. But here are the Jews dwelling among us, whose ancestors killed him and crucified him groundlessly. Let us take vengeance first upon them. Let us wipe them out as a nation; Israel's name will be mentioned no more. Or else let them be like us and acknowledge the son born of menstruation. [35]

This Christian sense of Jews as historic enemies is by no means limited to the broad introductory sections of these Hebrew narratives; the same theme recurs frequently in narration of specific incidents. Note, for example, the assault in Worms on the bulk of the Jewish community of that town, which had sequestered itself in the bishop's palace for safety: "The crusaders and burghers said: 'Behold those who remain in the courtyard of the bishop and in his chambers. Let us take vengeance upon them as well.'"[36] As the followers of Count Emicho burst through the city gates of Mainz, opened for them by burgher collaborators, the Hebrew narrative has them echoing this theme of Jewish enmity and requisite vengeance: "The enemies of the Lord said to one another: 'Behold—the gates have been opened by themselves. All this the Crucified has done for us, so that we might avenge his blood upon the Jews.'"[37]

Thus, wherever we turn, the Christian sense of Jews as historic enemies is manifest. The arousal of some northern European crusaders to do battle against the Muslim enemy stirred up parallel hostility against Jews, perceived as both worse than Muslims in their hatred of Christianity and readily at hand. This sense of the Jews as historic enemies of Christianity and Christendom constitutes the most damaging anti-Jewish stereotype reflected in the literature of the late tenth through the early twelfth centuries, exceeding in significance and impact the more realistic images of the Jews as newcomers, religious dissidents, business competitors, and allies of the barony. The power of this imagery probably accounts for the limited appearance or even the non-appearance of some of these other, more realistic characterizations of the Jews.

Looking ahead for a moment to the coming chapters, we might note one slight, but critical, twist to this imagery of the Jew as enemy. As we have just seen, the key element in this stereotype is the Jewish role in the Crucifixion. In a few instances, however, the perception of the Jew as historic enemy takes a yet more ominous turn, with the suggestion that acts of Jewish malevolence can be discerned in the present as well. As noted, medieval Christians and Jews tended to operate with an assumption of unchanging human character, meaning for medieval Christians that their Jewish contemporaries shared the same propensities as those who had called for the crucifixion of Christ a millennium earlier. Nonetheless, there is a crucial difference between perceiving Jews as historically disposed to acts of enmity and perceiving Jews as actually perpetrating acts of violence against their present-day Christian neighbors. What we have seen in the crusade materials is perception of the Jews as progeny of past enemies and hence disposed to anti-Christian animosity. On a very few occasions we also see allegations of present-day acts of hostility.

A curious late tenth-century incident in northwestern France involved anti-Jewish machinations by a onetime Jew caught up in rivalry with and hatred of Jewish neighbors. This fellow, Sehok ben Esther, contrived to destroy the Jews of Le Mans by convincing the count of Maine that these Jews had plotted against him. According to the Hebrew account, the agitator planted in the ark of the synagogue a waxen image. He then convinced the count of the nefarious designs of the Jews. "He went and said to the baron: 'Do you know what these people have done? They made a waxen image in your likeness, which they pierce with a sharp instrument on the three pilgrimage festivals of the year [Passover, Shavuot, and Succot], in order to destroy you. Indeed, thus their ancestors did to your god.'"[38] Reflected here are both the sense of Jews as historically ill disposed to Christianity and the perception of tenth-century Jews as living out that hostility. In effect, the plotter played on his certainty that the count of Maine would be fully prepared to see his Jewish subjects as hostile and ready to express their enmity in harmful acts undertaken against him.

A second reflection of this sense of active Jewish malevolence is found in two of the depictions of the early eleventh-century persecution already noted. Both Adhémar of Chabannes and Raoul Glaber speak of the role played by northern European Jews in bringing about the destruction of the Church of the Holy Sepulcher. Indeed, according to Raoul, Christian awareness of this heinous Jewish action set in motion the richly deserved persecution of the Jews.[39] Now, the historicity of the link between alleged Jewish plotting and the persecution of northern European Jewry is not our issue; the historicity of the plotting is similarly irrelevant to our concerns. Important for our purposes is the calumny itself. Two significant eleventh-century observers were convinced that anti-Christian actions by Jews were not confined to antiquity, that their contemporary Jewish neighbors were deeply implicated in ongoing harmful efforts.

A similar propensity to believe in Jewish malevolence is reflected in the agitation that led to the first 1096 assault against the Jewish community of Worms. Again, plotters played on the widespread Christian sense of Jewish malevolence. Early in the attack on the Jews of Worms, with the community divided into two groups, plotters fomented violence against the Jews who had opted to stay in their homes. "They took a trampled corpse of theirs, that had been buried thirty days previously, and carried it through the city, saying: 'Behold what the Jews have done to our comrade. They took a gentile and boiled him in water. They then poured the water into our wells in order to kill us.'"[40] This agitation was once more predicated on Christian willingness to believe the worst of the Jews, a readiness that in fact proved to be the case in Worms in the spring of 1096, as it had in Le Mans a century earlier. Expansion of the sense of Jews as historically hostile to the perception of contemporary Jews as steeped in anti-Christian animosity is of utmost significance, although there are but limited signs of such expansion prior to the middle of the twelfth century.

In sum, the Jews of northern Europe were the object of considerable popular antipathy. The images that underlay this animosity were to some extent grounded in the realities of the Jewish situation: The Jews were immigrants and had to bear the resentment newcomers generally face; they were the only legitimate dissenters in a religiously cohesive area; they were business competitors in the nascent towns of this early period; they were the sworn allies of the barony. Dwarfing this set of realities was the historic Christian legacy that portrayed Jews as implacable enemies of Christian faith and Christians. This powerful imagery, in combination with the realities of Jewish life in northern Europe, created the potential for serious anti-Jewish sentiment. Particularly ominous, although by no means widespread, was the perception of the Jewish immigrants as consumed by an animosity to contemporary Christianity and Christians which moved them to commit anti-Christian acts.

The five anti-Jewish themes noted—four related to the realities of Jewish life and one to traditional Christian teaching—break down into two fundamental groups. The first two—Jews as newcomers and Jews as religious dissidents—focus on Jewish otherness; the remaining three—Jews as competitors, Jews as allies of the barony, Jews as historic enemies—project an image of Jewish harmfulness. Of these two fundamental groups, the latter is surely the more potent. Christian conviction of Jewish hatred and harmfulness, whether rooted in contemporary realities or traditional teachings or both, was much more likely to provoke fear and loathing.

The impact of the anti-Jewish stereotypes, both realistic and traditional, was substantial, although the hostilities of the majority were normally held well in check. Again, recall that both secular rulers and churchmen were fully immersed in the life of this young society. Many of these leaders undoubtedly shared the prejudices so widely disseminated, yet nonetheless they remained by and large committed to safeguarding the Jews and in fact were generally successful in providing the protection that made continued settlement in northern Europe attractive all through the eleventh century and in fact well into the twelfth. Precisely how deeply rooted and widely spread anti-Jewish imagery was across northern Europe cannot now be fully known. It was probably omnipresent, but how significant a force it represented we cannot fathom. In any case, such anti-Jewish sentiment was not potent enough at this time to place the budding Jewry of northern Europe in serious jeopardy or to impede its rapid growth and development.

2

Real Change and
Reality-Based Imagery

Despite the sizable number of casualties associated with the crusader attacks on Rhineland Jews in 1096, the steady development of early Ashkenazic Jewry was by no means disrupted. The Jewish population of northern Europe continued to grow, partially through biological increase and partially through continued immigration. Worms, Mainz, and Cologne, where Jewish communities seem to have been obliterated in 1096, were quickly repopulated by new Jewish settlers. This continued Jewish immigration into northern Europe during the early decades of the twelfth century is particularly revealing. Immigrants are unlikely to make their way into an area where safety is uncertain or where serious decline is under way. The fate of the early Ashkenazic Jews during the Second Crusade is additionally illuminating. While crusader antipathy to the Jews developed almost instantaneously and while the Jews and their protectors were alarmed, the bloody Rhineland assaults of 1096 were not repeated. The efforts of the secular authorities and leading churchmen—in particular the spiritual leader of the Second Crusade, Bernard of Clairvaux—and the Jews themselves were successful in quashing incipient anti-Jewish violence.

During the first half of the twelfth century Jewish economic activity took a new turn. Despite the problems associated with this new specialization, moneylending, northern European Jewry seems to have been stronger and more prosperous during the twelfth century than it had been previously. Although Jewish cultural productivity lies outside the purview of this study, it affords yet one further index to the circumstances of mid-twelfth-century northern European Jewry. While the early foundations of Jewish cultural and spiritual creativity were sturdy, activity accelerated toward the end of the eleventh century, culminating in the brilliant achievement of Rabbi Solomon ben Isaac of Troyes (Rashi, d. 1105), whose extensive commentaries on both the Bible and Talmud quickly became authoritative, first within Ashkenazic Jewry and then beyond. The first half of the twelfth century shows no abatement of creative energy, despite the debacle of 1096. To the contrary, spiritual and intellectual innovation was, if anything, intensified. Both biblical and talmudic commentary were pushed in exciting new directions by scholars who were influenced by Rashi and were, in some important cases, biological descendants of the sage of Troyes. Innovative mystical speculation blossomed, and a new historical style made its appearance.[1]

These indices of growth and development belie the sense of 1096 as signaling the onset of decline for early Ashkenazic Jewry.[2] Evidence of augmented growth and development in Jewish life during the twelfth century should hardly come as a shock. The closing decades of the eleventh century and most of the twelfth century constitute a period of material and spiritual progress in western Christendom, a period whose widely acknowledged creativity has resulted in the designation "twelfth-century renaissance." Historians of medieval western Christendom have identified striking advances in the economy, in political organization, and in cultural creativity, advances that laid the foundations for eventual leadership by western and central Europe in world affairs. This view is captured in a striking way in the overall assessment of the English medievalist R. W. Southern:

For a thousand years Europe has been the chief centre of political experiment, economic expansion and intellectual discovery in the world. It gained this position during the period with which we are concerned [the mid tenth through the late twelfth century, with a focus on the late eleventh through the late twelfth century]: it is only losing it in our own day.[3]

Southern's sentiment would be seconded by most historians of medieval western Christendom. Against this backdrop of a dynamic majority society, the continued growth and development of early Ashkenazic Jewry is readily understandable.

Of late a new theme in the dynamism of the "twelfth century renaissance" has been sounded. Researchers working in diverse areas have come to see as part of this dynamism rejection and even persecution of outgroups in western Christendom. This tendency constitutes one of the central themes of the present study. The argument is that precisely this creative century, which fostered the rapid development of the immigrant Jewry depicted in the preceding chapter, spawned a set of destructive images fated to play a decisive role in the subsequent decline of early Ashkenazic Jewry and, further, to plague Jewish history from the twelfth century to the present.

Real Change

The economic upsurge of the late tenth through the early twelfth century intensified during the first decades of the twelfth century. Improved cultivation of the land and expanding artisanry meant satisfaction of an increasingly large population and production of more goods for exchange and sale. This resulted in more trade on both the local and international level. As northern Europe became better integrated into the rest of western Christendom and then into the eastern Mediterranean world, the thirst for goods developed, a yearning that only augmented trade could satisfy. The crusading ventures, which had little lasting political impact, played a more significant role in the maturation of the northern European economy.

The early Ashkenazic Jews, during this period of efflorescence, in effect shifted economic gears, moving vigorously into the money trade. Opportunities in finance reflect the same basic economic surge. Projects of all kinds became increasingly grandiose during the second half of the twelfth century and on into the thirteenth. Trading ventures became more expansive, necessitating considerably more capital. The same is true for localized military aggressions, for large-scale warfare within northern Europe, and for the international efforts that more often than not were carried out under the crusading banner. The brilliant building programs that have left us so many impressive remains similarly required large sums of capital. In a more general way, maturation of both secular and ecclesiastical authority meant a need for enhanced funding. The expanding economy provided the requisite background for the maturation of both church and state, whose development served in turn as stimulants to the growth of the northern European economy. The result of all these processes was the need for funding on a massive scale. For a variety of reasons Jews were attracted to the expanding money trade, playing a significant if fairly short-lived role in the rapid expansion of the northern European economy.

The burgeoning economy of the late tenth and eleventh century in northern Europe had attracted Jewish immigrants to an undeveloped area. From the meager evidence available for this early period, these Jewish immigrants appear to have been heavily involved principally in commerce. One of the critical issues for the future well-being of the new Jewish settlements was maintenance of economic strength. Could these Jews support themselves effectively through continued specialization in commerce? Alternatively, might they find another or other sustaining specialties? Economic diversification, the creation of varied economic outlets, would present the most positive prospect, at least theoretically. As the accelerated economic growth of northern European society opened up new opportunities, specialization in the money trade proved to be a profitable shift for the Jews of northern Europe, but one fraught with problematic ramifications.

A new Jewish economic specialization in the money trade is not meant to conjure up a vision of all Jews—or even a majority of Jews— engaged in moneylending. The earlier Jewish focus on commerce by no means meant that all immigrating Jews engaged in commercial activity; rather, while the immigrating Jews pursued diverse enterprises, commerce constituted the backbone of the Jewish economy, provided the profits that made Jewish life viable, and made the immigrating Jews so prized by the most progressive rulers of northern Europe. Similarly, from approximately the mid-twelfth century onward, while Jews continued to support themselves in multifarious ways, including commercial enterprise, moneylending took over as the prime specialization of the early Ashkenazic Jews, provided their most important source of profit, elevated key members of the community to positions of considerable wealth and power, and attracted once more the interest and support of major political authorities.

Let us attempt to track briefly the shift in Jewish economic activity. The transition from trade to moneylending was a fluid one. Many of the eleventh-century responsa, written exchanges to clarify points of Jewish law, indicate selling of goods on credit, and the move from such sales on credit to full-scale moneylending is a relatively small step. What were the dynamics that opened to the Ashkenazic Jews new opportunities in finance? Especially important was the fortuitous combination of enhanced economic activity and intensified ecclesiastical opposition to Christian usury. All across northern Europe, more expansive business enterprises were launched, larger armies were raised, and more impressive buildings were erected. In order to sustain all this activity, sizable sums of capital were required. In addition to the increasing need for capital, the discovery of new silver deposits in Germany during the early 1160s facilitated the circulation of coinage throughout Europe at precisely this juncture.[4] Business activity continued to increase markedly during the second half of the twelfth century.

The growth in business activity all across northern Europe came at the same time that a more active Roman Catholic church was pressing for major reforms, attacking abuses within ecclesiastical ranks and in Christian society at large. One of the major targets of the reform program was usury, first as practiced by members of the clergy and eventually as practiced by all Christians.[5] To the extent that the church was successful in its effort to check Christian usury, at a time when the need for capital was ever more urgent, it unwittingly paved the way for greater Jewish involvement in lending. Because of the Deuteronomic distinction between the taking of usury from a brother or fellow countryman—which was forbidden—and from a stranger or foreigner—which was permitted—Jewish usury fell outside the purview of the church campaign. The way was open for Jewish business activities that were lucrative and useful, although not highly appreciated in society at large. Once again, there is more here than simple Jewish response to economic opportunity. Many of the most progressive rulers of northern Europe saw great advantage to the societies that they ruled and to themselves in fostering Jewish moneylending. The original alliance between Jews and their lords was much strengthened by the emergence of moneylending as a Jewish economic specialty.

Let us begin our brief look at the new Jewish economic specialization by noting four mid-twelfth-century literary testimonies to the centrality of moneylending among the Jews. We shall quickly proceed to verify these perceptions, but they afford an interesting starting point for our discussion. Particularly fortunate is the diversity in these sources, two from the pens of Jews, one formulated by a sympathetic Christian observer, and one bearing a tone of undisguised hostility.

The first Jewish source is the chronicler of the fate of northern European Jewry during the Second Crusade, Ephraim ben Jacob of Bonn. Ephraim's Hebrew account moves geographically across Germany into

France and on into England. In his depiction of the fate of French Jewry, he details the death of one major leader, Rabbi Peter, and the violent assault on the outstanding figure in mid-twelfth-century northern French Jewry, Rabbi Jacob Tam. He proceeds to note:

In the remaining communities of France, we have not heard that a single Jew was killed or forcibly converted. But they did lose much of their wealth. For the king of France commanded: "Anyone who has volunteered to journey to Jerusalem shall have his debt annulled if he be indebted to the Jews." Most of the loans extended by the Jews of France are by charter; hence they lost their money.[6]

This description of the royal edict poses certain problems. It is a bit difficult to imagine at this moment a royal order forgiving crusaders the entirety of their debts to Jewish creditors.[7] Whether the depiction of the royal mandate is accurate or not, Ephraim of Bonn clearly perceived his contemporaries in northern France as relying heavily on governmentally supported moneylending in their economic activity. Detrimental royal interference in this moneylending would constitute, according to Ephraim, a grievous blow to these Jews of northern France.

The sympathetic Christian statement can be found in Peter Abelard's *Dialogue of a Philosopher with a Jew and a Christian*. In a statement highlighting Jewish zeal for observance of divine law and Jewish willingness to suffer on behalf of this divine law, Abelard has the Jewish protagonist lament his situation:

We can possess neither fields nor vines nor any land, since nothing can guarantee them against covert or overt attack. Therefore our sole resort is usury. It is only by practicing usury with non-Jews that we can maintain our miserable livelihood. Yet through this we provoke bitter hatred on the part of those who consider themselves gravely burdened.[8]

Again, this depiction should not be taken as absolutely accurate. We know very well that Jews, then as well as later, did possess and work fields and vines.[9] We also know that other options existed besides farming, on the one hand, and moneylending, on the other. Nonetheless, what Abelard seems to be saying is that such activity as farming was difficult and fraught with problems, making the option of moneylending the best available to an outsider group like the Jews.[10] In any case, his statement once more reflects a twelfth-century observer who saw the cornerstone of Jewish economic fortunes in moneylending.

The unsympathetic Christian observer is the key figure in Jewish fate

during the Second Crusade, Bernard of Clairvaux. Bernard's stance on
the Jews combined a firm insistence on the church's policy of protection of Jewish life with justifications for this policy that reinforced traditional imagery of Jews as enemies. Bernard's central role in assuring
Jewish safety was acknowledged by Ephraim of Bonn and has been fully
recognized by modern historians. In his letters calling Christian warriors to the crusade, Bernard conspicuously included a paragraph prohibiting anti-Jewish violence. Nonetheless, in the very letters in which
he sternly prohibited violence against the Jews, he buttressed his insistence on Jewish safety with imagery from Psalms that highlights the
Jew as enemy.[11] In fact, Bernard's negative imagery proceeds beyond
this traditional motif in a new direction. In the same letters he also
makes gratuitous reference to Christian usurers who "jew worse than
the Jews themselves" (*peius judaizare*), suggesting that, for Bernard,
usury was synonymous with Jews.[12] At a later point, we shall explore
the addition of this new theme to the traditional panoply of anti-Jewish
perceptions. For the moment, Bernard reinforces our sense of a significant shift in Jewish economic enterprise.

Our fourth and last testimony comes from a letter written in the
aftermath of an incident in Blois in 1171. In the wake of proceedings
that involved recourse to outdated procedures of judicial appeal and
the execution of more than thirty Jews, Jewish leadership in northern
France embarked on a vigorous effort at self-protection. One line of activity involved negotiations concerning the Jews of Blois themselves,
specifically burial for the martyrs, freedom for Jews who had been im-
prisoned, and permission to return to Judaism for youngsters who had
been forcibly converted. While the first goal does not seem to have
been achieved, the other two were. The Jewish negotiator, writing of
his successes, makes the following observations: "All the captives went
forth from the control of the wicked one [Count Theobald] with their
clothing and no more. For he confiscated all their possessions—debts
and funds."[13] Off-handed identification of meaningful Jewish possessions as "debts and funds" again suggests a new focus in Jewish economic activity.

The congruence in the perceptions of these four sources is striking.
Four observers, representing varied perspectives and assessing Jewish
usury in diverse ways, agree in suggesting the centrality of moneylending to the Jewish economy in northern France. While this consensus
is impressive, we must check these mid-twelfth-century perceptions

against independent data. Do these data in fact suggest that money-lending had become by the second half of the twelfth century the back-bone of Jewish economic life? Full evidence to chart Jewish business ac-tivity is of course unavailable. If, however, we proceed from west to east, from the newest settlement of early Ashkenazic Jewry in England to the older centers in France and Germany, we encounter a multitude of sources that point to accelerating Jewish specialization in money-lending.

The best evidence comes from the small and relatively new Jewish settlement in England. Data for Jewish business activities in England are by far the best available for this period, a tribute both to the early development of sophisticated record keeping by the English monarchy and to excellent preservation of these records. These materials have been widely published and extensively analyzed, the most useful studies being those of H. G. Richardson and Robert C. Stacey.[14] In these ma-terials we see lending taking place on varied scales ranging from the modest to the grand, with diverse Jewish lenders making loans to Christians from the bottom to the top of English society. In this multi-faceted lending activity, the royal government, with its ever more so-phisticated bureaucracy, played a central role. In fact, most of the specific information available on Jewish lending comes from the records of the royal bureaucracy, for example, in its confirmation or repudiation of loans. The overwhelming impression from this wide-ranging evi-dence is the significance of Jewish moneylending to the general English economy and the centrality of moneylending to the Jewish economy. What precise percentage of English Jews was involved in moneylending is essentially irrelevant. The crucial point is that moneylending was the mainstay of Jewish economic activity, the means by which the Jewish community as a whole maintained its economic viability and won the political support requisite to its survival.

An interesting perspective on the centrality of moneylending in Jew-ish economic well-being is provided by the careers of some outstand-ingly wealthy English-Jewish financiers of the twelfth and early thir-teenth century. While the activities of a number of these highly successful Jewish bankers are well documented, the most famous was surely Aaron of Lincoln (d. 1186), probably the wealthiest of all. Aaron's agents ranged far and wide in their business activity, and his loans were extended to private individuals, ecclesiastical institutions, the barony, and the crown. The death of Aaron, even with heirs, meant a major windfall to the royal treasury. In addition to Aaron's liquid assets, the king took over debts owed to him. In order to realize the moneys owed to Aaron, a special branch of the Exchequer was created, the *Scaccarium Aaronis*, which labored for years to clarify the obligations still owed to the deceased Jewish moneylender and to realize maximal revenue for the royal treasury.[15] While it is tempting to see Aaron as an anomaly, it is probably wiser to see him as an index of the importance of Jewish lending to Jewish economic life, on the one hand, and to the English economy, on the other. This economic specialization offered considerable opportunity for wealth and power, balanced by serious liabilities.

As broadly indicative of the significance of this Jewish moneylending, let us note the hostility to these business activities revealed by the anti-Jewish violence that broke out in England during the late 1180s and early 1190s.[16] Particularly striking is the fate of York Jewry. The story involved a most unfortunate confusion in communication between the Jews and the royal official who would normally have provided protection, a siege of the Jews of York sequestered in Clifford's Tower, and the eventual surrender by some of the besieged Jews, who expressed a willingness to convert. To this point the story fits a well-established pattern of crusade-related violence. What happened next is unprecedented. The Jews who had declared themselves ready for baptism were slaughtered upon their emergence from the fortification, an act unparalleled during our period. This massacre of Jews prepared to enter the Christian faith clearly indicates the impact of factors other than normal crusading zeal. This extraneous factor is revealed in the next step taken by the rioters, who then made their way to the York cathedral, invaded the basement in which loan documents were kept, and proceeded to destroy the records of indebtedness. This explosion of anti-usury sentiment subsequently resulted in the establishment in England of a more sophisticated system of record keeping, intended to forestall repetition of the violent disruption that had taken place in York.[17]

The story of the York violence leads us in one last direction, and that is the cooperation—perhaps collusion is the better term—between successful Jewish lenders and the royal authorities in England. We have already noted that support of the authorities was vital to the Jewish immigrants who were prepared to make their way into northern Europe. When the shift in economic specialization from commerce to moneylending took place, the authorities came to play a yet more preponderant role in Jewish affairs. Here I must digress for a moment to identify a major distinction in styles of moneylending.

The essential problem in moneylending involves repayment of moneys disbursed by the lender. Repayment is the central anxiety of the creditor. Since funds leave the lender's possession, how can he be assured that sums owed him will be returned? The most primitive technique for securing repayment of a loan is deposition with the lender of objects at least equal in value to the loan and the projected interest. Thus, should payment not be forthcoming, the lender would hold in his possession an object that would substitute for the sum lost. The pawnbroking style of moneylending enabled the creditor to assure himself of repayment of a loan in the most direct manner, with minimal involvement by the authorities. But the advantages of simplicity and self-sufficiency were counterbalanced by certain liabilities. Two disadvantages of the pawnbroking system are particularly noteworthy. First, it is a tedious way of doing business. Physical objects have to change hands, be stored, and then be returned or sold. Mobility, always a desideratum in business affairs, is limited. Moreover, deposition of physical objects restricts the scope of both lending and profit. Rarely were objects of great value available to secure large loans. The significant collateral most commonly available during the Middle Ages, real estate, could not be used for securing loans in pawnbroking style since land could not pass physically into the hands of the lender at the time of the loan. Thus, pawnbroking was ultimately limited to a relatively low level of business, one in which profitability was restricted.

In contrast, there was and is a second system for securing repayment of loans, a system far more flexible and lucrative. The essential innovation involved introduction of real estate into the lending business through governmental participation in the process. If powerful authorities were willing to become party to the lending business and to assure that moneys disbursed would eventually be recouped, then large sums could be lent against the promise of governmental assistance. These authorities would, if necessary, secure for the Jewish creditor possession of land put up as collateral for the obligation. This system could operate only when and where governments emerged that were sufficiently powerful to afford Jewish lenders such assistance and when and where Jewish creditors had sufficient confidence in governmental protection to warrant disbursement of funds against the promise of eventual intervention. Not all authorities were perceived as having the requisite power to buttress this sophisticated lending business. Only strong and effective rulers were so perceived—indeed Jewish lenders were ineluctably attracted to the very strongest political authorities, rulers who could intervene in disputes even with barons and secure their compliance, such figures as the kings of England and France. Where such authorities were available and willing to involve themselves in Jewish financial affairs, then an entirely new level of Jewish business was achieved. This is the kind of moneylending so copiously reflected in the archives of twelfth- and thirteenth-century England.

To be sure, the involvement of political authorities was hardly disinterested. Complex lending arrangements included considerable profit for the Christian partners in this Jewish moneylending business. This new partnership with the political authorities intensified Jewish reliance on them. Now, in addition to depending on rulers for protection from physical violence, Jewish moneylenders were dependent on the selfsame authorities for the success of their business affairs. Potential pitfalls were numerous, and some liabilities in fact rapidly materialized.

While the evidence from England for the centrality of moneylending to Jewish economic life is incontrovertible, it might well be objected that the English situation was anomalous and in no way reflects the realities of Jewish life in the larger and older centers of early Ashkenazic Jewry. Does the evidence for France and Germany sustain the sense of preponderant Jewish involvement in moneylending? The first point to note is that the evidence for reconstructing French- and German-Jewish business activity in the latter half of the twelfth and on into the thirteenth century is minuscule in comparison with the rich records from England. More precisely, French data are meager and German data are almost nonexistent. Nonetheless, our limited sources provide much the same picture already encountered for England, with some modifications.

We have already noted four broad testimonies to the centrality of moneylending among Jews during the middle decades of the twelfth century. All four reflect conditions in France. The German-Jewish Ephraim ben Jacob was explicitly depicting the fate of French Jewry during the Second Crusade; the two Christian observers, Peter Abelard and Bernard of Clairvaux, seem to have been generalizing on the basis of their French experience; the letter written in the aftermath of the

Blois incident clearly shows us northern French circumstances. To these four mid-twelfth-century testimonies, we can add two more, from the early decades of the thirteenth century.

The royal biographer Rigord, in his depiction of the first years of the reign of Philip Augustus, describes in detail the harsh anti-Jewish steps taken by the young monarch.[18] According to Rigord, these draconian measures, which culminated in an expulsion of Jews from the royal domain in 1182, were undertaken by the king in his role as protector of Christian society, a role that Rigord goes to great length to portray by specifying the Jewish misdeeds that purportedly aroused royal ire. The depiction of both royal actions and alleged Jewish crimes focuses on Jewish involvement in the money trade. That involvement and its supposedly harmful consequences loom large in the catalog of Jewish misdeeds, and royal actions centered on eliminating (and profiting from) indebtedness to the Jews. Once more we need not accept the portrait as exact; nonetheless, Rigord clearly saw the Jews as sustaining themselves primarily through moneylending.

Our second source affords a radically different type of evidence, the iconographic depiction of Jews in the earliest extant versions of the lavishly illustrated *Bibles moralisées*. Two such manuscripts have been subjected to rigorous analysis by Sara Lipton, who finds the image of the Jew in the money trade as the dominant iconographic representation. In her words: "The single most common iconographic attribute associated with Jews is the moneybag."[19] The pictorial evidence supplied by these two early thirteenth-century manuscripts supplements nicely the literary testimonies adduced thus far.

In addition to these general impressions of Jews as moneylenders, we have some corroboration in French governmental edicts and treaties from the late twelfth and early thirteenth century. Constant reference to Jewish moneylending in these materials must reflect its importance in the lives of the Jews. A few instances will suffice. From France we have first Robert of Auxerre's description of baronial regulations imposed during the last years of the twelfth century:

For since the lord Fulk [the reforming preacher Fulk of Neuilly] demanded the complete extirpation of sins and the implanting of virtues and utterly abhorred usurers, he detested the Jews in all ways, because many of us were weakened by infinite and heavy usuries. Hence, through his instigation and through the efforts of the bishops, it was brought to pass that half of all debts owed to the Jews were to be repudiated and half were to be paid at decreed terms.[20]

Yet more striking are the arrangements made by King Philip Augustus on readmitting Jews to his domain after the expulsion of the early 1180s. A series of treaties was struck, the purpose of which was to protect in some measure the returning Jews and to protect in greater measure the monarch's investment in these Jews. Let us note one such treaty document.

Let all whom the present letter reaches know that we have conceded that we shall retain in our land none of the Jews of our most beloved and faithful nephew, Theobald count of Troyes, unless with the verbal consent of that count; and that none of our Jews will be permitted to lend money to anyone or to seize anyone or anything in the land of the aforesaid count, unless with the verbal consent of the aforesaid count. The same Count Theobald conceded to us that he will retain none of our Jews in his land, unless with our verbal consent; and that none of his Jews will be permitted to lend money to anyone or to seize anyone or anything in our land, except with our verbal consent.[21]

While this document does not mean that all Jews were moneylenders, moneylending does emerge as the most significant Jewish economic activity. Finally, when we reach evidence that approaches royal legislation concerning the Jews, the important edicts of 1206 and the following three decades, they in fact turn out to be a series of regulations imposed on Jewish moneylending.[22] Again, this does not imply that moneylending was the sole Jewish economic activity; it does indicate, however, the importance of finance in Jewish economic life.

While the picture for the older and larger Jewish community of France is hardly as compelling as for the better documented Jewry of England, it does seem reasonable to conclude, despite the paucity of materials, that a shift took place in northern France as well and that early involvement in trade gave way to growing dependence on moneylending, with all the complex implications of such dependence. By the first decades of the thirteenth century, we begin to find evidence in France for a class of wealthy Jewish bankers, although this evidence is nowhere near as full as that for England.[23] Finally, we must note that the style of moneylending in France was—like that of England—clearly the more sophisticated lending against land that required governmental support, with all the advantages and disadvantages this style of lending entailed.

Let us now turn our attention to Germany, where the transition into moneylending proceeded more slowly and in somewhat different fashion. Here the evidence is scanty. Business records are almost nonexistent; government documentation is exceedingly slim, nowhere near even the limited evidence available for Capetian France; and even literary reflections of Jewish economic activity are sparse. We might begin by recalling Ephraim of Bonn's testimony to the centrality of sophisticated Jewish moneylending for the economy of French Jewry. The tenor of Ephraim's observation—its explanation of the impact on the French Jews of the supposed royal edict absolving crusaders of debts—suggests that his German-Jewish audience was relatively unfamiliar with this style of moneylending. Along the same lines, Ephraim's account of the York massacre shows no awareness of the special character of that particular assault and the role that governmentally sponsored moneylending played in it.[24]

As indicated, there was little governmental regulation of Jewish affairs in twelfth-century Germany. We might note, however, the imperial charter of 1157, extended to the Jews of Worms. Striking in this charter is the absence of the new economic reality discernible farther west. The key stipulations involve trade and money changing, with usury conspicuously absent:

They [the Jews of Worms] may have the free right to exchange silver with anyone, throughout the entire city, except before the minter's house or anywhere else the minters set for exchange. Within the bounds of our kingdom they may travel freely and peacefully in order to carry on their business and trade, to buy, and to sell. No one may exact from them tolls or demand any public or private levy. If a stolen item be found in their possession and if the Jew claims that he bought it, he shall substantiate by an oath according to his law how much he paid and how much he would accept, and he shall return the item to him to whom it belonged.[25]

Reflected here is the earlier economic reality of the eleventh century. While it is possible that an archaic privilege, no longer reflective of current economic realities, might have been ceremonially granted by the emperor, the likelihood of such an arrangement is slim. Much more plausible is the conclusion that in fact economic realities were slower to change in Germany. Differential economic development, with England and France outstripping neighboring Germany, was already well under way by the twelfth century.

Nonetheless, development in Germany did eventually take place, although at a slower pace. To indicate the eventual primacy of moneylending among German Jews, let us have recourse to the well-known charter issued by Duke Frederick of Austria to his Jews in 1244.[26] The entire tone of this document reflects new economic realities. Of the thirty paragraphs that constitute the charter, more than a third (eleven to be precise) have to do with moneylending. Of these, one spells out the legal rate of interest (paragraph no. 30), one addresses lending against landed property (no. 25), and nine deal with deposition of pledges in simple pawnbroking transactions (nos. 2–7, 23, 27, 28). The charter suggests that in mid-thirteenth-century Austria Jews were seriously engaged in moneylending and that in most cases they lent against pawns.

In comparison with the system already in practice in England and France, the Austrian arrangements seem quite primitive. Here too the authorities were solidly ranged on the side of the Jewish lenders—probably for much the same reasons—but the system has simply not proceeded to the level of sophistication encountered farther west. The bulk of the stipulations in the 1244 charter deal with lending secured by deposition of a pawn; only one clause addresses lending against land, and that clause establishes no more than the most abstract support for such transactions. Given the complexity of the bureaucratic arrangements established much earlier in England and France, our sense of the rudimentary nature of these imperial provisions of 1244 is more than justified. The combination of economic backwardness and lag in sophisticated governance combined to leave German Jewry at a more primitive state of economic development.

We have thus far established the sense, all across early Ashkenazic Jewry, of a transition from commerce as the mainstay of Jewish economic life to moneylending as the key to economic viability. This shift took place more rapidly and more completely in the western lands, with the support and collusion of the political authorities. While we can make no accurate survey of Jewish economic well-being during the eleventh through the thirteenth centuries, the move into moneylending seemingly brought the wealth of early Ashkenazic Jewry to its height. Evidence from both England and France of successful Jewish financiers is most impressive, particularly in England. To be sure, not all Jews were wealthy on that scale. Clearly, however, the wealth of Aaron of Lincoln and his peers had to trickle down into the Jewish community at large and enrich that community considerably.[27] The impression of a community increasingly well-off suggests that the shift in enterprise was not forced on the Jews and that the change was not—at least immediately—for the worse. Thus, I have been depicting transition, not deterioration. Yet in the long run this economic shift moved the Jews of northern Europe from one specialization to an even more precarious specialization rather than in the direction of greater diversification. This change thus bore within it the seeds of serious economic problems, which were not long in materializing. In a nutshell, the more precarious business specialization meant that, were governmental support to waver or fail, the foundations of the Jewish economy would be quickly eroded.

Our discussion of the transition from early Ashkenazic specialization in commerce to the more lucrative and more precarious money trade leads to a few brief observations about the relationship of this shift to intensification of the alliance between the Jews and the ruling class. As already noted, the more advanced style of moneylending so obvious in England and France presupposed the active involvement of the authorities. In effect, earlier dependence on the lords of northern Europe for physical safety was now reinforced by Jewish reliance on the same authorities for direct support of moneylending. The links that bound the Jews and their protectors were now doubly intensified: The rulers and the Jews were caught up in a more complicated web of dependencies. Intensification of this relationship brought the Jews more fully into the orbit of authorities that were now far more sophisticated in their approach to governance and in their ability to control and exploit the various forces and groupings over which they ruled.

Once more, the authorities—the stronger party—seem to have concluded that support for Jewish lending would bring general economic benefit to their domains and at the same time would afford considerable immediate revenue for baronial and royal coffers. Thus, Jewish profits seem to have come at a considerable price: yet closer involvement with and dependence on the political authorities, a potentially damaging liability. I have already noted such identification with the ruling class as one of the early anti-Jewish themes in northern Europe. The move into moneylending and resultant intensification of the link with the secular authorities had to deepen the animosity created by a perception of the Jews as lackeys of the ruling class.

Reality-Based Imagery

We have already seen that two of the realistic motifs in anti-Jewish hostility, the sense of the Jews as newcomers and as religious dissidents, are extremely difficult to track in the earliest period of

Jewish settlement in northern Europe. The image of the Jew as new-comer might be expected to have diminished, as Jewish roots in north-ern Europe deepened. Such is suggested by the following interesting passage in Rigord of St. Denis:

At this time, a great multitude of Jews lived in France; it had assembled there over a lengthy prior period from diverse parts of the world, because of the tran-quillity and liberality of the French. The Jews had heard of the vigor of the kings of the French against their enemies and their great scrupulousness toward their subjects. Therefore, their elders and experts wise in the laws of Moses, who were called by the Jews *didascali* [teachers], decided to come to Paris.[28]

An interesting passage. On the one hand, Rigord still evokes recollec-tion of the Jews as onetime immigrants; at the same time, he acknowl-edges the length of their stay in northern France. Overall, we are prob-ably justified in hypothesizing that the negative stereotype of the Jew as newcomer receded somewhat with the passage of time but that it by no means disappeared.

It is widely agreed that the twelfth century saw marked intensifica-tion of religious identity in both the Christian majority and the Jewish minority in northern Europe. On the majority side the Roman Cath-olic church improved its organizational structure and committed itself to more effective promulgation of its teachings throughout every stra-tum of Christian society. In the view of many scholars the First Crusade represents, above all else, an initial outburst of popular religiosity in western Christendom. Expressions of intense religious sentiment on every level of Christian society proliferated during the course of the twelfth century.[29] Similar tendencies are observable within the Jewish minority. Here too the First Crusade shows an outburst of religious enthusiasm as profound as that manifested by the Christian crusaders. Jews responded to the crusader assaults with violent repudiation of Christianity and its imagery. Jews subjected to forcible conversion publicly denounced Christianity and damned its beliefs and symbols. Rather than submit to forced conversion, many Jews took up arms and slaughtered themselves and their kin. The religious and intellectual cre-ativity noted earlier manifests, in more tranquil terms, the same in-tensification of Jewish identity.[30] Given both the enhanced sense of Christian identity within the majority and the augmented commitment to Jewish identity among the minority, perceptions of Jews as dissidents probably deepened during the twelfth century.

Similarly, the remaining two realistic motifs—harmful Jewish economic activity and Jewish alliance with the authorities—show signs of intensification. To be sure, these motifs are obviously intertwined. Jewish economic activity and Jewish alliance with the authorities were intimately linked to one another, as we have seen, and were so perceived in popular imagery concerning the Jews. Despite this intertwining, I shall examine each theme independently, acknowledging all the while the web of connections linking them.[31]

The shift in Jewish economic activity in northern Europe from commerce to moneylending seems to have resulted in considerable Jewish economic advantage, balanced by substantial liabilities. One liability was the promotion of popular hostility, which can be explained in a number of ways. The simplest explanation is the normal human propensity to resent repayment of borrowed sums. We should be careful not to overstate this natural inclination. The excellent research of Joseph Shatzmiller has shown us that moneylenders were on occasion appreciated for their human qualities and for the assistance they provided. In general, however, pressures associated with indebtedness and the pain associated with repayment of loans tend to transform moneylending into one of the least sympathetic human professions.[32]

To this normal human negative reaction to moneylending and the moneylender, we can add at least two more explanations for popular anti-Jewish attitudes. The first derives from ecclesiastical censure of moneylending and the exemption of Jews from that censure. As noted, moneylending, or more accurately the charging or paying of usury, was increasingly viewed by the medieval church and by medieval society as a serious sin and crime. Jews were exempted in clearly articulated fashion from the prohibition of taking or giving usury by the projection of Christians and Jews as estranged from one another. Since Deuteronomy 23:20–21 prohibited lending at interest among brethren or fellow countrymen but permitted such lending to the stranger, permission for Jewish usury was in fact rooted in the technical definition of Jews as "strangers," distanced from their Christian neighbors. Those aware of the legitimate basis for Jewish involvement in usury surely absorbed a negative picture of the Jewish "other."[33] I probably should not overstate the significance of this rather intellectualized rationalization for Jewish pursuit of usury. For many medieval Christians were oblivious to the justification for Jewish moneylending and thus the more normal reaction of common folk would have been to condemn Jewish usury along with Christian usury. Particularly during the latter decades of the twelfth century, when the ecclesiastical campaign against Christian usury reached its zenith, popular revulsion for an activity viewed by the church as a sin probably stigmatized the Jews as well. To put these two possible Christian reactions together: either there was understanding of the special circumstances of the Jews, in which case the perception of Jewish otherness was exacerbated, or there was no real appreciation for these special circumstances, in which case Jews would simply be seen as perpetrating one of the major crimes on the societal scene.

Finally, we should note that scholars such as Lester K. Little and even more strongly Jacques Le Goff project medieval usury as involving "the labor pains of capitalism." According to Le Goff, "The sudden eruption and spread of the monetary economy threatened old Christian values. Capitalism, a new economic system, was ready to take shape. If it did not require new technology to get started, it at least made wholesale use of practices that had always been condemned by the church."[34] Neither for the first time in their history nor for the last, Jews—in part because of their general marginality—strongly identified with the new order, thereby attracting the animosity of those committed to the old order and profoundly resentful of the new. The hostility aroused by Jewish usury was multifaceted and intense.

A variety of sources from the late twelfth and early thirteenth century regularly present the image of the deceitful Jewish moneylender inflicting harm on society. Let us note an important letter written in 1208 by the powerful pope Innocent III to the count of Nevers. Innocent III, so central to expansion of papal power, was deeply affected by his schooling experience in Paris and his attitudes clearly reflect some of the major anti-Jewish themes generated during the second half of the twelfth century across northern Europe.[35]

It has been reported to us that certain princes do not have their eye upon the Lord, before whom all things lie exposed and obvious. Since it is unseemly for them to exact usury, they receive Jews into their villages and towns, so that they [the princes] appoint them [the Jews] their agents for the collection of usury, since they [the Jews] are not afraid to afflict the churches of God and oppress the poor of Christ. Moreover, when Christians who had taken a loan from the Jews have paid them back the principal and more besides, the appointees and servants [the Jews] of those authorities [the Christian princes], after seizing the pledges and casting these Christians into prison, compel them to pay most exorbitant usury. Thus are widows and orphans robbed of their inheritance, and churches defrauded of their tithes and other traditional subventions. For the

Jews retain seized castles and villas and utterly refuse to reply to the prelates of the churches concerning parochial law.[36]

This is a striking litany of complaint. Far from a careful legal brief, the letter is rather an inflammatory indictment of Jewish moneylenders and their baronial protectors.

Innocent III begins by casting aspersions in a general way on Jewish moneylending. While he was certainly aware of the Jewish right to usury, by beginning his letter with reference to the shamefulness of Christian usury the pope raises some sense of stigma associated with Jewish pursuit of such activity. More pointedly, he delineates a set of alleged Jewish misdeeds: demands for repayment after repayment had already taken place,[37] illicit seizure of pledges and imprisonment of debtors, refusal to pay the normal dues owed for properties seized from Christian debtors. The result, according to the pope, was inordinate harm inflicted on Christian society: Widows and orphans were robbed of their inheritance and churches were deprived of moneys legitimately theirs. The portrait is consistent and distressing. Through their money-lending Jews cause extensive damage to the Christian society that hosts them. On the one hand, traditional imagery of Jewish enmity toward Christians surely played some role in the elaboration of these charges. On the other, normal disdain for the moneylender and his activities clearly reinforced stereotypes of Jewish enmity.

A slightly earlier letter from the same pope to King Philip Augustus of France repeats the twin accusations of Jewish misdeed and Christian suffering.

Know then that news has reached us that in the French kingdom the Jews have become so insolent that by means of their vicious usury, through which they extort not only usury but even usury on usury, they appropriate ecclesiastical goods and Christian possessions. Thus seems to be fulfilled among Christians that which the prophet deplored with respect to Jews, saying: "Our heritage has been turned over to strangers, our houses to outsiders."[38]

Innocent III's complaints about Jewish moneylending are again expressed forcefully. They involve in part reforms for which the church successfully agitated: prohibition of compounded interest, of appropriation of ecclesiastical goods, of distraint of Christian property. Beyond his specific complaints, which in fact the church acted on over time, the pope purveyed a broader image of the harm inflicted by these Jewish moneylenders, in this case the general accusation that they were taking over the Christian patrimony. This exaggerated specter could and did raise considerable fear—in all likelihood exaggerated—of Jewish lending and its impact.[39]

Some of the early animosity toward northern European Jewry was clearly occasioned by perception of the Jews as bound in tight alliance with the ruling authorities, at the expense of other elements in majority society. Particularly significant was burgher resentment of Jewish ties with those external forces at whose expense the urban municipalities were attempting to expand their powers. As the link between the Jews and their lords grew, so did popular resentment. The Jews of the late twelfth and early thirteenth century were more fully bound to the centralized authorities than they had ever been before, and they were among the most clearly subservient elements in society. For those chafing at limitations imposed by increasingly powerful rulers, the Jews, allies of those authorities, earned even greater resentment.

Not surprisingly, anti-Jewish hostility and violence came to be regularly associated with antigovernment sentiment. The case was particularly extreme in England, where foreign barons had invaded and conquered. The Norman newcomers had brought in their wake foreign Jewish allies whom they had supported extensively. With the Jewish move into moneylending, the alliance between the monarchy and the Jews became yet more obvious and intense. Successful and useful Jewish moneylending could simply not be carried on without the vigorous involvement of the royal bureaucracy. The research of H. G. Richardson has suggested convincingly that this Jewish lending had considerable economic and social impact on English society, in particular by facilitating transfer of lands from unsuccessful magnates to the new and more effective possessors of funds.[40] This process, in all likelihood beneficial for English society as a whole, was of course exceedingly painful for those whose failures were magnified by growing indebtedness. Thus, the violence perpetrated against the Jews of England during the late 1180s and early 1190s was clearly and correctly perceived by the English rulers as an assault on royal authority itself. In a vicious cycle, the Jews were resented and attacked for their close ties to the authorities; the authorities intervened vigorously to protect "their" Jews; the negative perception of a royal-Jewish alliance was thereby reinforced. The impact on the negative image of the Jewish minority had to be considerable.

The above-cited complaint of Pope Innocent III, from the year

1208, articulates this sense of anger at the alliance binding Jews to their baronial lords. The pope paints a picture of a remarkably harmful collaboration: "Since it is unseemly for them [the rulers] to exact usury, they receive Jews into their villages and towns, so that they [the rulers] appoint them [the Jews] their agents for the collection of usury." The Jews in effect do the dirty work of Christian princes. We might recall the more neutral observation of Rigord of St. Denis that the Jews had been attracted to northern France because of the excellent reputation of the kings of France. It seems fair to conclude that the augmented alliance between the Jews and their royal and baronial protectors did in fact result in enhanced animosity toward that alliance, an animosity that tended—not surprisingly—to vent itself on the weaker partner.

Real changes in Jewish life thus entailed a deleterious alteration of prior and broadly negative imagery of early Ashkenazic Jewry. Had these changes in circumstance and alterations in imagery been the only developments of the middle decades of the twelfth century, early Ashkenazic Jewry would surely have fared much better than it did. But we have already noted that in its earliest phase this young Jewry was stigmatized more by traditional Christian imagery of the Jew as enemy than by reality-grounded perceptions. Unfortunately for the early Ashkenazic Jews—and for their successors as well—the image of the Jew as enemy underwent significant intensification in its own right.

3

Intensified Perceptions
of Jewish Enmity:
Diverse Testimonies

During the middle decades of the twelfth century, the shift in Jewish economic activity and the deepening of group identity within the Christian majority and the Jewish minority combined to strengthen prior perceptions of the Jews of northern Europe as economically and politically harmful and as religiously and culturally dissident. In some measure, these changes in reality and perception reinforced the traditional Christian sense of the Jew as enemy; at the same time, independent developments, rooted largely in the group psyche of majority society, intensified the traditional Christian sense of Jewish enmity. This heightened sense of Jewish hostility can be discerned at every level of society, from the lowest to the highest. We shall begin our study of this intensified perception of the menace of Jews by examining a few representative testimonies from the mid-twelfth through the early thirteenth century, drawn from both the Christian majority and the Jewish minority.

A Paradigmatic Pair:
Bernard of Clairvaux and Peter the Venerable

Two spiritual giants of the twelfth century, Bernard of Clairvaux and Peter the Venerable, provide fascinating evidence for intensification of the image of the Jew as enemy. By opening my investigation of altered perceptions of Jews with these two great figures I by no means intend to suggest change that took place only at the highest levels of society and filtered downward. I begin with these two important churchmen because they offer us a convenient and striking introduction to the change in peception we wish to track.[1]

Bernard of Clairvaux (d. 1153) was profoundly aware of the potential of crusading zeal to develop into anti-Jewish aggression and he has been widely recognized as a major force in obviating such violence during the Second Crusade. The most eloquent statement of his role in saving Jews from repetition of the bloody 1096 assaults appears in a work by a Jewish contemporary, Ephraim ben Jacob of Bonn. In this broad account of the events of 1146–1147, written some time after the incidents themselves, Ephraim pays full tribute to the abbot of Clairvaux. While well aware of successful intervention by the secular authorities and of prescient steps taken by the Jews themselves, Ephraim focuses on Bernard, identifying the specifics of Bernard's argument against violence and emphasizing the disinterested quality of Bernard's intervention. Ephraim's praise for the abbot of Clairvaux is enthusiastic and unstinting.[2]

Ephraim of Bonn's positive portrait of Bernard, however, has been altered considerably in modern scholarship. Bernard's views of Jews have been most fully explored by the historian David Berger, who while acknowledging Bernard's protective stance during the crisis period of 1146–1147, argues that a close look at Bernard's writings shows harsh condemnation of the Jews, with heavy emphasis on the traditional theme of Jewish enmity:

A general appraisal of Bernard's actions during the Second Crusade and the reasons he gives for them together with an examination of his anti-Jewish sermons and letters and his role in the Anacletus schism leads to the conclusion that he was an unusually strong opponent of the destruction of Jews, yet an equally strong spokesman for anti-Jewish stereotypes and prejudices. . . . Bernard himself was not led to violence by his prejudices, but the hatred which he preached was fanning the flames of violence in lesser men. The great Christian protector of twelfth-century Jewry sowed seeds which would claim the life of many a Jewish martyr.[3]

While the section of Bernard's crusade letter that relates to the Jews has been widely quoted, it merits scrutiny because it affords us a broad introduction to the range and complexity of Bernard's thinking on the

Jews. Bernard was a master of careful formulation, and this argument too shows all the sophistication of thought and style for which he is renowned. This crucial statement on the Jews constitutes the closing element in Bernard's broad missive of exhortation to the crusade. After his moving appeal to the warriors of western Christendom to join the holy undertaking, Bernard concludes by noting a danger associated with the enterprise, the danger of untoward anti-Jewish violence.

Bernard begins his famous letter with a frightening depiction of the actions of the Muslim enemy, portrayed as devastating the Holy Land and threatening Jerusalem itself. Bernard treats this appalling disaster as a divinely appointed occasion for pardon and glory: "I call blessed the generation that can seize an opportunity of such rich indulgence as this, blessed to be alive in this year of jubilee, this year of God's choice. The blessing is spread throughout the whole world, and all the world is flocking to receive this badge of immortality."[4] The Christian warriors to whom Bernard addresses the letter are known for their vigor of arms but have wasted much of their valor on internecine strife. Now they must turn their courage and strength in a divinely ordained direction. If they do so, their rewards will be immeasurable.

At this juncture the Jews are introduced, in an essentially protective context. The warrior caste of western Christendom has been lauded and has been invited to take up its arms in a sacred mission. The vigor and enthusiasm of those committed to the crusade is, for Bernard, wondrous and praiseworthy. There is, however, a danger: "We have heard with great joy that the zeal of God burns within you. But it is necessary in all things that the restraint of knowledge not be absent." The enthusiastic commitment of the crusading warriors might lead to misplaced aggression. While Bernard does not make specific reference to the attacks of 1096 or the brewing agitation of 1146, these clearly aroused his insistence on the restraint of knowledge.

He spells out unequivocally the precise demands of restraint of knowledge: "The Jews are not to be persecuted, killed, or even put to flight." We might, at this point, recall the rationale that underlay the slaughter of Jews in 1096 and the agitation to anti-Jewish action in 1146. The argument of some crusaders was that Jews are Christendom's worst enemy and that, as such, they should be the first objects of Christian wrath. Bernard's unequivocal prohibition of anti-Jewish violence rejects categorically the second half of this argument: The Jews are not to be the first objects—or the objects at all—of Christian

wrath. Why not? In responding to the grounds for violence against
Jews in 1096 and 1146, Bernard does not, at least at the outset, contest
the notion of Jewish malevolence. Indeed, he accepts it in a striking
way, as we shall shortly see. Historic Jewish enmity was highlighted by
the crusaders of 1096, by the Cistercian monk Ralph who agitated for
attack on Jews in 1146, and by Bernard himself. The shared sense of
Jewish enmity, however, has divergent implications. For the crusaders
of 1096 and for the monk Ralph, Jewish enmity justified bloodshed,
but for Bernard historic Jewish hostility could not be met with violence, primarily because Scripture overtly prohibited such persecution.
God outlawed violence because he had another plan. Bernard cites
Psalm 59 at considerable length in order to lay bare this divine plan.

Before following Bernard's careful explication from Psalm 59 of the
divine plan, let us pause for a moment to consider the setting of the
psalm and its broadest meaning. Psalm 59 depicts the protagonist as
surrounded by enemies but secure in God's protection. The tone of the
psalm is set in its opening verses:

> Save me from my enemies, O my God;
>   secure me against my assailants.
> Save me from evildoers;
>   deliver me from murderers.
> For see, they lie in wait for me;
>   fierce men plot against me
>   for no offense of mine,
>   for no transgression, O Lord;
>   for no guilt of mine
>   do they rush to array themselves against me.

Thus, by making Psalm 59 the initial basis for his prohibition of anti-
Jewish violence, Bernard—far from challenging the prevailing notion
of Jewish enmity—in fact buttressed that sense of hostility considerably. As had been claimed in 1096, the Jews were an implacable enemy,
a foe that had murdered, plotting groundlessly against a guiltless figure. For Christian readers attuned to the intertextual message of
Bernard's letter, this perception of Jewish malignancy was powerfully
reinforced by the source he chose as the starting point for his insistence
on nonviolence.

If Jews were in fact the enemy portrayed in Psalm 59, why then were
the crusaders of 1096 wrong in the bloody conclusion they drew from
their sense of Jewish hostility? For Bernard the answer lies in a careful

reading of Psalm 59 against the backdrop of traditional ecclesiastical doctrine concerning the Jews. The critical verse for Bernard, as for others, was 59:12: "Do not kill them lest my people be unmindful." God, whose mysterious ways Bernard had emphasized in the opening sections of his letter, might well have called for swift and direct revenge against the foe portrayed in the psalm. But he did not, preferring instead a more protracted punishment with pedagogic implications. Bernard, basing himself on the complete verse, spells out God's message in the psalm in the following terms: "They [the Jews] are for us living words, for they remind us always of the divine passion. They are dispersed into all areas so that, while they suffer the appropriate punishment for such a crime, they are everywhere the witnesses of our redemption." This doctrine is, of course, not original with Bernard. What is striking, however, is his utilization of this doctrine in precisely the circumstances described. Faced with the danger of yet another crusader slaughter of Jews, Bernard accepted and reinforced the traditional teaching of Jewish enmity, while arguing that God, who had provided unusual opportunities for Christian heroism and reward through the victories of the Muslims, had devised a special punishment for the Jews, which must not be altered through inappropriate human actions.

Had he stopped at this point, Bernard would have made an effective case for peaceful treatment of the Jews. He chose not to stop there, however, perhaps out of a perceived need to buttress his case in the face of excessive zeal, perhaps out of a desire to reflect some of the traditional complexity of church thinking vis-à-vis the Jews. Continuing his exegesis of Psalm 59, Bernard sets out a second argument against anti-Jewish violence, a rationale that maintains the essential framework of Jewish enmity while mitigating some of the harshness associated with the humiliating divine punishment. Bernard argues that the same psalm speaks of this enemy eventually, despite his potent hatred, returning at evening, which means for Bernard "a reconsideration on their part." This too was an element in the complex divine plan. If one component of that plan was to prove the truth of Christianity through Jewish subjugation and suffering, another was to show humanity the endless bounty of divine love, which had a place for even the worst of enemies. This eventual reconsideration, conversion, and salvation would be precluded by slaughter; therefore anti-Jewish violence was forbidden.

At this juncture in his complicated argument, Bernard abandons his biblical text, Psalm 59, and adduces a reasonable consideration. This shift in tack shows his feel for the emotions of his audience. Having begun by arguing that zeal might well lead Christians astray, Bernard opposes to that zeal the clear and unequivocal stipulation of God's word—Jews were not to be persecuted. Such a divine injunction brooked no objection. Here was God's command and plan. Having highlighted an unarguable divine injunction that in fact acknowledged the crusader sense of Jewish antipathy, Bernard proceeded to a somewhat softer scriptural argument and then—anticipating diminishing passions in his audience—proceeded from the biblically grounded case for eventual Jewish reconsideration to a similar argument from reason, an argument quite important for our purposes: "If the pagans were similarly subjugated to us, then, in my opinion, we should wait for them rather than seek them out with swords. But as they have now begun to attack us, it is necessary for those of us who carry a sword purposefully to repel them with force." Jewish subjugation, however, is for Bernard a fact. And this brute reality requires appropriate Christian restraint. While this argument would not have made a good opening position, given the passions Bernard was seeking to quell, it follows nicely from his previous point.

In his ever more positive case for the physical safety of the Jews, Bernard closes with an appeal that tempers some of the sense of Jewish enmity with which he began. While at the outset Bernard seemed to accept the crusader view of Jews as the profoundest enemies of Christendom, by the end of his case he is pleading for the special positive status of the Jews. Were Muslims to live peacefully under Christian rule, they too would be spared attack; this restraint is all the more appropriate "for those from whom we have a law and a promise, from whom we have our forefathers, and from whom we have Christ of the flesh." In a remarkable way Bernard has now diluted the sense of the Jews as the profoundest enemies of Christianity, the sense with which he first argued for their safety.[5]

A few closing observations with respect to Bernard. The complexity of Bernard's thought and style are both manifested in this analysis. One could ask if the movement from a harsh foundation for Jewish security to a more sympathetic rationale isn't a reflection of Bernard's truest feelings, the harshness simply being a way of winning over hostile readers and listeners. I would not go quite so far, given the thrust of the Berger study. Let it suffice to note the complexity of Bernard's thinking without aspiring to more.

With Peter the Venerable (d. 1156) we enter a new arena. For Peter, caught up in battling a variety of enemies of the Christian faith, Jews were yet more important. There is widespread agreement that Peter represents a significant watershed in polemical argumentation against the Jews, and his importance in this sphere has occasioned numerous studies. Alongside the study of Peter's polemics has come attention to his broad view of Jews, capped by a recent and valuable analysis by the French scholar Jean-Pierre Torrell, whose collaborative study of Peter the Venerable is the fullest yet available.[6]

Our focus will remain Peter's overall perception of Jews, seen in the context of crusader thinking and the complex views of Bernard of Clairvaux. Peter clearly shared the popular sense of the Jews as enemies, admitting little of the moderation discernible in Bernard. Expressions of Peter's perception of Jewish enmity abound. The Torrell study suggests that three texts are key to an analysis of Peter the Venerable and the Jews: Peter's depiction of an episode in the life of Matthew of Albano in his *De miraculis*, Peter's polemical work *Adversus Iudeorum inveteratam duritiem*, and Peter's letter to King Louis VII concerning the Second Crusade. In each of these works, we find harsh indictment of Jews.

As numerous analysts have noted, Peter's polemical tract against the Jews is unusually sharp in tone. Torrell notes three themes in Peter's excoriation of the Jews: (1) the repetition of traditional biblical reproaches of Jewish blindness and stubbornness; (2) the use of animal imagery, much of which can similarly be traced to biblical antecedents; (3) the use of broad expressions of contempt for Jews as philistine, blaspheming, satanic. Given our concern with the eleventh- and twelfth-century imagery of Jewish enmity, we might note that in Peter's tract there is recurrent reference to this theme, very much along the lines that we encountered in Bernard of Clairvaux, although without Bernard's complication of the stereotype. Like Bernard, Peter accepts the notion of the Jews as the worst of enemies: "Who would restrain the hands of our people from your blood, but for the commandment of Scriptures?"[7] The commandment of Scripture is once more that drawn from Psalm 59. Again, the crusader premise is accepted, with rejection of its behavioral implication. While slaughter of such enemies might make human sense, God ordered otherwise.

The story of Matthew of Albano adds a further twist to the enmity theme. According to Peter, Matthew, on taking responsibility for the

administration of Saint-Martin-des-Champs, learned that the priory
was heavily in debt to certain Jewish creditors. He ordered that these
debts be immediately discharged and that commercial contacts with
Jews henceforth be avoided. When the monks argued the necessity for
borrowing from Jews, Matthew responded vehemently:

With what countenance, with what conscience can I approach the altar of
Christ the savior, with what countenance can I attempt to speak with his sweet
mother, while I have pandered to their blaspheming enemies? How can I please
them if I become a friend to their worst enemies? How can I dare invoke them
or beseech them with the same mouth with which I have flattered their enemies, with respect to monetary affairs or anything else? [8]

Here the notion of the Jew as enemy takes a more foreboding turn.
While in no way condoning violence, Peter's laudatory depiction of
Matthew's actions suggests that the Jewish enemy should be isolated,
by monks at least. Had this line of behavior become normative, Jewish
circumstances would have become untenable. In this source we see re-
inforcement of the traditional malevolent stereotype of Jews with the
newer image of the Jewish moneylender. Matthew's story offers us a
striking proof of the potential dangers for Jewish imagery in the mid-
twelfth-century shift into the money trade. Negative images reinforcing
each other—in this case the traditional stereotype of the Jewish enemy
and the newer perception of the Jewish usurer—are especially potent.

The most interesting and revealing of the three sources for our purposes is Peter's letter to King Louis VII of France. Like Bernard, Peter
was fully cognizant of the crusading rationales of 1096, accepted the
imagery of Jewish enmity, yet repudiated violence against Jews. Despite
these parallels, what most impresses us is the contrast between the two
great abbots. The differences between them begin with the very place
of the Jews in these two well-known letters. As we have seen, Bernard's
letter was intended to rally the warrior class of western Christendom to
the new crusade; the Jewish issue was added at the end of the missive,
in order to forestall anti-Jewish violence. Peter's letter to King Louis
VII, in contrast, was written in order to move his monarch to appropriate anti-Jewish actions. While he too speaks of the importance of the
crusade and the glory of crusading, his essential purpose was to arouse
the king of France to take what Peter saw as requisite action against his
Jewish clients. Bernard adds the issue of the Jews as a protective after-
thought; Peter's letter was generated by his anger over the Jews and his

commitment to seeing them properly punished in a way that would provide support for the crusade.

The intensity of Peter's anti-Jewish animus is best appreciated by citing the central portion of his letter in its entirety. After speaking in praise of the crusading venture, the abbot raises a distressing question:

But what value in pursuing and attacking the enemies of the Christian faith in remote and distant lands, while the Jews, wretched blasphemers far worse than the Saracens, not far away from us but in our midst so freely and audaciously blaspheme, abuse, and trample on Christ and the Christian sacraments with impunity? In what way does the zeal of God consume the sons of God, if the Jews, the worst enemies of Christ and Christians, thus escape utterly unaffected? Indeed, has the mind of the king of the Christians forgotten that which was formerly said by a certain saintly king of the Jews? "O Lord, you know that I hate those who hate you and loathe your foes. I hate them with total hatred." The Saracens are to be detested, although they believe like us that Christ was born of a virgin and agree with us on many matters concerning him, because they deny that he is God and the son of God, which is more important, and deny his death and resurrection, in which the totality of our salvation lies. Thus, how much more are the Jews to be despised and hated, who, believing nothing concerning Christ and the Christian faith, reject, blaspheme, and deride that virgin birth and all the sacraments of human salvation.

I do not say these things so that I might sharpen the royal or Christian sword against the necks of these execrable [Jews]; since I bear in mind that it is said concerning them in the divine psalm, with the prophet saying the following in the spirit of God: "God will show me victorious over my enemies. Do not kill them lest my people be unmindful." Indeed, God does not wish that they be killed or destroyed entirely; rather, for the purpose of greater torment and ignominy, [he wishes that] they be preserved for a life worse than death. Cain, after the spilling of fraternal blood, said to God: "Anyone who finds me will kill me." It was said to him: "God does not say, as you think, that you shall die; rather, you shall be a sufferer and a wanderer upon the earth, which opened its mouth to accept the blood of your brother from your hand." Thus did the most just severity of God enact concerning the damned and damnable Jews from that time of the passion and death of Christ, and so shall be done through the end of the present world order. Since they spilled the blood of Christ—their brother in the flesh—they are enslaved, afflicted, anxious, suffering, and wanderers on the earth, until, according to the prophet, the miserable remnants of this people, when the fullness of the nations is realized, will be converted to God. Then, according to the Apostle, "All Israel will be saved."[9]

Peter the Venerable's lengthy and unmitigated excoriation of the Jews stands in marked contrast to the briefer, more restrained, and more nuanced statement by Bernard. While both see the Jews as the

enemies of Christ, Bernard's formulation is modest; Peter by contrast
expands relentlessly on Jewish malevolence. In his view the Jews are
clearly far worse than the Muslims, indeed the very worst enemies of
Christianity and Christendom. Peter embellishes Jewish guilt for the
Crucifixion with the potent imagery of the fratrical Cain and the punishment called down upon him. Jewish malignity is associated with and
projected back into the very beginnings of human history.[10]

More striking yet is Peter's assessment of contemporary Jewish behavior. Bernard, while accepting and reinforcing the traditional notion
of Jewish enmity, portrayed contemporary Jews as inherently hostile
but in actuality quite docile; according to Bernard, the Jews—living in
peaceful submission to Christian rule—should be left to live in their
state of subjugation. This is far from Peter's view. For Peter the Jews are
not in fact living in peaceful submission but daily express their enmity
in acts of blasphemy and abuse and they must surely be punished, albeit
not through physical violence. Indeed, it is yet more illuminating to
compare and contrast this stance on the part of Peter with the 1096 rationale for crusader aggression. Peter's hostility goes beyond even that
of 1096, while still rejecting violence. As we recall, the 1096 rationale
simply posited the Jews as hostile enemies because of their role in the
Crucifixion. Peter does more. He sees the Jews of his own age as maintaining the hostility of their ancestors in concrete ways. For Peter not
only did Jews a millennium earlier call for Jesus's crucifixion but the
Jews of his own day and age continued to "blaspheme, abuse, and
trample on Christ and the Christian sacraments," to "reject, blaspheme, and deride that virgin birth and all the sacraments of human
salvation." Historic hostility has here been transposed into contemporary enmity, not by simple attribution of past guilt to a present generation but rather through accusation of ongoing, unremitting Jewish
hatred.

Peter agreed with Bernard in prohibiting anti-Jewish violence. The
essential thrust of his letter, however, was to argue to King Louis VII
that the Jews should not be untouched by the crusading enterprise,
that they ought to contribute materially to the success of the great undertaking. In effect, he proposed that Jewish ill-gotten financial gains
be forcibly contributed to the crusade. In consonance with his portrait
of ongoing Jewish blasphemy and contempt, Peter's complaints about
Jewish economic life focus on the exploitation of business activities as
vehicles for abuse and blasphemy. The central complaint in Peter's let-

ter to King Louis VII involves the accusation that Jews receive stolen ecclesiastical vessels and vent their hatred upon them.

He [the thief] hands over the vessels of Christ's body and blood to those who killed him and spilled Christ's blood, who heaped contumely and injury upon him when he was among the living to the extent that they could and who now, as he is seated in the glory of eternal divinity, do not cease wounding him with verbal blasphemies to the extent that they dare. The sacred vessels, held captive among them as I have indicated, as in olden times [other sacred vessels were held captive] among the Chaldeans, suffer shame, even though they are inanimate. Indeed, Christ feels the Jewish abuse of these insensate vessels sacred to him.

To be sure, Peter's proposal is restricted to economic measures: Because of the ill-gotten nature of their gains, Jews should be forced to contribute heavily to the upcoming crusade. Yet the underlying issue is surely not economic; the underlying issue is the alleged contemporary Jewish hatred and abuse of Christianity.

Bernard and Peter offer us valuable insight into broad developments on the twelfth-century scene. Perceptions of the Jews as enemies had surely been exacerbated as a result of the crusading movement and the passions it engendered. For some, including the 1096 attackers of the Jews and Bernard of Clairvaux, the sense of Jewish enmity remained largely traditional; for others, here represented by Peter the Venerable, the traditional sense of historic Jewish enmity was transformed into something far more immediate: Jews were perceived as exploiting every opportunity to vent their age-old hatred of Christianity in the contemporary setting. Far from living in peaceful submission, as suggested by Bernard, the Jews Peter described were engaged in acts of clandestine opposition. A central vehicle for the expression of purported Jewish enmity was economic activity. Here, the new Jewish specialization in moneylending combined with the augmented sense of Jewish animosity to reinforce each other. The stereotype of the enemy Jew deepened the mistrust generally felt toward those in the money trade, and the new Jewish economic specialty—never very popular in any case—reinforced the traditional sense of the Jews as hostile. Beyond the sphere of economic activity, Peter's letter reveals a broader sense of the Jews as physically hostile and dangerous, ever ready to vent their wrath on Christianity and its sacred symbols. This pervasive sense of the Jews as hostile in the here and now lay at the core of the deteriorating image of the Jew in northern Europe. This pervasive sense of the Jews as actively

hostile was to enter the mainstream of Western anti-Jewish sentiment and plague Jewry the world over from the twelfth century to the
twentieth.

In the views of Bernard of Clairvaux and Peter the Venerable we see
sharply etched a critical transition in the broad perception of the Jewish
minority in twelfth-century northern Europe, the transition from the
traditional imagery of the historic Jewish enemy to the yet more dangerous stereotype of the contemporary Jewish enemy, bent on expressing his hostility wherever and whenever opportunity might present itself.

Rigord of St. Denis: Biographer of King Philip Augustus of France

Our examination of Bernard of Clairvaux and Peter the
Venerable has revealed a new sense of present-day Jewish hostility toward Christianity and Christians. In order to flesh out the broad and
ill-defined sense of Jewish malevolence expressed by Peter the Venerable, let us look briefly at Rigord of St. Denis's account of the early
years of the distinguished reign of King Philip Augustus. The adroit
young king of France took a number of radical steps against the Jews of
the royal domain during the very first years of his rule.[11] For his biographer Rigord, these anti-Jewish steps were important and laudable.
Rigord, anxious to portray his ruler as "the most Christian king," goes
to considerable lengths to reveal the mind-set of the young monarch
and describes the Jewish misdeeds that inspired the young French sov-
ereign to punish them, as it were, measure for measure.[12] Whether
these alleged misdeeds in fact influenced the thinking of Philip Augustus or were imputed to him by his biographer is for the moment of
no real concern to us. What Rigord provides is a rich and detailed late
twelfth- and early thirteenth-century depiction of the Jews and their
purported crimes.

Rigord begins by describing the royal arrest of the Jews and
confiscation of their goods in 1180. According to Rigord, this action
was undertaken because of royal outrage with Jewish behavior.

He [Philip Augustus] had often heard from the young men who lived with him
in the royal palace and had committed scrupulously to memory that the Jews

who lived in Paris, hidden in underground caverns, each year on Easter day or during the sacred and sad week, murdered a Christian in contempt of the Christian faith, seemingly as a sacrifice. For a long time, they had persisted in the diabolical iniquity of such evil. In the time of his [Philip's] father, they had often been seized and executed by fire. St. Richard, whose body rests in the Church of the Holy Innocents in the Field in Paris, thus murdered and cruci-fied by the Jews, went blessedly in martyrdom to the Lord. Indeed, we have heard that—to the honor of the Lord—many miracles have been accomplished through the prayers and intercessions of St. Richard, at the Lord's doing.[13]

More royal actions were to follow, including the forgiving of Jewish loans, with a fifth part paid to the royal treasury, and the subsequent expulsion of Jews from the royal domain. According to Rigord, both these actions were set in motion by Philip's anger with Jewish lending and the abuses it occasioned. These abuses involved persecution of Christian debtors through distraint or imprisonment, unwarranted accumulation of wealth by the Jews, and "judaizing," that is to say, adopting Jewish behaviors, by Christian servants working in the homes of these well-to-do Jews. Yet more offensive to Rigord (and allegedly to the king) was blasphemous Jewish handling of ecclesiastical objects turned over as pledges. Out of his righteous indignation over these usury-related crimes the monarch eventually expelled his Jews.[14]

Discernible here are the central themes already noted in Peter the Venerable. In the eyes of Rigord, Jews were involved in economic en-terprises that enabled them to vent hatred upon Christian society and Christianity. Usury in and of itself brought harm upon Christians and illegitimate wealth to the Jews. More important yet, through usury Jews gained possession of ecclesiastical objects and expressed their rage by abusing them, a reflection of their underlying hatred of the Chris-tian faith. This same alleged animosity moved Jews to vent their hostil-ity on Christians as well as Christian objects. For Rigord the Jews of his days practiced on their neighbors the murderous acts first undertaken by their ancestors against Jesus. Jews were much more than the descen-dants of Jesus's murderers. For Rigord murder by Jews was a twelfth-century occurrence, and a common one at that.

The Jewish Perspective

A reservation often expressed about research into the twelfth century is that source materials come from only one segment of the Christian populace, those relatively few clerics who were literate. As a result, one can argue, we have today a rather skewed portrait of the Christian majority and its views on a wide range of issues. But this reservation is not in fact completely warranted, for the Jews of twelfth-century northern Europe have left precious sources of their own which enable us to understand developments in the Christian majority from an alternative point of view. One such valuable source, an unusual catalog of actions against Jews, provides a rich set of anti-Jewish images, some standard and some innovative.

The editor of this rich catalog was Ephraim ben Jacob of Bonn, whose chronicle of Jewish fortunes during the Second Crusade has already been cited. In addition to his report on the Second Crusade, Ephraim of Bonn also left us a listing of eleven anti-Jewish incidents, stretching in time from 1171 through 1196.[15] The data presented in this Jewish record afford us yet another perspective on the anti-Jewish imagery current during the second half of the twelfth century, affording us a better sense of the representativeness of observations of individual Christian thinkers and writers such as Bernard of Clairvaux, Peter the Venerable, and Rigord of St. Denis. Let me then simply provide a résumé of the valuable listing compiled by Ephraim of Bonn:

1. An incident at Blois in France, in 1171. In this incident, a Jew was accused of depositing the body of a Christian youngster in the fast-running waters of the Loire river. The accusation fell into a complex political and romantic situation in Blois, where the count—a major figure in northern French political life—was conducting an affair with a Jewish woman. The opponents of this relationship utilized the accusation against the entire Jewish community of Blois. The witness to the alleged deposition of the body was put to the ordeal and when his testimony was seemingly vindicated, more than thirty Jews were condemned to death by burning and were executed. Subsequently, the count was bribed in order to spare the rest of the Jews of his county from any harm.[16]

2. An incident at Boppard in the Rhineland, in 1180. As two ships proceeded down the Rhine river from Cologne to Boppard, the Christian crew on the second discovered the body of a young Christian girl on the river bank. These crew members pursued Jews who had been traveling on the first ship into Boppard and eventually brought them to the river, urged them to baptism,

and—when the Jews refused—drowned them in the Rhine. One of the Jews thus killed was subsequently dragged publicly from town to town, further arousing wide-ranging public hostility toward the Jews. Eventually, the emperor and the archbishop of Cologne were paid to provide protection for the endangered Jews.

3. An incident at London, in 1189. At the crowning of the new king of England, Richard Lion-Heart, a number of Jewish notables mingled with the crowd, arousing considerable animosity. Unbeknownst to the king, this animosity escalated into full-scale rioting, spurred by the false rumor that the king had sanctioned anti-Jewish violence. Approximately thirty Jews were killed, with a smaller number taking their own lives, apparently to avoid baptism.[17]

4. An incident at York, in 1190. Threatened by crusaders preparing to depart for the Third Crusade, the Jews of York congregated in their synagogue. Approximately sixty Jews took their own lives, but others were slaughtered by the crusaders. Ephraim reports the sum total of casualties as one hundred and sixty. The homes of the Jews of York were plundered and destroyed.[18]

5. An incident at Brie-Comte-Robert, in 1192.[19] A Jew was killed by a Christian, who was in some way a vassal or serf of the king of France. The aggrieved Jews approached the countess of Brie and secured the hanging of the murderer, which took place symbolically on the festival of Purim. The enraged king—Philip Augustus—came to Brie-Comte-Robert and executed all Jews of the town over the age of thirteen by burning.[20]

We also possess a report of this incident by the royal biographer Rigord, a report so strikingly different in perception that it is worth detailing as a foil to the Jewish account.[21] According to Rigord, the Jews of Brie-Comte-Robert falsely accused a Christian of theft and murder and bribed the countess to hand the falsely accused Christian over to them. This unfortunate Christian was led by the Jews through the town, hands bound and crowned with thorns. He was subsequently hung from a cross.

6. An incident at Cologne, in 1171.[22] Two Jewish traders who had come to the Cologne fair to pursue their business were unjustly accused of passing counterfeit coins. Through payment of a

substantial bribe, the accused Jews were saved from terrible punishment.

7. Brief and cursory reference to the dangers attendant upon the Third Crusade, with emphasis on the energetic intervention of the emperor Frederick I on behalf of the Jews and the resultant suppression of anti-Jewish violence.[23]

8. An incident at Neuss in the Rhineland, in 1186. A deranged Jew publicly slew a Christian girl, thereby arousing fury against the Jews and resulting in the immediate killing of the guilty Jew and six others and the plundering of their homes. Even this violent retribution did not assuage popular outrage. The corpses of the dead Jews were publicly displayed. A few days later passions had still not subsided. The mother of the deranged killer was buried alive; his uncle was drawn and quartered and publicly displayed; and four Jewesses were forcibly converted. The Jews were fined by the bishop; they subsequently paid to have the corpses cut down and transported for burial in Xanten, farther down the Rhine river. The Jewesses forcibly converted eventually returned to the Jewish fold.

9. An incident in Austria, in 1196. A wealthy and high-ranking Jew, extremely close to the duke of Austria, discovered one of his servants, who had taken the crusading vow, to have stolen from him. Imprisonment of this crusader by the Jew set off a hue and cry on the part of the crusader's wife, resulting in an assault on the wealthy Jew, his death, and the death of some fifteen other Jews as well. The duke, hearing of this violence, executed two of the ringleaders of the assault.

10. An incident at Speyer, in 1196. The body of a Christian youngster was found outside the town of Speyer. This discovery immediately gave rise to the accusation that Jews were responsible for the girl's death. The corpse of a recently deceased Jewess was exhumed and hung naked in the marketplace, with a mouse curled in her hair. The Jewess's father was successful in having the authorities return the girl to her grave. On the morrow the home of the local rabbi was attacked and the rabbi was killed, along with eight other Jews. Jewish houses in Speyer were burned, with the Jews taking refuge in their synagogue. After dark they were secreted out of Speyer and escorted to safety. Duke Otto of Burgundy, in the absence of his brother the em-

peror Henry, took immediate and harsh vengeance on the bishop and burghers of Speyer. When the emperor returned, he fined the malefactors heavily, forwarded the funds to the Jews, and assisted them in rebuilding their homes and synagogue.

11. A second incident at Boppard, this time in 1196, only seven days after the incident in Speyer. This Boppard incident is depicted in cursory fashion, with mention only of the killing of eight Jews, motive unspecified, and the subseqent punishment inflicted once again by Duke Otto and his brother the emperor.

This diverse catalog of incidents provides valuable data on the deteriorating image of the Jews. In this list crusading and the negative stereotypes it evoked still play a central role in stimulating anti-Jewish animosities; economic issues are occasionally mentioned; yet surely the dominant theme is the alleged murder of Christians by Jews, reflecting a sense of the Jews as continuously vindictive and dangerous.

4

Intensified Perceptions of Jewish Enmity: Principal Themes

From the beginning of their sojourn in northern Europe the early Ashkenazic Jews were plagued by the hostility of their Christian neighbors. This animosity was based in part on real characteristics that these early Ashkenazic Jews exhibited: their newness to the area, their uniqueness as the only legitimate religious dissenters, their commercial activities, their alliance with the political authorities. The antipathy was also rooted in traditional imagery that portrayed Jews as the historic enemies of Christianity and Christendom. In the middle decades of the twelfth century the shift in Jewish economic activities from commerce into the money trade earned positive economic results for both the Christian majority and the Jewish minority but had negative implications for the Jewish image in majority society. In addition, during the first half of the twelfth century, the perception of Jews as enemies deepened with a new sense of the Jews' continuing, active hostility to the Christian faith and to the Christian society that hosted them. We must now take a closer look at the principal themes in the Christian majority's increasingly widespread and intense perception of Jewish enmity.

The Jew as Blasphemer and Murderer

Of all the northern European anti-Jewish stereotypes, the one that predominated, both prior and subsequent to the middle of

the twelfth century, was the historic Christian notion of the Jews as enemies of God, the Christian faith, and the Christian community. While
the roots of this perception extend back into the earliest stages of
Christian history, we cannot simply identify the attitude as traditional
and constant.[1] Such conventional themes undergo change, sometimes
losing significance and sometimes growing in importance. Is it possible
to identify such change in the workings of this traditional perception of
the Jews?

As we have seen, the popular crusading assaults on Rhineland Jewry
were predicated on identification of Jews as historic enemies of Christianity and Christendom, indeed as the oldest and profoundest of enemies. This sense led the radical crusading bands to conclude that a
lengthy journey to do battle against the lesser foe, the forces of Islam,
made no sense, that their struggle ought to commence with the immediate enemy who was also the archenemy. During the second half of
the twelfth century, as reflected strikingly in the writings of Peter the
Venerable, the earlier sense of historic Jewish animosity and historic
Jewish crime was transformed into the notion that contemporary Jews
acted out that selfsame hatred for Christianity and Christians. There
developed during this period a conviction that Jews hated Christianity
and their Christian neighbors to the point of doing harm to both the
Christian faith and its practitioners, harm that had no rational motivation. This assumption involved far more than an allegation of historic
hostility; it projected twelfth-century Jews as embittered and aggressive, eager to take action against Christian contemporaries.

The key anti-Jewish theme bequeathed to posterity from the earliest
phase of Christian history was Jewish culpability for the Crucifixion.
Because of the Christian's special conception of Jesus as both divine
and human, Jewish opposition to Christ, culminating purportedly in
his death, constituted a crime both against God and man, against the
Christian faith and the human bearers of that faith. While the implications of this dual affront were not readily drawn until the High Middle
Ages, this understanding of the nature of Christ and of the Jewish
crime against him held the potential for an eventual stereotype of the
Jew as both blasphemer and murderer.[2]

Let us begin with the stereotype of Jewish assault on Christianity and then proceed to the imagery of Jewish violence against Christians. Hatred of the symbols of rival faiths is common in the history of
religions. Such hatred has been pronounced over the long course of

Christian-Jewish relations but was especially notable from both sides during the First Crusade assaults. The enraged crusaders went out of their way to desecrate Jewish symbols, while the beleaguered Jews are regularly portrayed as blaspheming the symbols of Christianity.[3] Indeed, one of the special forms of Jewish martyrdom singled out by Jewish chroniclers of the 1096 events involved Jews who seemingly accepted baptism in order to gather a crowd of Christian onlookers before whom they then publicly denounced Christianity, perishing of course in the process.[4] Even when the special tensions of 1096 had abated and Jewish authors wrote of the Christian attacks and the Jewish responses, they liberally sprinkled their narratives with damning indictments of Christianity and its symbols, indictments intended obviously for Jewish eyes only.[5] These intense expressions of hatred for the symbols of the rival faith might well be explained as resulting from the extraordinary religious exhilaration associated with the First Crusade. Certainly prior to the middle decades of the twelfth century, Christian perceptions of the Jews were not marked by this profound sense of the Jews as regular blasphemers.[6]

What is so striking as we proceed into the middle decades of the twelfth century is the intensified sense of Jewish enmity with a heightened focus on purportedly regular Jewish abuse of Christian symbols. Peter the Venerable highlighted alleged Jewish blasphemy (see above, pp. 47–51). In the story of Matthew of Albano Peter's hero speaks of the Jews as "blaspheming enemies." In his letter to King Louis VII of France, Peter himself speaks of the Jews as "wretched blasphemers" who regularly "blaspheme, abuse, and trample on Christ and the Christian sacraments" and as enemies who "reject, blaspheme, and deride . . . all the sacraments of human salvation." According to Peter, in earlier times the Jews had inflicted their hatred directly on Jesus; in Peter's own day, he believed, they continued to harbor the same contempt and hatred, which they expressed in their verbal abuse of Jesus and his faith and in their physical abuse of objects sacred to him.

Rigord of St. Denis, writing early in the thirteenth century, echoes Peter (see above, pp. 52–53). By Rigord's day the Jews had completed their transition into moneylending and, according to Rigord, ecclesiastical vessels thereby fell into Jewish hands and were scandalously mistreated. According to Rigord, this blasphemy against sacred objects in their possession moved King Philip Augustus to the culminating stage of his early anti-Jewish actions, the expulsion of the Jews from the royal domain. Historic Jewish enmity was thus transformed into clear and present danger.

We have already noted the intertwining of the negative image of Jews in business, and especially of Jews in moneylending, with the traditional perception of the Jew as enemy. Most of the medieval criticisms of Jewish usury focus on the harm that it inflicts on Christians of all classes and on the sacred symbols of Christianity. The new Jewish economic specialty was therefore problematic not only in and of itself but also as yet another vehicle by means of which Jews vented their hatred on unsuspecting Christians and their religion. Christians were harmed by the usurious transactions themselves; Christianity was harmed through Jewish possession of sacred vessels and the abuses to which Jews then subjected these objects.

While this heightened sense of blasphemy surely reflects significant intensification of the imagery of Jewish enmity, yet more striking is the concomitant emergence of the stereotype of the Jews as physically harmful to their Christian neighbors, lying in wait to murder Christians when opportunity might arise. Let us note the appearance of this new fear in the *Annales Herbipolenses,* the annals of the town of Wurzburg. The following incident took place in early 1147, as the crusaders gathered in Wurzburg.

During the month of February, as noted, crusaders streamed into the city [of Wurzburg]. On February 24 an amazing incident took place. The body of a man was found, cut up into many pieces. Two large pieces were discovered in the Main river, one among the mills toward the suburb called Bleicha and another toward the town of Thunegersheim. The remaining pieces were found in a ditch opposite the tower that is generally called Katzinwichus. When all the scattered pieces of the body were gathered together, it was taken to an inn within the town and there was buried in the forecourt of a church. As if this gave them just cause against the Jews, both citizens and crusaders, suddenly seized by a frenzy, invaded the homes of the Jews and assaulted them, killing indiscriminately old men and young, women and children, without pause and without mercy. A few [Jews] were saved through flight. Fewer, in hopes of avoiding [death], were baptized. Very few are known to have remained in the [Christian] faith, when peace was restored. Signs were said to occur at the grave of the body. The dumb were said to speak, the blind to see, the lame to walk, and other signs of this kind. Thus, the crusaders began to honor the man as if a martyr, carrying around relics of the body, and demanded that he—whom they called Theodore—should be canonized. The pious bishop of the city, Siegfried, along with the clergy, resisted their misguided demands. They [the crusaders] began to assault the bishop and the clergy. Since they intended to stone the bishop, they forced him to the protection of fortified towers. The canons, out of fear of their assailants, did not dare, even on the most holy evening of the Last Supper, to ascend to the choir or to chant matins. At last Easter came and the crusaders began their journey. Thus, the tumults in the city were quieted, and all became peaceful.[7]

This is a remarkable portrait of group stereotyping. The backdrop to the incident is crusading fervor. The author sees the crusaders and the excitement they generated as lying behind the unfortunate incidents he depicts. Discovery of a mutilated corpse resulted in a widely shared perception of the Jews of Wurzburg as murderers and occasioned a frenzy of bloodletting against the supposed culprits. This assumption of Jewish guilt promoted the further conviction that the Christian victim had been martyred, meaning that the alleged Jewish violence was religiously motivated. This led to a clash with the ecclesiastical authorities, who rejected the allegations. To be sure, the anti-Jewish stereotypes reflected in the Wurzburg incidents were not shared throughout Christian society. The ecclesiastical leadership opposed these anti-Jewish views and paid a price for its opposition. The author of our account likewise rejected the allegations, clearly appalled by the Christian behaviors he reports. Underlying this story, however, is the widespread perception of "citizens and crusaders" that the Wurzburg Jews were guilty of murderous animosity toward their Christian neighbors.

From Wurzburg of the 1140s let us turn our attention westward to the English town of Norwich during the same decade. Here we encounter a similar story, drawn from a rather different source, Thomas of Monmouth's *Life and Miracles of St. William of Norwich*. In both Wurzburg and Norwich discovery of a corpse ignited a popular sense that local Jews had committed murder. This assumption then led to a conviction, at least among some, that the Christian victim had been martyred and that miracles were performed by this saintly martyr. Whereas the Wurzburg annalist was shocked by the behavior he describes, Thomas of Monmouth sought to accentuate the stereotype of the Jewish murderer, embellishing it with striking flourishes.[8]

Thomas's work is in one sense hagiographic, a depiction of the beauty, dignity, suffering, martyrdom, and miracles of a saint. In another sense it is engaged polemic. For in Norwich the populace was divided on the question of the sainthood of the lad William. Thomas's *Life* thus constituted an extended argument for sainthood, based essentially on three considerations: William's unusual personality, reflected in a sweet childhood; his martyrdom; the miracles accomplished by him after his death. Of these three arguments, the middle one was critical to Thomas's case for sainthood. Without a martyr's death, William's claims to sainthood would have been fatally vitiated. In this sense, then, the role of the Jews is essential to the polemical case advanced by Thomas. As we shall see, however, Thomas's arguments for the Jews as the villains of the story go well beyond the formal requirements demanded by their role.

Thomas seems to provide us with corroborating evidence of new popular perceptions of the Jews as murderers of Christians. Methodologically, we must be a bit cautious in dealing with Thomas's account. Even a casual reading suggests a high level of embellishment and a low level of reliability. The historian of antisemitism Gavin I. Langmuir has subjected Thomas's account to careful analysis and has shown the many flaws associated with Thomas's case for Jewish ritual murder. In fact, Langmuir concludes that Thomas of Monmouth himself, writing six years after the murder of William, was the initiator of the charge that the Jews slew the lad in ritualistic fashion.[9] To utilize such a flawed text to elicit evidence of broadly held popular views is thus risky. Nonetheless, it seems rather clear from Thomas's account that when the body of the lad William was discovered in the woods outside Norwich, a measure of popular suspicion fastened immediately on the Jews as murderers. Let us look closely at the discovery of the corpse.

Thomas describes this discovery as taking place in a number of stages. The first was a near discovery, not a full discovery. An eminent citizen of Norwich, Aelward Ded, early on Good Friday morning encountered the Jews allegedly secreting the body of William out of town, suspected something amiss, touched the sack, and felt it to be a body. The Jews immediately bolted, but Aelward inexplicably went about his business. Subsequently, the Jews revealed their secret to Sheriff John (another detail hard to believe), who elicited from Aelward Ded an oath that he would not reveal this secret, at least until he lay on his deathbed.[10] While too much should not be made of this garbled and implausible account, it at least suggests that one townsman did not rush immediately to the conclusion that Jews had murdered a Christian.

The first real discovery of the corpse was made by the nun Legarda, who saw the body being attacked by ravens, who were unsuccessful in their attempts to devour the flesh of the dead lad.[11] No immediate suspicion of Jewish involvement is reflected in this episode either.

The second actual discovery of the corpse was made by the forester Henry de Sprowston, alerted by both a prior vision and the intervention of a peasant (who entertained no suspicions of the Jews either). But Henry, on inspecting the corpse, immediately came to the conclusion that Jews were involved: "Becoming aware that he [the lad] had been treated with unusual cruelty, he [Henry] now began to suspect, from the manner of his treatment, that it was no Christian but in very truth a Jew who had ventured to slaughter an innocent child of this kind with such horrible barbarity."[12] Given Langmuir's meticulous case for concoction of the ritual murder allegation by Thomas himself in 1150, what Henry of Sprowston thus suspected was simply that Jews had savagely killed this Christian youngster.

According to Thomas, rumor traveled quickly into town, the folk of Norwich gathered in the streets, and "it was asserted by the greater part of them that it could only have been the Jews who would have wrought such a deed, especially at such a time [the Easter season]."[13] Thomas thus seems to show us that the finding of the corpse of a young Christian boy, not yet identified as William, immediately convinced at least some—but certainly not all—the burghers of Norwich that Jews had committed the murder. In this respect Thomas's *Life* reinforces the Wurzburg annalist's sense of a new popular perception of Jews as murderers.

Thomas in fact provides corroboration for a second element in the Wurzburg story, the sense that the killing of Christian victims involved hatred of them as Christians. Subsequent to the discovery of the corpse of the boy, an ecclesiastical synod was held in Norwich under the leadership of Bishop Eborad. At this convocation the priest Godwin, William's uncle, rose to accuse the Jews. He made clear, according to Thomas of Monmouth, that he had risen "to plead not so much a private or domestic cause, as to make known to you an outrage done to the entire Christian community." Godwin argued specifically that the act had been committed out of the Jews' unrelenting hatred for Christianity and Christians: "I accuse the Jews, the enemies of the Christian name, as the perpetrators of this deed and the shedders of innocent blood."[14] Again, Langmuir has argued convincingly that prior to 1150 there was as yet no accusation of crucifixion. There was, however, a sense of the Jews as more than simply responsible for murder; they were alleged to have committed this foul deed as an outrage against Christianity and Christendom, hence the unusual recourse to an ecclesiastical court for redress. The matter was quickly moved out of the jurisdiction of the ecclesiastical synod, but its initial hearing in that setting reveals the special religious twist to this allegation of murder.[15]

Thomas of Monmouth's own view of the Jews is harsher and certainly more detailed than that of the burghers of Wurzburg and Norwich. As proven by Langmuir, Thomas, anxious to reinforce the sense of William as more than a victim of Jewish crime, made a case for the martyrdom of the Norwich boy which involved more than an accusation of Jewish murder, even out of hatred for Christianity and Christians. Let me present the heart of the allegations advanced by Thomas of Monmouth for the alleged crime of the Jews of Norwich in 1144.

He [the young William of Norwich] was treated kindly by the Jews at first; ignorant of what was being prepared for him, he was kept till the morrow. But on the next day, which in that year was the Passover for them, after the singing of the hymns appointed for the day in the synagogue, the chiefs of the Jews, assembled in the home of the aforesaid Jew, suddenly seized hold of the boy William, as he was having his dinner and in no fear of any treachery, and mistreated him in various horrible ways. For while some of them held him behind, others opened his mouth and introduced an instrument of torture which is called a teazle, and, fixing it by straps through both jaws to the back of his neck, they fastened it with a knot as tightly as it could be drawn.

After that, taking a short piece of rope about the thickness of one's little finger and tying three knots in it at certain distances marked out, they bound that innocent head with it from the forehead to the back, forcing the middle knot into his forehead and the two others into his temples, the two ends of the rope being most tightly stretched at the back of his head and fastened in a very tight knot. The ends of the rope were then passed round his neck and carried round his throat under his chin, and there they finished off this dreadful engine of torture in a fifth knot.

But not even yet could the cruelty of the torturers be satisfied without adding even more severe pains. Having shaved his head, they stabbed it with countless thorn-points and made the blood come horribly from the wounds they made. And so cruel were they and so eager to inflict pain that it was difficult to say whether they were more cruel or more ingenious in their tortures. For their skill in torturing kept up the strength of their cruelty and ministered arms thereto.

And thus, while these enemies of the Christian name were rioting in a spirit of malignity around the boy, some of those present adjudged him to be fixed to a cross in mockery of the Lord's Passion, as though they would say: "Even as we condemned Christ to a shameful death, so let us also condemn this Christian, so that, uniting the Lord and his servant in a like punishment, they may retort upon themselves the pain of that reproach which they impute to us."

Conspiring therefore to accomplish the crime of this great and detestable malice, they next laid their bloodstained hands upon the innocent victim and, having lifted him from the ground and having fastened him upon the cross, they vied with one another in their efforts to make an end of him. In doing these things, they were adding pang to pang and wound to wound and yet were not able to satisfy their heartless cruelty and their inborn hatred of the Christian name. After these many and great tortures, they inflicted a frightful wound in his left side, reaching even to his heart, and, as though to make an end of all, they extinguished his mortal life, so far as it was in their power. Since many streams of blood were running down from all parts of his body, they then poured boiling water over him to stop the blood and to wash and close the wounds.[16]

The depiction is chilling, and I have quoted it in its entirety in order to afford a full sense of the author's profound animosity and his sense of the inhuman perversity of the Jews. Without belaboring this distasteful material, we must nonetheless identify the key elements in Thomas's extreme sense of Jewish malevolence. These include (1) the contemporary expression of Jewish hatred—like Peter the Venerable, Thomas of Monmouth sees twelfth-century Jews as engaged in the same hateful acts as were their forefathers more than a thousand years earlier; (2) the immediacy and directness of this Jewish hostility— rather than hating Christians in the abstract or venting their animosity through magic or even through the poisoning of wells,[17] these Jews, it is claimed by Thomas, savagely abused a specific, living Christian; (3) the selection of an innocent and sweet Christian youngster as the victim, one who had done the Jews (or anyone else for that matter) no harm and who was incapable of properly protecting himself; (4) the depravity of the Jews in fiendishly and endlessly torturing the unfortunate victim, a reflection of the intensity of their hatred and the depths of their inhumanity; and (5) the relating of these activities to the Jewish holiday of Passover, on which the depicted activities allegedly took place. The result of all these interwoven strands is a lavishly detailed and chillingly inhuman portrait of the Jews.

Two further elements in Thomas of Monmouth's depiction of the alleged murder of William deserve mention. The first is the dream reported by William's aunt Leviva after she was informed of the death of her nephew. According to Thomas, on receiving this terrible news, Leviva recalled a dream in which Jews attacked her, broke her leg with a club, and then tore the leg off her body and ran away with it. This is a curious image but one that again attests to a sense of intense and inhuman Jewish malevolence.[18]

Finally, we must note the information purportedly passed on to Thomas of Monmouth by a certain Theobald, a convert from Judaism to Christianity. This information deepens the connection between the Jewish actions alleged by Thomas and normative Jewish religious doctrine.

As a proof of the truth and credibility of the matter, we now adduce something we have heard from the lips of Theobald, who was once a Jew and afterward a monk. He indeed told us that, in the ancient writings of his fathers, it was written that the Jews, without the shedding of human blood, could neither obtain their freedom, nor could they ever return to their fatherland. Hence it was laid down by them in ancient times that every year they must sacrifice a Christian in some part of the world to the Most High God in scorn and contempt of Christ, that so they might avenge their sufferings on him, since it was because of Christ's death that they had been shut out of their country and were in exile as slaves in a foreign land.[19]

According therefore to the testimony of this Theobald, more was involved in the alleged assault in Norwich than simple human depravity; the Jews of Norwich were purportedly fulfilling a key tenet of Jewish religious tradition, built into the fundamental Jewish dream of restoration.

Thomas of Monmouth is an insignificant figure whose stature hardly approaches that of Peter the Venerable or Rigord of St. Denis. He also did not express an accepted consensus. Indeed, he wrote his account of William of Norwich precisely in order to convince some of his fellow Christians sceptical of the claims associated with the William cult; his depiction was intended to buttress the contention that William had died the death of a Christian martyr. Thomas of Monmouth has been cited as an extreme instance of the anti-Jewish imagery circulating in northern Europe during the middle decades of the twelfth century. If, however, we strip away the excesses of Thomas's account—the pathological cruelty he attributes to the Jewish torturers of the lad William— and recall the broad assumptions about the Jews reflected in Thomas, as in the Wurzburg annals, we are left with additional firm testimony to the new mid-twelfth-century perception of Jews steeped in hostility toward Christianity and Christians. Peter the Venerable, the Wurzburg annalist, Thomas of Monmouth, and Rigord of St. Denis, with marked differences of style and with differing personal views of the reasonability of the new stereotype, nonetheless provide us with solid evidence of the new perception of everyday Jewish animosity and malevolence.

When we turn once more to Ephraim of Bonn's valuable listing of persecutions of Jews (see pp. 54–57), we find that six of the eleven incidents he reported arose from warranted or unwarranted perceptions of Jews as causing physical harm to their Christian neighbors. In three of these incidents physical harm was in fact inflicted: In the Austrian incident of 1196, a wealthy Jew brought about the imprisonment of a crusader on charges of theft; in the Brie-Comte-Robert incident of 1192, Jews were involved in some way or other in the death of a Christian; in the Neuss incident of 1186 Ephraim acknowledges Jewish culpability in the death of a Christian, although he depicts the Jewish killer as deranged. More striking yet are two incidents in which mere discovery of a corpse sufficed to set off charges of Jewish murder and to unleash persecution. Such was the case in Boppard in 1180 and in Speyer in 1196. The Blois case is even more extreme, for there no corpse was ever discovered. The mere assertion of deposition of a corpse convinced many of Jewish guilt and allowed others to exploit this propensity to fasten responsibility on the Jews.

Indeed, the Blois incident and its aftermath provide our most striking insight into Jewish anxiety about these new Christian perceptions of murderous Jewish hostility. Profoundly frightened that the actions of Count Theobald of Blois might reinforce the image of Jews as murderers, the Jewish leadership of northern France sought the assistance of key political figures in combating the pernicious new stereotype.[20] Thus, with great enthusiasm, the leaders of Paris Jewry reported to their brethren on a successful meeting with King Louis VII. The most important element in this productive negotiation was the royal promise that "even if a body be discovered in the city or in the countryside, I shall say nothing to the Jews in that regard."[21] A more cursory report indicates a parallel approach to the count of Champagne, brother of Count Theobald. According to this brief account, the count "was distressed over the matter, saying: 'We have not found in the Jews' teachings that it is permitted [for them] to kill a gentile.'"[22] The royal and baronial pronouncements were extremely gratifying to the Jewish leadership; the fact that such reassurance was necessary indicates how widespread the presupposition of Jewish culpability had become. Many Christians had obviously come to believe that Jewish teaching sanctioned or even commanded the killing of Christians and were thus disposed to greet the discovery of a Christian corpse with the assumption of Jewish responsibility.

Were Jews themselves aware that the allegations of murder posited some kind of Jewish religious obligation and enthusiasm? In reporting the Wurzburg incident as part of his account of the Second Crusade and its impact on the Jews, Ephraim of Bonn notes explicitly that the anti-Jewish attack was fueled by the conviction that the Christian victim was a martyr (that is, murdered for his religion) and that subsequent to his death he performed wonders.[23] The report on the meeting with King Louis VII has the king telling the Jews about the supposed martyr Robert, allegedly killed by the Jews in Pontoise and buried as a saint in Paris.[24] We have noted the count of Champagne proclaiming in favor of his Jews that "we have not found in the Jews' teachings that it is permitted [for them] to kill a gentile," specifically rejecting the allegation that killing was related to Jewish law. While Jews were aware of this added claim of a religious foundation to the purported murders, what the Jews of the mid-twelfth century seem to have been most concerned to combat was the more general Christian sense of Jews as murderers.

This presupposition of murderous Jewish hostility was not just the prerogative of the lower classes but spread throughout all classes of Christian society. Particularly striking is the following notice in a papal letter of 1205 to King Philip Augustus: "Settled among Christians, they repay their hosts badly. When the opportunity presents itself, they surreptitiously kill Christians. It was recently said to have happened that a certain poor student was found dead in their latrine."[25] This papal allegation of murder forms part of a letter of general complaint about Jewish behavior, a document filled with assertions of Jewish enmity toward the Christian society that hosted them.

Thus, while the notion of Jewish enmity gave rise to allegations of Jewish economic crimes and Jewish blasphemy, the most important new stereotype was that of the Jew as murderer. The traditional understanding of the Jews as enemies took on stark contemporary meaning; many Christians came to see Jews as consumed by hatred, poised to exploit every opportunity afforded them to take Christian lives. Both Christian and Jewish sources concur in highlighting the perception of the murderous Jew as the dominant new stereotype of the second half of the twelfth century. Seen against the traditional allegation that the

Jews were responsible for the Crucifixion, which conviction lay at the core of the crusader anti-Jewish violence, this new stereotype involved a double deepening of anti-Jewish imagery: Now contemporaries sensed an immediacy in the purported Jewish malevolence and a direct assault on Christians rather than the more remote Roman-era demand for the execution of Jesus.[26] The new stereotype represents a marked deterioration of the Jewish image, which became increasingly more anxiety-provoking and hence more potent. Indeed, this broad perception of the Jews as murderers lent itself to rich imaginative embellishment.

Imaginative Embellishments

The imagery of the Jews as simultaneously blasphemers and murderers is rooted in the fundamental Christian perception of Jesus as both divine and human and the parallel assumption of the Jews as opposed to him on both levels. The notion that Jews murder Christians out of their hatred of the Christian faith involves in and of itself a considerable leap of imagination. The richly imaginative environment of the twelfth century, however, moved minds to embellish the notion of Jewish enmity in far more radical directions.

The first of these imaginative embellishments was Thomas of Monmouth's argument that the Jews murdered William of Norwich in ritualized fashion, reenacting their historic crime of crucifixion. We have noted similar embellishment by Rigord of St. Denis in his depiction of the Brie-Comte-Robert incident, where he has the Jews bribing the local ruler, leading the Christian victim through town with hands bound and crowned with thorns, and eventually hanging the victim on a cross. During a period when the cult of the suffering Jesus was intensifying, connecting historic Jewish enmity and purported contemporary Jewish aggression through recapitulation of crucifixion obviously appealed to many minds and imaginations in Christian society.[27]

The claim of ritualized murder by Jews seems to have taken a second, albeit less popular form. We again recall that Thomas of Monmouth's formerly Jewish informant makes mention of the notion "that every year they [the Jews] must sacrifice a Christian in some part of the world to the Most High God in scorn and contempt of Christ." What the ex-Jew Theobald seems to be conjuring up here is an image of the literalist Jews re-creating their cultic system through the sacrifice of a Christian. The same imagery is introduced by Rigord of St. Denis in his report of the rumors that King Philip Augustus had supposedly heard as a child and come to believe. The notion of Jews ritually sacrificing Christians never made quite the same headway as did the parallel allegation of Jews reenacting the historic crime of crucifixion.[28]

The sense of Jews as implacable enemies in the abstract and vicious murderers in concrete terms expressed itself over time in a variety of further imaginative accusations, each distinct from the other yet all linked by the common theme of Jewish hostility. During the thirteenth century the broad sense of Jewish hostility took two new directions. The better known of these two directions is the blood libel, the charge that first emerged in the middle decades of the thirteenth century and continued to plague the Jews of the Western world down into the twentieth century. The blood libel accuses the Jews of using the blood of Christian youngsters to perform rituals associated with the Passover celebration, specifically its central wine rituals. There are many dimensions to this allegation: It reflects the centrality of blood in the original Passover story (seen as sacred and authoritative in both Judaism and Christianity) and the related significance of wine in Passover commemoration; it absorbs folkloristic elements widely reported in a variety of cultures; in ways not yet fully understood it touches deep psychological predispositions, hence its remarkable tenacity. The dimension of most significance for our purposes is this accusation's undoubted emergence from the twelfth-century sense of Jews as aggressively hostile. Whereas the more widespread of the twelfth-century imaginative embellishments of this core notion focused on the imagery of Jewish reenactment of the Crucifixion during the Easter season, the thirteenth-century blood libel shifts from the Christian celebration of Easter to the Jewish celebration of Passover.[29] This newer claim proved the more alluring to the majority. The first index of this attraction is the longevity of the allegation, which remained prominent from the thirteenth century to the twentieth. While the crucifixion allegation never seems to have become dangerous enough for Jews to devote energy to combating it, the blood libel did touch a nerve both among the Jews and their ecclesiastical and secular protectors, who made strenuous efforts to protect the Jews from this potent new slander.[30]

The less widely known of the two new thirteenth-century allegations was the host profanation charge in which Christians claimed that Jews, again because of their hatred for Christianity, reenacted the historic crime of deicide by venting their spleen on the host wafer, which contained the body and blood of Christ. The host profanation allegation brings us back to the starting point of this chapter, to the way in which the dual nature of Christ engendered Christian perceptions of Jewish enmity toward both the Christian faith and its practitioners, creating stereotypes of the Jews as blasphemers and murderers. The host profanation allegation projects Jews as committing blasphemous acts against the host wafer and inflicting physical harm on the body of Christ contained therein.

A number of modern observers have related the development of this charge to elevation of the doctrine of transubstantiation to a role of central significance in thirteenth-century Christian theology. This allegation then becomes most curious for it presupposes Jewish acceptance of the doctrine of transubstantiation, a doctrine that the Jews of medieval western Christendom saw as one of the most perverse deficiencies of Christian faith. Medieval Jewish polemical works, written for Jewish readers in an effort to assure them of the indisputable truth of their own tradition, are unanimous in singling out even the more general notion of the Incarnation as an utterly unacceptable teaching, one sufficient in itself to nullify the Christian faith.[31] While Jewish attitudes toward the Incarnation and transubstantiation undermine the host-profanation allegation, the charge of profanation flows in a natural way from the perceptions we have been examining. As the Christian sense of Jews as blasphemers intensified, Jewish abuse of the host became an increasingly more reasonable inference. Simultaneously, Jews perceived as murdering Christian youngsters out of spiteful hatred of Christianity and of Christ, could easily be assumed to vent this same hostility in more direct fashion on that object in which the body of Jesus could be found. The allegation of torture of the host was every bit as immediate and damning as torture of a young child. So here we again encounter another spin-off of the intensified twelfth-century sense of Jewish enmity and malevolence.[32]

While I cannot make a foolproof case—by modern social science criteria—for an increasingly negative popular image of the Jews as enemies in late twelfth- and early thirteenth-century northern Europe, by the standards of medieval studies I have probably not done too badly. The immediacy of the perceived Jewish malevolence; the threat posed by alleged Jewish economic crimes, blasphemy, and above all murders;

the diffusion of these negative stereotypes through all levels of Christian society; proliferation of diversified and demeaning imaginative embellishments—all these elements reinforce the general argument for a deepening sense of the Jew as enemy, beginning with the middle decades of the twelfth century. The transition from the crusading anti-Jewish rationales of 1096 to the revised version of these arguments encountered in Peter the Venerable captures the essence of the change. Jews for Peter were no longer merely the heirs of those who had opposed Jesus and brought about his death; they were in his own day active in their continued opposition to and hatred of the faith and the community that Jesus had founded. Jews had been transformed from a historic enemy into a present-day threat of real proportions.

5

The Deteriorating Jewish
Image and Its Causes

The Jews who immigrated into northern Europe during the closing decades of the tenth century and throughout the eleventh met with considerable popular animosity, rooted in part in their immigrant and minority status and in part in traditionally negative Christian thinking vis-à-vis Jews. During the middle decades of the twelfth century new negative stereotypes emerged, intensifying majority perceptions of this Jewish minority as different and threatening. Can we now identify the critical factors contributing to the deteriorating image of the early Ashkenazic Jews?[1]

The Jewish Minority

Throughout this study my analysis of anti-Jewish perceptions has begun with the realities of Jewish life. I have noted twelfth-century changes that contributed to deterioration of the Jewish image. To invoke once more my prior categories, the sense of Jewish newness diminished as the Jews became more firmly settled in northern Europe; at the same time, however, the enhanced commitment of Jews to their tradition and identity magnified the Christian perception of Jewish dissidence. More striking is the augmented sense of Jewish harmfulness. Jewish involvement in the money trade intensified the Christian focus on alleged economic ills caused by Jews; moreover, the same shift to moneylending heightened Christian awareness of the Jewish alliance with the political authorities.

The critical development in twelfth-century anti-Jewish imagery involved deepening perceptions of Jews as enemies, perceptions profoundly rooted in the Christian legacy which antedated the migration of Jews into northern Europe. To be sure, Jewish involvement in moneylending and the growing Jewish alliance with the authorities may have served in some measure to heighten Christian fears of Jews. Jewish activities, such as usury, viewed negatively in and of themselves, were increasingly seen as tools utilized by Jews for damaging their neighbors. Yet a question remains. How do we account for the most pernicious of the new stereotypes which projected the Jews as blasphemers and murderers? Were there more specific developments in Jewish life that strengthened the sense of Jews as enemies, eager to harm Christianity and Christians whenever possible?

An interesting suggestion relevant to this query has recently been advanced by the Israeli researcher Yisrael Yuval. In a stimulating essay Yuval has argued for the development in Ashkenazic Jewry of what he calls "vengeful messianism," a belief that redemption of the Jews would be accompanied by the destruction of their enemies. Yuval suggests that some Ashkenazic Jewish behaviors, such as cursing Christianity, were intended to hasten this process of redemption and destruction. Yuval focuses in particular on Jewish martyrdom as a method of advancing the onset of divine revenge. Yuval's claims lead him in a striking direction. He proposes that the Jewish martyrdoms of 1096, which in the eyes of both contemporary and subsequent Jewish observers constituted the most admirable of Jewish and human behaviors, were accurately perceived by twelfth-century Christians as acts intended to bring about the destruction of Christendom and he concludes that these Jewish martyrdoms thus led directly to the new twelfth-century perceptions of Jewish enmity. According to Yuval, majority perceptions of the real meaning of the 1096 Jewish behaviors planted in Christian minds an awareness of the profound Jewish hatred of Christianity and Christians and gave birth to such notions as the crucifixion accusation.[2] Yuval's suggestions, if correct, do in fact locate the twelfth-century stereotypes of Jewish enmity, to an extent at least, in the realities of Jewish belief and behavior.

What do we make of these proposals? The first problematic aspect of

Yuval's suggestions is the focus on the eschatological. For Yuval the Jewish martyrdoms of 1096 were essentially actions intended to hasten the onset of messianic deliverance, with its anticipated blessings for Jews and punishments for Christendom. This seems to me a fundamental misreading of the events of 1096. The Jews unexpectedly assaulted by a spontaneous coalition of popular German crusaders and Rhineland burghers do not seem to have been driven by a desire to hasten the messianic advent. They seem to have been concerned, above all, to achieve safety for themselves and their families. When all efforts to save themselves failed and the only remaining options were conversion or death, these Jews seem to have been moved by a visceral rejection of Christianity and an unshakable commitment to the God of Israel. The belief system that sustained the wrenching choice of death over conversion was complex and included hopes for eventual divine reaction to the events of 1096, meaning reward for the Jewish martyrs and punishment for the Christian malefactors. To transform this hope, which is but one element in the complex belief system that underlay the Jewish martyrdoms of 1096, into the driving force that stimulated them seems unwarranted. Likewise, the conviction of reward and punishment in the writings of the Jewish authors who memorialized the martyrs does not mean that the 1096 Jewish behaviors were in any sense eschatologically driven. The most that Christian observers might have drawn from the events of 1096 would have been a sense that under terrible duress Jewish rejection of Christianity was intense and resolute.[3]

Let us briefly examine the 1096 Jewish behavior within the non-eschatological, here-and-now framework I have emphasized. To the extent that this Jewish behavior might have become known, it would have heightened the perception of Jewish otherness. Jews willing to die and to kill family members out of loyalty to the Jewish faith and rejection of the Christian alternative were surely profoundly "other." In addition, the sense of Jews as blasphemers would have been augmented as well. Jews in many instances responded to the 1096 assaults by blasphemous repudiation of Christianity. One of the major Jewish martyr types was the figure who seemingly agreed to conversion and then took the opportunity of an assembled crowd to denounce Christianity, perishing of course in the process. In a few instances Jews are portrayed as defending themselves physically by taking up arms against their Christian attackers or—alternatively—killing Christians in a quest for Jewish honor. In this sense the Jewish behavior of 1096 might be said—in a more realistic way—to have contributed to heightened majority perceptions of Jewish dissidence and Jewish enmity.

Yet even this more realistic and more limited suggestion as to the impact of 1096 Jewish behavior on twelfth-century Christian perceptions is problematic. While Jewish observers at the time and subsequently have been deeply impressed with 1096 Jewish resistance and martyrdom, the murderous assaults were quite limited in time and place, as was the resolute Jewish rejection of Christianity highlighted in the medieval Hebrew narratives and in modern historiography. The Jewish responses that involved blasphemous abuse of Christianity and the taking of Christian lives were rather rigorously restricted to the major Rhineland communities of Worms, Mainz, and Cologne. We know of no such reaction in 1096 in England, France, or elsewhere in Germany, raising the related questions of the extent of such behavior and resultant Christian awareness of these unusual Jewish actions. While murderous Christian assaults and extreme Jewish responses are central to the remarkable Hebrew 1096 narratives, they make no appearance whatsoever in the Latin eyewitness accounts of the successful crusading armies and only minimal appearance elsewhere in Christian sources. The Jewish reactions of 1096 may have had some realistic impact on twelfth-century Christian perceptions, but such impact had to be extremely limited. Nowhere in the twelfth-century sources cited have we encountered any reference to such Jewish behavior. It is unlikely that many Christians in the aftermath of the First Crusade were aware of either Christian aggression or militant Jewish response.[4]

The focus thus far on Jewish behavior, while useful and appropriate, must now be supplemented by consideration of the parallel deterioration in image of other outgroups. Heretics, lepers, and homosexuals as well as Jews all seem to have been perceived in increasingly negative terms at precisely the same time, suggesting that majority circumstances and sensitivities count for more in understanding the deteriorating images of these minority groups than the behavior of the minorities themselves. Indeed, that other outgroups suffered parallel deterioration in image alerts us to a general consideration: Prejudice and persecution are ultimately grounded far more in the circumstances of the persecuting majority than in the behavior of the persecuted minority.[5] This is not to say that minority circumstances can be neglected. All through this study I have attempted to portray the anti-Jewish hostilities of northern Europe against the backdrop of Jewish life and its contours. At the same time, in order to comprehend the declining image of the Jews in mid-twelfth-century northern Europe, we must attend more fully to the social, psychological, and spiritual realities of majority life at this critical juncture. A brief look at the broader development of intolerance in mid-twelfth-century western Christendom and the explanations proposed by major recent researchers offers a convenient entrée into these realities.

General Decline in Outgroup Images

The pivotal place of the twelfth century in the development of medieval western Christendom has long been acknowledged. We have noted the economic surge that made this century so important. Widespread reference to a "twelfth-century renaissance" indicates that the significance of this period extends far beyond the sphere of economics. Of late some medievalists have begun to argue that alongside the advances in material and spiritual life during this vibrant period, there were less salutary developments as well, particularly affecting minority groups, which found themselves increasingly marginalized.

Two important contributions, that of the late John Boswell on the fate of homosexuals in western Christendom and the wide-ranging theses of R. I. Moore on the simultaneous rejection of diverse minority groups on the twelfth-century scene, provide some sense of the work under way in this field. The findings of these scholars reveal the extent of parallel outgroup marginalization and help to explain the increasingly negative outgroup stereotypes.[6]

John Boswell, in his widely acclaimed study *Christianity, Social Tolerance and Homosexuality,* analyzed the changing circumstances of Europe's homosexual population from antiquity through the fourteenth century, with particular emphasis on the High Middle Ages.[7] Boswell suggests that in popular parlance the adjectives "medieval" and "intolerant" are almost synonymous, a perception he finds utterly erroneous. According to Boswell, the period designated medieval included subperiods of considerable tolerance and others marked by a high level of intolerance. Boswell notes that most scholars see the eleventh and early twelfth centuries as an era of "openness and tolerance in European society, times when experimentation was encouraged, new ideas eagerly sought, expansion favored in both the practical and intellectual realms of life." By contrast, "most historians consider that the thirteenth and fourteenth centuries were ages of less tolerance, adventurousness, acceptance—epochs in which European societies seem to have been bent on restraining, contracting, protecting, limiting, and excluding."[8] Thus for Boswell the late twelfth century marks a point of transition for the homosexuals of western Christendom from an earlier openness and acceptance to increasing identification, opposition, and persecution. Boswell, it should be noted, is regularly sensitive to parallels between the fortunes of homosexuals and the fate of other outgroups, often adducing in particular the Jews.

The broadest and most radical view of the emergence of intolerance in medieval European society is that of the English medievalist R. I. Moore in his provocative study *The Formation of a Persecuting Society: Power and Deviance in Western Europe, 950–1250.*[9] Moore certainly shares the general sense of European vitalization which is common among present-day medievalists; he goes much further than others, however, in his assessment of the underside of the late tenth through the late thirteenth centuries. Moore notes early on that the era with which he deals constitutes "one of the most vigorous and creative periods"[10] in the history of European society. Nonetheless, he points out that this period shows more than a bit of intolerance against outgroups; for Moore, "whether we choose to see the epoch since 1100 as one of progress or decline, to step back a little further is to see that around that time Europe *became* a persecuting society. Even if it had not remained one, the reasons for such a change would be worth exploring."[11] The implication is, of course, that Europe has in fact remained a persecuting society, making study of the development of this crucial tendency all the more pertinent. For Moore as for Boswell the onset of new persecutory patterns can be traced to the twelfth century.

While Boswell's study focuses on homosexuals, noting throughout useful parallels between perceptions and treatment of homosexuals and other outgroups, Moore addresses intolerance and persecution as wide-ranging phenomena in medieval western Christendom, accelerating tendencies that did incalculable harm to numerous minorities in society. Moore discusses in particular three targets of majority hostility and persecution: heretics (who were the object of his earliest research), Jews, and lepers, with occasional further observations on homosexuals and prostitutes. Moore goes far beyond Boswell in his sense of parallels, since his focus is "the formation of a persecuting society." Indeed, after brief examination of heretics, Jews, and lepers, Moore proceeds to argue the interchangeability of the three, concluding: "For all imaginative purposes heretics, Jews and lepers were interchangeable. They had the same qualities, from the same source, and they presented the same threat: through them the Devil was at work to subvert the Christian order and bring the world to chaos."[12] Moore's claim of interchangeability clearly exceeds Boswell's sense of parallels.

The reason for Moore's rather extreme stance is his conclusion that the specific characteristics of the minority objects of intolerance and persecution are relatively insignificant; the key to comprehending intolerance and persecution lies overwhelmingly in understanding the majority, its tensions and needs. Here is Moore's own summation:

The parallels not only in the chronological evolution of persecution but between the forms which it took and the beliefs which engendered it must undermine that approach [the approach that attempts to see realistic bases for accelerating persecution]. The coincidence is too great to be credible. That three entirely distinct groups of people, characterized respectively by religious conviction, physical condition, and race and culture, should all have begun at the same time and by the same stages to pose the same threats, which must be dealt with in the same ways, is a proposition too absurd to be taken seriously. The alternative must be that the explanation lies not with the victims but with the persecutors. What heretics, lepers and Jews had in common is that they were all victims of a zeal for persecution which seized European society at this time.[13]

This is a powerful statement that must be submitted to careful scrutiny.

The assertions of Boswell and Moore find considerable support in the present analysis of a deteriorating Jewish image. Indeed, our close study of the Jews allows for more precise delineation of the time frame of deterioration, with the middle decades of the twelfth century showing recurrent evidence of increasingly negative majority perceptions of the Jewish minority. Boswell and Moore focus their explanations for deteriorating images and heightened persecution on majority society and the developments it underwent. I shall examine the explanations they advance as a starting point for further discussion.

Both Boswell and Moore suggest that the declining fortunes of Europe's outgroups were largely a result of changes in governmental authority. Both scholars are concerned with the role of elite and powerful groups in society in generating negative stereotypes of outgroups and then in taking the necessary steps to counteract the purported dangers posed by these groups. Boswell explains the rise in persecution as follows:

The transition from tolerance to hostility . . . had little if anything to do with the dichotomy described above [the distinction between rural and urban patterns of organization]; it was almost wholly the consequence of the rise of corporate states and institutions with the power and desire to regulate increasingly personal aspects of human life. Minorities in states invested with substantial power over the private lives of citizens inevitably fare only as well as the central authority wishes.[14]

Moore advances a more radical position on governmental responsibility. For Moore change in perception and treatment of outgroups is rooted in what he calls "the transition from segmentary society to state,"[15] a state with its own concerns and interests. One of the major techniques for buttressing the power of this new-style state, according to Moore and the Weberian sociological view he adopts, is the identification of threats to society, which the power elite then attacks. Thus for Moore the anti-heretic, anti-Jewish, anti-leper thrusts that manifested themselves during the latter part of the twelfth century owed far less to genuinely popular concern than to the machinations of a power elite anxious to expand its own authority through identification and repression of alleged threats to the public good. Moore summarizes his position with respect to heretics and Jews in the following terms:

In short, despite the simple piety which we are encouraged to imagine at the heart of everyday life in the Europe of the cathedrals, and despite the invidious position which Jews unquestionably occupied in its political and financial structures, it seems necessary to conclude that heretics and Jews owed their persecution in the first place not to the hatred of the people, but to the decisions of princes and prelates. In neither case [heretics and Jews] have we found the grounds to justify the description of the persecutor merely as the agents of society at large, at least if our conception of society is one which includes the great majority of its members.[16]

Now we are in a position to understand Moore's insistence on the interchangeability of the various persecuted outgroups. They are interchangeable because the persecution was thoroughly contrived, in some instances even fabricated. Rather than a popular if exaggerated reaction to the real characteristics of heretics, Jews, and lepers, the intolerance and persecution of the late twelfth and thirteenth centuries were created by those in power for their own purposes. The specific threats allegedly posed by heretics, Jews, and lepers were at most secondary, the pegs on which power-hungry ecclesiastics and princes hung their efforts at expanded power and authority.[17]

Both Boswell and Moore—the latter far more sharply—identify the authorities of western Christendom and their quest for augmented power as responsible for the new isolation and persecution of out-groups. Although the sources regularly adduced in study of the new persecutory tendencies attribute fear and hatred to the masses, Moore argues that this attribution of outgroup rejection to the masses was in effect a ploy on the part of those in power. Controlling the "media," as it were, these authorities, through their dominance of literacy, attempted to mask their true objectives, which were primarily self-aggrandizement and enhanced control of the societies they ruled.

My above analysis of the deteriorating image of Jews during the second half of the twelfth century affords us a special opportunity to test the Boswell-Moore emphasis on the role of power elites in fostering anti-outgroup imagery. With respect to the Jews we are not dependent on the voices of the authorities and their lackeys. We have in our possession materials from the Jewish side, evidence that is in no way beholden to the bearers of power in European society.

What then does this evidence reveal? It strongly suggests that increasingly negative perceptions of the Jews manifested themselves at every level of society, but flowed particularly from the lower classes. The perception of Jews as murderers which first surfaced in Wurzburg and in Norwich, for example, quite clearly emanated from the masses, with the authorities opposing these popular views more or less effectively. The incidents depicted by Ephraim of Bonn show the same anti-Jewish imagery rooted in the masses. In these instances it is impossible to make a case for generation of negative stereotypes by the authorities.

Indeed, the twelfth-century Jews themselves regularly saw the problem as deriving from the masses, with the authorities of both church and state perceived as protectors. These Jewish perceptions are reflected in both the writings of the Jews and in their actions. Ephraim of Bonn, for example, whom I have cited regularly, repeatedly emphasizes the protective stance of the authorities. In his account of the fate of the Jews during the Second Crusade and throughout his valuable listing of late twelfth-century persecutions, Ephraim lavishly praises diverse authorities of church and state for their protective stance vis-à-vis Jews.

That a keen observer like Ephraim was regularly misled by the authorities seems highly unlikely.

Yet more striking is the evidence of twelfth-century Jewish actions. Stunned by the executions ordered by a power-bearer, Count Theobald of Blois, the Jews of northern France turned to the count's peers for the protection they desperately needed, and the Jews were delighted when the king of France and the count of Champagne provided reassurance. The pattern of regular Jewish dependence on the authorities remained unchallenged, despite occasional failures on the part of these authorities. In the face of this Jewish evidence, it seems impossible to maintain the notion of a conspiracy on the part of the authorities, masked by their control of the "media" as they then operated.[18]

This perspective on the deteriorating image of the Jews leads in a number of directions. In the first place, it now seems unacceptable to make the objects of the growing contempt of majority society interchangeable, as does Moore. The Jews were not in fact perceived by their neighbors in precisely the same way as heretics, lepers, and homosexuals were perceived, nor were they treated in precisely the same manner. What seems more reasonable is to posit deteriorating images and enhanced persecution of all these groupings as flowing in part from the real aspects of their existence and in part from the needs of the persecuting majority, with considerable emphasis on the latter. The real and psychic needs of the majority constituted the driving force in the increasing ostracization and persecution. These new tendencies were, however, pegged to the specifics of minority life. The deteriorating image of the Jews was fueled by the anxieties of the majority in developing western Christendom; the precise forms of the new imagery were shaped by the prior legacy of anti-Jewish thinking and the real changes that took place in Jewish life.

Thus, the evidence provided by the deteriorating image of Jews affords considerable grounds for rejection of what Moore calls a Weberian explanation for the persecutory tendencies of the second half of the twelfth century. To be sure, I will consider in subsequent chapters the accelerating anti-Jewish actions of the power elites across northern Europe. These actions, however, will be shown largely as flowing from popular anti-Jewish attitudes. The authorities seem to have played little role in generating these anti-Jewish perceptions. When authority figures like Peter the Venerable did play a role in fostering anti-Jewish attitudes, they do not seem to have been moved by the yen for power; figures like Peter the Venerable seem to have been moved by the anxieties and fears evident all through majority society, and they expressed these fears in particularly strident tones.

Both Boswell and Moore offer a second broad explanation for accelerating sentiment against outgroups. Moore's suggestion relies on classical sociological theory:

All this might suggest that the appearance of persecution in Western Europe provides a striking illustration of classical deviance theory as it was propounded by the father of sociology, Emile Durkheim. On his view the purpose of defining individuals or groups as deviant (the idea of deviance embracing both crime as formally delineated by law and other kinds of behaviour generally held to violate social norms and values) is by excluding some to reinforce the unity of the rest. The exercise is particularly necessary at times of rapid social change and increasing differentiation, when the redefinition of social values and the reaffirmation of social unity is called for.[19]

Boswell makes much the same kind of suggestion, although his statement is less sociologically impersonal and introduces some of the intense feelings and fears involved.

A tendency of humans to dislike or mistrust what is different or unusual adds a certain visceral force to this belief in the rightness of majority sentiment. Especially when difficulties beset a population already inclined to value conformity for its own sake, those who are perceived as willfully different are apt to be viewed not only as mistaken (or "unnatural") but as potentially dangerous. It seems to have been fatally easy throughout most of Western history to explain catastrophe as the result of the evil machinations of some group distinct from the majority; and even when no specific connections could be suggested, angry or anxious people have repeatedly vented their negative emotions on the odd, the idiosyncratic, and the statistically deviant.[20]

The suggestion of a society in flux seeking to maintain its cohesion by ostracizing diverse outgroups makes good sense. It is widely agreed that twelfth-century western Christendom was very much a society in flux. With respect to the Jews specifically, we have seen that the perception of Jews as newcomers and as religiously different played a role in early anti-Jewish imagery in northern Europe. The twelfth-century strengthening of Jewish identity has already been cited as a realistic factor in the deterioration of the Jewish image. To suggest that the Christian majority of twelfth-century northern Europe, caught up in the affirmation of its own Christian identity and at the same time beset by burgeoning social differentiation, became increasingly aware of others and increasingly threatened by them seems altogether reasonable.

A New Cultural Climate and Enhanced Concern with Otherness

The sense of the twelfth century as a pioneering epoch of exciting material and cultural advance during which new intellectual and spiritual avenues were explored has been widely shared ever since the publication more than half a century ago of Charles Homer Haskins's *The Renaissance of the Twelfth Century*.[21] New sources of information became available to western Europeans through widening spheres of travel and commerce and the recovery of ancient literary texts. Innovative patterns of scientific and philosophical reasoning developed alongside altered esthetic sensitivities and expressions. Such broadening of human experience and knowledge inevitably heightened awareness of a variety of others, living both outside the orbit of western Christendom and within. While it is fashionable to project widening knowledge and experience as liberating, leading to augmented respect for the varied patterns of human existence, such in fact is by no means the historical record. As often happens, increased awareness of diversity gave rise during the twelfth century to defensiveness and fear.[22] Moreover, some of the exciting new cultural directions heightened negative attitudes toward others in general and toward the Jewish other in particular.[23]

The first such innovative cultural direction we might note is the growing commitment to rational philosophy which looms so large in the history of Western speculation. The emphasis on reason, its powers, and the extent to which it might undergird both the life of society and the dictates of traditional religion represents an important step in the direction of much modern sensibility. Yet as noted in a penetrating observation by the late medievalist Amos Funkenstein, this stress on rationality, which might have meant enhanced openness and tolerance, actually became a factor in growing intolerance of non-Christians.[24] Given the twelfth-century sense that reason would buttress the teaching of Christianity, a sense further augmented by the sophisticated speculation of the thirteenth century, the conviction that non-Christians were ultimately nonrational was for many inescapable. To the extent that comprehending the truth of Christianity was either a divinely dispensed grace or at least the fortuitous result of being born into the Christian fold, nonbelievers had to be the object of condescending pity; to the extent that Christian truth was deemed obvious to anyone pursuing rational truth with a measure of desire and objectivity, then nonbelievers were condemned as willful disbelievers. In this way the rationality of the period—surely a positive development from the modern perspective—regularly generated deepening distrust of those who dissented.

While Christians might readily criticize other groups and their failure to heed the dictates of reason, with respect to the Jews the criticism was far more intense. The Jews were after all the people who shared with Christians—and, from the Christian perspective, misunderstood— the message of divine revelation, the correct reading of which they obstinately refused to acknowledge. In the schools of twelfth-century northern Europe the Bible, long at the center of Jewish and Christian thinking and the Jewish-Christian rift, was studied in exciting new ways by both Jews and Christians. Intensified focus on the literal sense of the biblical text held the potential of bringing Christians and Jews together, and in very limited ways it did so. Christians, for example, increasingly consulted with Jews learned in Hebrew.[25] Yet the search for the plain meaning of the biblical text ultimately meant that those not assenting to this reading were viewed as either intellectually or morally deficient. So long as Jews—from the Christian perspective—were simply mired in their own wrongheaded traditions, they could again be the objects of condescending pity. To the extent that the meaning of biblical texts should have been readily apparent to any reasonable reader, Jewish resistance to the obvious and incontrovertible message of the Bible had to become a source of bewilderment, dismay, and suspicion.[26] Once more a major new development in the intellectual environment of northern Europe turned out to have harmful implications for perceptions of the dissident Jewish minority.

Finally, the growing intellectual horizons of the late twelfth century meant Christian engagement with rabbinic literature. Once more, what might have been illuminating and liberating turned out to arouse Christian sensitivities and to reinforce the Christian perception of Jewish error. It is striking that Peter the Venerable, who was among the first to advocate and advance direct Christian knowledge of Muslim

and Jewish religious classics, was led to vituperative dismissal of the religious literature of both these alternative traditions.[27]

In whatever intellectual direction we turn—enriched philosophic
speculation, intensified study of the Bible, engagement with the internal traditions of such dissenting groups as the Jews—the picture is consistent: The new intellectual horizons did little to lead in the direction
of greater toleration of dissidence; by and large the new intellectual
proclivities served to arouse defensiveness in the majority and to reinforce suspicion of outgroups.

The Durkheimian explanation of intensified intolerance of outgroups, used by both Moore and Boswell, seems helpful in explaining
to some extent the deterioration of the Jewish image in northern Europe. Yet one finding in my foregoing analysis of anti-Jewish imagery
does not seem well addressed by this Durkheimian approach, and that
aspect is the heavy Christian emphasis on Jewish harmfulness which
constitutes the most striking aspect of the deteriorating Jewish image in
northern Europe. As I have noted, the Boswell formulation associates
otherness with perceptions of danger. Boswell connects suspicion of
dissidence and fear of harm: "It seems to have been fatally easy throughout most of Western history to explain catastrophe as the result of the
evil machinations of some group distinct from the majority." Yet he immediately indicates that the connections between anxiety over otherness
and fear of harm are in many instances not at all obvious: "Even when
no specific connections could be suggested, angry or anxious people
have repeatedly vented their negative emotions on the odd, the idiosyncratic, and the statistically deviant." Given this uncertain connection,
we might pursue the sources of the fear of Jewish harm a bit further.

Surely dissidence could always lead to one obvious type of harm to
the majority, and that is the impact of dissident thinking and behavior
on the majority. I noted earlier that the Roman Catholic church, which
made explicit allowance for Jewish dissidence, set up safeguards against
any untoward Jewish impact on the majority. Jews were rigorously
prohibited from proselytizing among their Christian neighbors. In
fact fears did develop during the late twelfth century of the potential
impact of heretical and Jewish thinking on the majority. But, as we
have seen, the sense of Jewish harmfulness that developed during the
middle decades of the twelfth century was more direct, involving above
all suspicion of Jewish blasphemy against the symbols of Christianity
and Jewish aggression against Christians. Were there aspects of cultural

change that contributed directly to this fear of Jewish harmfulness? More important, were there vulnerabilities within majority society that triggered such fears?

Northern Europe and Its Anxieties

We might begin this discussion of the sources of Christian fear of harm from Jews by considering yet another major cultural and spiritual change that negatively affected the Jews. The restless energy and intellectual curiosity that sparked new philosophic speculation, innovative study of the Bible, and the beginnings of serious interest in the religious traditions of Islam and Judaism were also directed outward into the realm of nature and inward into the realm of the human psyche. The twelfth century shows sharply heightened awareness of the complexities of nature and human experience. Once more, these tendencies became part of the Western movement toward modernity and modern sensibilities, and once more they reinforced anti-Jewish stereotypes.

Numerous observers have cited the growing humanization of Jesus and the enhanced focus on his earthly experience. These tendencies have been noted in literary sources as well as in artistic representation.[28] Once again, however, positive developments—at least from the modern perspective—bore negative implications for the image of Jews.[29]

At the core of Christian-Jewish tensions lay a problematic dyadic relationship, viewed in traditional Christian thinking as Christ the victim versus his Jewish attackers. As interest in human experience deepened, new understandings bore greater negative implications with respect to Jews as a result of the enhanced humanization of the victim figure in the traditional Christian-Jewish dyad and also as a result of the effort to comprehend more profoundly the aggressors.

Let us begin with the humanization of the victim. As sensitivity to the human experience and qualities of Jesus increased, a key element of his humanity that was emphasized was his suffering. Just as the call to the crusade, with its emphasis on the Holy Sepulcher, had as an inevitable concomitant the stirring up of animosity against those who had allegedly been responsible for laying Jesus in his grave, so too did enhanced concern with Jesus's humanity and his suffering accentuate the guilt of those responsible for his anguish.

We can see this dynamic at work in Thomas of Monmouth's depiction of the suffering of the young William. Thomas rather strongly identifies the saintly William with Jesus, portraying the torture and crucifixion of the young lad in excruciating detail. The primary goal of this lavish account of Jewish cruelty may not have been vilification of the Jews. Arguably, what Thomas of Monmouth was most concerned to convey was the gruesome suffering of his hero, with the purpose of highlighting William's martyrdom, in particular through an identification with the suffering Jesus. Accepting for a moment that the goal of Thomas's elaborate description was emphasis on the nobility and heroism of William of Norwich, that emphasis demanded a concomitant highlighting of the bestiality of his tormentors. Thus, in a curious and lamentable way a major spiritual development of the period had damaging implications for the Jews.

Deepening sensitivity to human experience had yet a second negative implication for the Jews. As is well known, philosophers and theologians from the twelfth century on vigorously debated the question of the intentionality of human actions. This new interest represents, again from a modern perspective, a considerable advance over the more behavioristic attitudes of the prior centuries. No longer was action the critical dimension of human experience and the sole basis for evaluating human behavior. This more sensitive age probed the intentions that lay behind action and behavior. Once more, this development boded ill for the Jews. In a careful study of the motif of the Jews as killers of Christ, the historian Jeremy Cohen has tracked marked deterioration in the image of the Jew. In effect, concern with human motivation deepened the traditional sense of Jewish culpability.[30] Now attuned to human feelings and intentions, scholars analyzed the feelings, intentions, and nature of the Jews who had been responsible for the death of Jesus. While the purported act of deicide had always been judged reprehensible, the more that Christians focused on this act as a reflection of thinking and feeling persons, the more they would be ineluctably drawn to questioning the nature of such persons and, almost inevitably, to judging them with greater severity. This advance in spirituality thus had serious repercussions for Jews.

Beyond these intellectual and spiritual developments that enhanced the perception of Jewish malevolence, were there broader tensions that might have induced irrational fears and perceptions of Jews and other minority groups as well? As so often happens, a society discomfited and anxious is led to exaggerate dangers lurking about and within it, to identify alleged threats, and to exaggerate these threats to the point that one can no longer speak of reasonable responses to real forces. We might recall once more Boswell's sense that "angry or anxious people have repeatedly vented their negative emotions on the odd, the idiosyncratic, and the statistically deviant." We therefore must ask whether there is evidence of disequilibrium and fear in northern European society of the twelfth century which might have led Christians to identify and isolate an outgroup that had traditionally been viewed as harmful.

Let us begin our search for factors contributing to societal disequilibrium and anxiety in the realm of the realistic. At least two major factors can be discerned. The first and less obvious of the factors was the accelerating rate of change. Although it is impossible to be as precise as social scientists would be in dealing with a contemporary societal situation, we find broad agreement among medievalists that the rate of change in societal life in northern Europe accelerated markedly during the middle decades of the twelfth century. To be sure, the direction of this change was by and large positive. What must be stressed, however, is that even positive change can be disruptive. While many members of society may benefit from change, a minority adversely affected by even positive change always exists. In fact, we need not think simply of positive and negative change. The status quo, however problematic, has the virtue of familiarity; new circumstances, however beneficial, are uncomfortable in their very newness. It hardly seems amiss to suggest that rapid change itself meant some loss of societal equilibrium, a measure of enhanced anxiety, and therefore augmented concern with dangers real and fancied.

A more obvious factor in increasing societal anxiety was the existence of real challenges and dangers, both external and internal. Let us begin with the former. For approximately one hundred and fifty years, from the late tenth through the mid-twelfth century, a fairly lengthy stretch of time from the perspective of an individual life span, northern European civilization had been maturing and expanding at the expense of its neighbors. Particularly stunning were the remarkable successes associated with the First Crusade. While modern historiography has downplayed the long-term significance of the victories of 1095–1099, the emotional importance of Jerusalem was enormous and the crusading achievements were perceived as the hand of God at work in favor of a powerful and divinely favored Christendom. The impact of the reverses of the mid- and late twelfth century was considerable. Confu-

sion, consternation, and anxiety followed the fall of Edessa and in particular the failure of the grand army organized by St. Bernard of
Clairvaux. Something was clearly amiss on both the terrestrial and
heavenly level.[31] But even before these defeats the very successes of the
eleventh and early twelfth centuries had created an awareness of the
difficulty of the enterprise. Christians now had far greater appreciation
of the vastness of the Muslim world and considerable fear of its massive
resources. Naive optimism began to give way to a more realistic appraisal of the forces ranged against Christendom. This new awareness
of external threat surely played a role in the anxieties that beset European society.

It might well be objected that in fact the Christian world was
stronger in relation to the Muslim sphere than it had been before the
mid-twelfth century. This hardheaded appraisal is for our purposes beside the point. What counts for us is the twelfth-century understanding
of circumstances. An unreasonably self-confident western Christendom
now found itself beset with serious misgivings about its external enemies. In such a state of disequilibrium, societies often turn against perceived threats within their midst. The tendency to magnify the dangers
from minor threats that can in fact be readily contained is a constant of
both individual and societal response to feelings of insufficiency and
loss of control. So it seems to have been in mid-twelfth-century northern Christendom. Enhanced awareness of external threat galvanized
concern for a variety of alleged internal dangers, which had the virtue
of being far more controllable than the powerful Muslim world lurking
beyond the borders of the Christian West.

A second danger threatened mid-twelfth-century western Christendom, and that was the internal danger of dissension and dissidence.
While from a modern perspective (and to some extent even from a medieval perspective), new ideas and ideals have the capacity to revitalize,
in traditional societies such new notions are often perceived as threatening the core of authoritative belief by which a society, in particular, a
religious society, orients itself. Despite Moore's lumping together of
heretics, Jews, and lepers, I would argue that in fact heretics did constitute a real challenge to the stability of at least the established church.
One might contend that the definition of heresy was unduly narrow or
that the means chosen to repress perceived heresy were ultimately
counterproductive. Nonetheless, a threat did exist, one that in conjunc-
tion with the external danger from the Muslims upset the equilibrium

of society. Perception of the internal threat fostered insecurity that in turn focused attention on a number of minority groups, among them the Jews. Thus, perceived external and internal dangers raised the anxiety level in mid-twelfth-century northern Europe, disquieting broad segments of the populace and predisposing many to a level of fear and hostility toward outgroups which would not have been manifest in stabler circumstances.

Majority awareness of this variety of external and internal threats tended inevitably to produce conflation of these perceived foes. Perhaps most notably, Jews were seen as heretics, and heretics as Judaizers, although other conflations are notable as well.[32] It would be an error to take these conflations too seriously. Concern about heretics did not directly generate anti-Jewish perceptions, nor did concern about Jews occasion anti-heretic imagery. Anxiety about one group did not directly create fear of the other. Rather, disequilibrium and insecurity were induced by a multiplicity of alleged external and internal foes; conflation of the divergent enemy groups served to reinforce the sense of danger.[33] This conflation should be seen, above all, as metaphorical manipulation, a tendency on the part of anxious members of the majority to heighten the overall feeling of crisis and to highlight the heinousness of particular outgroups by association of one with the other.[34]

Awareness of the complications of the human psyche aroused distress from yet another set of dangers—less tangible perhaps than the dangers posed by external enemies and internal dissidents, but real nonetheless. Members of mid-twelfth-century northern European society found themselves frightened by more than real developments; they were also upset by the dangers increasingly perceived as lurking within the complex human psyche.

While the mechanisms are murky, the implications were palpable. The complications of human thinking meant a fresh look at mankind's potential for both beneficent and malevolent behavior. Thomas of Monmouth's portrait of Jewish cruelty is in part an offshoot of this troubling new sense of the human capacity for both good and evil. One of the striking manifestations of this new sense is an increasing awareness of the ubiquity of evil and its central location in the human heart. In his major recent investigation of witchcraft the medieval historian Jeffrey Burton Russell, in a chapter entitled "Demonology, Catharism, and Witchcraft, 1140–1230," speaks of the new personal experience of God and Satan, or good and evil:

The result [of a series of economic and social changes] was a great transformation in man's view of the supernatural. The saints, the Virgin, and God himself
were progressively humanized. The stiff, composed, majestic Christ of the Ro-
manesque crucifixes yielded to the suffering, compassionate Christ of Gothic
art. Christ the awesome and remote Creator was replaced by the brother and
lover of men, and his new gentleness was supplemented by the tenderness and
warmth of the cult of the Virgin. The very same impetus humanized Satan.
Christ, the Virgin, Satan—all three were no longer remote principles but immediately present, every moment, in the bustle of the day and in the stillness of
the night. The eternal Principle of Evil walked in solid, if invisible, substance
at one's side and crouched when one was quiet in the dark recesses of room
and mind.[35]

Once more, while there is much that is generally appealing in the trans-
formations depicted by Russell, this shift held appalling implications for
the image of European Jewry. To the extent evil was increasingly perceived as lurking in the recesses of the human psyche, troubled and
frightened Christians marked Jews (and others as well) with a new intensity as potentially dangerous forces operating within an ever-more-
threatened Christian society.

It may well be objected at this point that in fact all societies are
afflicted by a measure of insecurity so that appeal to societal anxiety as
a critical factor in generating fear of outgroups explains nothing. I
would reject such an objection. To begin with the realm of the individual, where the social sciences have given us far more insight, most researchers agree that all human beings exhibit some level of insecurity,
yet that has not led either theoreticians or practitioners to shy away
from labeling extreme levels of anxiety pathological. By extension, all
societies exhibit some measure of insecurity, but this should not preclude our identifying certain societies as highly, perhaps even patholog-
ically, insecure. Of course, no real guidelines are available for assessing
levels of societal insecurity. Students of this period have, however,
identified significant developments that engendered a sense of dislocation and anxiety in the northern European populace of the late twelfth
and early thirteenth century. A fearful population would have been
likely to project some of its discomfort on small, readily identifiable,
and easily controlled minorities in its midst.[36]

While some aspects of Jewish behavior contributed to deterioration
of the Jewish image in late twelfth- and early thirteenth-century northern Europe, ultimately the critical shift took place within the collective
psyche of the Christian majority in this rapidly maturing area. New

knowledge of a more diverse world produced defensiveness with respect to others, and new patterns of thinking, by and large positive in
their central thrusts, focused concern on dissidence and increasingly
projected an image of the Jews and others as recalcitrant, unable or unwilling to acknowledge universal truths that should have been irresistible. More important yet, some of the new intellectual and spiritual
tendencies enhanced the perception of Jewish malignity, while dangers
real and imaginary heightened the anxieties of the majority and spurred
a search for enemies immediate and potential. Given the earlier legacy
of Christian thinking about the Jews and the realities of Jewish life in
this area, it was almost inevitable that the heightened anxieties and the
frantic effort to identify sources of threat would fasten intensely, although not exclusively, on Jews. The discomfort engendered by rapid
social change, by real dangers from outside the Christian realm and
within it as well, by new awarenesses that ultimately proved distressing
and threatening attuned members of the majority to alleged dangers
posed by such minority groups as the Jews. While the sense of danger
was not chimeric, the danger perceived was exaggerated beyond the
realm of the reasonable.

No single factor by itself explains the deterioration of the image of
Jews which we have tracked. A combination of factors influenced these
deleterious developments. And the existence of such a multiplicity of
factors at work reinforces my conclusion that deterioration did not result from an organized campaign initiated by elites to achieve ulterior
ends. Wide-ranging changes in the material and spiritual life of northern Europe combined to raise new fears and to focus attention on the
supposed profound threat posed by a number of small and relatively
weak outgroups, not the least of which was the Jews.

6

The Deteriorating Jewish Image and Its Effects: Ecclesiastical Policies

This study began with an emphasis on the immigrant status of the early Ashkenazic Jews. The exciting development of northern Europe attracted Mediterranean Jews northward for the first time in significant numbers. One of the puzzles associated with the history of this new Jewry concerns the rather abrupt shift in its fortunes. It is clear that early Ashkenazic Jewry flourished through the eleventh century and well into the twelfth century, despite the anti-Jewish violence associated with the First Crusade. Yet by the middle and end of the thirteenth century, the fortunes of this young Jewry had declined markedly. By the close of the thirteenth century the youngest branch of early Ashkenazic Jewry, the Jews of England, had been expelled, and the Jews of France were soon to follow. German Jews remained in place, but their circumstances were dolorous. This change in fortune raises at least two important questions: When did decline first manifest itself in serious dimensions? And what were the major factors in this fairly precipitous transition from growth to decay? I wish to argue that the deteriorating image of the Jews of northern Europe played a considerable role in the changes that overtook this young Jewry.

The Jews of northern Europe had never been well received by the Christian majority. Immigrant Jews encountered considerable animosity, to some extent the normal lot of newcomers, to some extent triggered by the special characteristics of Jewish life in the north, and to some extent the result of the historically negative image of Jews in

95

Christian tradition. Despite such resistance, however, early Jewish settlement went well, largely because of the protective stance of the political
authorities, whose growing power in the twelfth and thirteenth centuries afforded northern European Jews more effective protection from
popular animosity. But the political authorities themselves also became
the source of significant decline in Jewish circumstances by constrict-
ing, exploiting, and in some case expelling their Jewish clients. Thus, in
effect I am arguing that deterioration of the Jewish image in northern
Europe eventually influenced treatment of the Jews by their baronial
and royal lords, resulting in policies that sapped the strength of early
Ashkenazic Jewry.

One additional and important factor must be introduced in pursuing this argument: the role of the Roman Catholic church. The church,
while not directly controlling Jewish circumstances in northern Europe, exercised considerable influence on the fate of the Jews. Serving
as guardians of Christian tradition and often expressing popular griev-
ances in Christendom, the policies of the church exerted constant pressure on the secular establishment. To the extent that ecclesiastical leadership lobbied for constraints on Jewish life, it represented a force that,
while not automatically and immediately effective, exerted palpable influence over time. Absorption of the increasingly negative image of
Jews by the leadership of the church could and in fact did lead to shifts
in ecclesiastical policy which put new pressure on the ruling class and
eventually had major impact on Jewish life.

Our first task is to identify shifts in ecclesiastical thinking and policy
that stimulated baronial and royal reconsideration of policies vis-à-vis
the Jews. A word of orientation is in order. During the early period
of Jewish settlement in northern Europe, from the late tenth through
the mid-twelfth century, ecclesiastical policy played a relatively limited
role in the circumstances of Ashkenazic Jewry. The Jews clearly did not
represent a high priority to a church caught up in strenuous efforts
aimed at its own reform and consolidation. As we proceed through the
twelfth century, however, the range of issues that church leaders vigorously addressed was continually expanding, as churchmen sought to
identify in ever widening spheres the goals of Christian living and to
press for their implementation in both personal and corporate life.
Among these expanded priorities, the Jews came to occupy a recogniz-
able position.

While care should be exercised not to exaggerate the importance of the Jewish issue to the church, at the same time it should not be minimized. The Jews represented an age-old challenge to Christendom; now the church determined to spell out its earlier stance in the fullest possible detail; most important, the church committed itself to pressing for implementation of requisite policies vis-à-vis Judaism and the Jews. As the intensifed negative perceptions of Jews were absorbed by church leaders, a shift in ecclesiastical policy toward limitation of Jewish behavior was inevitable.

My earlier analysis of anti-Jewish imagery in northern Europe identified two central thrusts to this perception: Jews as different, either as immigrants or as religious dissidents, and Jews as harmful, in the traditional sense or as a result of their economic, political, and social behavior. The Roman Catholic church traditionally acknowledged the Jewish right to otherness, but prohibited any Jewish behavior that might adversely affect Christian society. In the most general way, then, we might anticipate that as the popular perception of Jewish harmfulness deepened, ecclesiastical policy would necessarily absorb, reflect, and reinforce such imagery.[1]

Ecclesiastical Policy:
Traditional Concerns and Their Extension

Long before southern European Jews first began to immigrate into the reaches of northern Europe, the Roman Catholic church had enunciated a clear yet complex policy for Jews living within the boundaries of Christendom. In its most concise form this policy stipulated that Jews enjoyed the right to a safe, secure, yet limited and conspicuously secondary place in Christian society, with the leadership of the church committed to the enforcement of both the protections and the limitations.

Since much of this chapter focuses on the limitations, traditional and innovative, demanded by the church, let us begin with the protections the church was committed to assuring. As stipulated in the broad *Constitutio pro Judeis*, confirmed by popes from the twelfth century on, Jews were entitled to security of person and property, to protection from forced baptism, and to safeguards for their Jewish rituals.[2] We have already encountered ecclesiastical commitment to upholding these Jewish rights at a number of junctures. Pehaps the most striking was Bernard of Clairvaux's insistence on Jewish safety during the Second Crusade which he based on this fundamental church doctrine.

Bernard's invocation of the doctrine of Jewish right to physical safety may well have enhanced commitment to this notion in northern Europe. And just as Bernard had insisted on safety for the Jews during the Second Crusade, so too did ecclesiastical leadership reiterate this traditional stance on the eve of the Third Crusade. A valuable Jewish account of events at the famed Court of Christ, held in Mainz in late March 1188, indicates that the taking of the cross by the emperor and many of his barons occasioned serious danger for the Jews. Yet the emperor, his retinue, and the assembled ecclesiastical dignitaries went to extraordinary lengths to protect those Jews in immediate danger and to unequivocally invoke the traditional policy of security for Jews. According to our firsthand Jewish source, "The bishops condemned anyone raising his hand against the Jews in order to harm them and indicated that his crusader status would not aid him."[3] To cite but one more example of ecclesiastical protection in the face of crusaders, Pope Gregory IX issued moving appeals for protection of endangered Jews in the wake of devastating attacks in western France in 1236. The papal letters are remarkable in the poignancy of their depiction of Jewish suffering.[4] All of these appeals for protection of Jews were rooted in the same policy that had inspired Bernard of Clairvaux as well almost a century earlier.

The innovative anti-Jewish allegations that began to spread during the middle decades of the twelfth century served as a new source of danger from which ecclesiastical leaders attempted to shield the Jews. Since I have drawn attention repeatedly to the Blois incident of 1171, let us note further the efforts of a major prelate on behalf of that Jewish community in the aftermath of the execution of more than thirty Jews as the result of the unsubstantiated charge of murder. A private letter, written in all likelihood by a well-placed Jewish negotiator named Nathan ben Meshullam, details the successful Jewish appeal to the archbishop of Sens, who was the brother of Count Theobald of Blois, brother-in-law of the king of France, and one of the highest ranking ecclesiastical leaders in northern France:

Yesterday I came to the archbishop of Sens, to seek to extricate the prisoners from the prison which belongs to his brother, the wicked count, and those righteous ones who were forcibly converted. I paid him one hundred and twenty pounds, along with one hundred pounds for the count; I have already deposited surety. He has already signed a pledge that the former be freed from imprisonment. With regard to the lads who were forcibly converted, he will request that they return to the Lord. Then they [the Jewish prisoners] left joyously. All the prisoners left the control of the wicked one with their clothing alone, and nothing more, for he held everything that they owned—debts and money. He further signed a pledge of benefit to us—that they will henceforth not bring claims against Jews groundlessly. All these things the Lord has done on our behalf.[5]

As the allegations against the Jews matured and took new forms, the Jews in their growing anxiety turned recurrently to both the temporal and spiritual leaders of western Christendom for protection from the ever-intensifying spate of slanders. The thirteenth-century accusation that seems to have been adjudged by the Jews themselves as the most threatening was the blood libel slander, and at the first surfacing of this charge they turned to both their temporal lords and the leadership of the church for assistance. Pope Innocent IV addressed a vigorous letter to the archbishops and bishops of Germany, indicating receipt of the Jewish complaint, exonerating the Jews of the new charges, and ordering intercession with the secular authorities on behalf of endangered Jews. Not accidentally, this letter of 1247 echoes much of the argumentation and symbolism of the missive written by Bernard of Clairvaux slightly more than a century earlier.[6]

Concern about this new slander was sufficent to warrant reissue in 1247 of the *Constitutio pro Judeis* by Pope Innocent IV, with a brief but significant addition. Pope Innocent appended to the list of prohibited infringements on Jewish rights the following: "Nor shall anyone accuse them of using Christian blood in their religious rites, since in the Old Testament they are instructed not to use blood of any kind, let alone human blood. But since in Fulda and in several other places many Jews were killed because of such a suspicion, we, by the authority of these letters, strictly forbid the recurrence of such an occurrence in the future."[7] This prohibition of the blood libel accusation in a broad papal guarantee of Jewish rights is eloquent testimony to the dangers associated with these damaging new allegations and to the traditional church commitment to shield Jews from infringement of their fundamental rights.

Church emphasis on the legitimate rights of Jews, despite their otherness, was balanced, of course, by parallel insistence on limitation of harmful Jewish behavior. The oldest and most traditional church concern involved possible Jewish subversion of Christian belief, especially

through relationships in which Jews exercised power. The classic relationships of concern to the church—Jews as owners of Christian slaves,
Jews as spouses of Christians, Jews exercising political authority over
Christians—were almost nonexistent in northern Europe. Rather, the
church in the late twelfth and thirteenth century became worried about
relationships that generated what it viewed as excessive contact between Jews and Christians in situations that had the potential of luring
these Christians away from their ancestral faith. The Third Lateran
Council of 1179 categorically prohibited employment of Christians in
Jewish homes.[8] Pope Innocent III, who will figure prominently in this
chapter and who spent critical formative years in Paris under the influence of the reforming ecclesiastical circles of northern France, reiter-
ated this concern in a letter of 1205 addressed to the king of France:

It was decreed in the Lateran Council [the Third Lateran Council of 1179]
that Jews are not permitted to have Christian servants in their homes, either
under pretext of nursing their children or for domestic service or for any other
reason whatsoever, but that those who presume to live with them shall be ex-
communicated. However, they [the Jews] do not hesitate to have Christian servants and nurses, with whom they at times work such abominations as are more
fitting that you should punish than that we should specify.[9]

The principle of obviating problematic Christian-Jewish relations was
well established in early church legislation regarding Jews, but the
principle was open to a variety of interpretations and to considerable
extension.

One striking extension of the principle of prevention of contact was
decreed by the Fourth Lateran Council in 1215:

In certain provinces of the church, divergence in clothing distinguishes Jews
from Christians and Saracens from Christians; however, in certain [provinces],
there has arisen such confusion that no differences are discernible. Thus, it
sometimes happens that by mistake Christians mingle with Jewish or Saracen
women, and Jews or Saracens with Christian women. Therefore, lest they, under the cover of error, find an excuse for the grave sin of such mingling, we decree that these people [Jews and Saracens] of either sex and in all Christian
lands and at all times be readily distinguishable from others by the quality of
their clothing. Indeed, this very legislation is decreed for them [the Jews] also
by Moses.[10]

This decree illustrates the way a traditional policy could be intensified
through the use of new and more extreme techniques for achieving
older purposes. The imposition of distinguishing Jewish garb followed

almost naturally from earlier church policy of limiting contact between Christians and Jews. While there was nothing new in principle about the requirement of distinguishing Jewish garb, the result of the new regulation was certainly altered circumstances for the Jews of western Christendom.

There was a second kind of harm the church traditionally feared from the Jews, and that was denigration of Christianity. Jews were utterly forbidden to engage in criticism of the ruling Christian faith. In prior centuries this fear took the form of limiting any Jewish behavior that could be construed as openly or even obliquely derogatory to Christianity. In the High Middle Ages we find the church again reiterating traditional prohibitions and instituting wide-ranging new limitations.

As an instance of reenforcing prior regulations, let us again cite the valuable papal letter of 1205, addressed to King Philip Augustus.

Indeed, blaspheming against the name of God, they publicly insult Christians, [saying] that they [the Christians] believe in a peasant hung by the Jewish people. To be sure, we do not doubt that he was hung for us, since he carried our sins in his body on the cross. However, we do not acknowledge that he was a peasant, either by manners or by birth. Surely, they themselves cannot deny that physically he was descended from priestly and royal stock and that his manners were distinguished and proper. Furthermore, on [Good] Friday the Jews, contrary to former practice, publicly run about through streets and squares and everywhere assemble, as is their custom, and deride Christians because they adore the crucified one on the cross and, through their improprieties, attempt to disturb them from their worship.[11]

Medieval Jews despised the faith of the Christian majority and expressed their animus in terms as vigorous as those used by Christians in denouncing Judaism. The rules governing Jewish presence in western Christendom, however, made overt expression of this hostility utterly intolerable.

The Fourth Lateran Council also broadly addressed this general principle in an edict against blasphemous behavior which echoes Pope Innocent III's letter of 1205.

Moreover, they [the Jews] shall go out in public as little as possible on the days of lamentation [preceding Easter] or the Sunday of Easter. For, as we have heard, certain of them do not blush to proceed on such days heavily ornamented and do not fear poking fun at Christians who display signs of grief at the memory of the most holy Passion.[12] We most strictly forbid that they dare to break forth into insults against the Creator and Redeemer. Since we must not shut our eyes to insults heaped upon him who washed away our sins, we order that such presumptuous persons shall be duly curbed by fitting punishment meted out by the secular rulers, so that they dare not blaspheme against him who was crucified for our sake.[13]

In the sphere of purported Jewish blasphemy, surely the most significant innovation lies in the assault on the Talmud and related rabbinic literature. The specific grounds for eventual condemnation of the Talmud involved blasphemy against Christianity and rabbinic teachings that promoted socially harmful Jewish behavior toward Christians. Let us attend, for the moment, to the former, to alleged blasphemy against Christianity. Prohibition of such Jewish blasphemy constitutes no innovation whatsoever. What is new is Christian awareness of traditional Jewish literature and the conclusion that some forms of prohibited activity could be found in that authoritative corpus.[14]

The case against the Talmud promoted an innovative investigation of rabbinic literature and a series of moves against it. With both papal and royal support an ex-Jew named Nicholas Donin charged in a public trial held in Paris in 1242 that the Talmud was full of blasphemies against Jesus and Mary, the central figures in Christianity. The allegations were substantiated to the satisfaction of the ecclesiastical tribunal that heard the case, and the Talmud was condemned to destruction. Large numbers of Talmud volumes were burned in Paris in 1244. While the principle underlying investigation of the Talmud was rooted in traditional ecclesiastical policy, the specific steps taken in northern France were new and their results were deleterious both immediately and in long-range terms. Zealous enforcement of a radical version of the papal-royal campaign seems to have had significant impact on the once flourishing center of rabbinic studies in northern France.[15] It is difficult to be sure of the direct influence of the papal-royal campaign, however, since King Louis IX was at the same time instituting a parallel set of actions against the foundations of Jewish economic life as well.

Beyond the immediate impact of this new thrust, the campaign against the Talmud dramatically reinforced the stereotype of Jewish malevolence that lies at the core of this study. In a real sense, we find in this campaign against the Talmud a vicious cycle. The growing perception of Jews as ranged in ongoing hostility against Christianity and Christians made the ecclesiastical authorities highly receptive to the charges leveled by the ex-Jew Nicholas Donin; the presentation of talmudic material by Donin served to reinforce suspicions that talmudic literature and by extension normative Judaism were at their core profoundly hostile to Christianity and Christians.

In sum, the essential Christian policy concerning the Jews offered protection and demanded limitation. The fundamental limitations demanded were intended to obviate harmful behavior on the part of Jews. As the sense of Jewish enmity toward Christianity and Christians deepened during the middle decades of the twelfth century, the stereotype of the malevolent Jew had to influence traditional ecclesiastical thinking. Even in those areas of traditional church concern—Jewish influence on the beliefs and practices of Christian neighbors and denigration of the Christian faith—ecclesiastical programs of the late twelfth and early thirteenth century show heightened fear of Jewish misdeed, broader suspicion of harmful Jewish activity, and harsher measures to obviate such damaging behavior.

Heightened Rhetoric and Innovative Concerns

Although we have seen that fear of harmful Jewish behavior lay at the core of the arrangements made for Jewish life in Christendom, from the middle of the twelfth century on this sense of pernicious Jewish activity intensified and expressions of concern about Jews by ecclesiastical leaders became more strident. Indeed, our introduction to this new sense of Jewish enmity, a perception that cut across all levels of northern European society, came from the pen of Peter the Venerable, one of the key figures in mid-twelfth-century western Christendom whose anti-Jewish rhetoric was vigorous and intense. One other major late twelfth-century ecclesiastical leader merits discussion for his anti-Jewish rhetoric, particularly because he was the most powerful pope of this epoch.

It is widely agreed that the pontificate of Innocent III (1198–1216), set the stage for the power of the papacy as it was expressed and perceived through the following centuries. As I have already noted, Innocent III spent his formative years in Parisian intellectual circles and developed a profound sense of a Christendom imperiled by both external and internal foes. He was a militant crusading pope and an implacable foe of those branded heretics. Not surprisingly, his sense of the

Jews as a serious threat to Christian society was recurrently expressed in his rhetoric and in his programs.[16]

We might begin by noting that Pope Innocent III added to his predecessors' version of the *Constitutio pro Judeis* both a derogatory preamble and a demeaning conclusion. The latter is particularly revealing for our purposes. After detailing the protections to which Jews are rightfully entitled, he concludes: "We wish to place under the protection of this decree only those who have not presumed to plot against the Christian faith."[17] While this is a perfectly reasonable condition, one that accords with traditional ecclesiastical policy, it is nonetheless striking that Pope Innocent III found it necessary to add this qualification.

The pope's sense of the Jews as potentially harmful is obvious from the outset of his papal reign. Flamboyant expressions of concern with Jewish malevolence dot his letters. Note first the opening of a papal letter of 1205, addressed to the archbishop of Sens and the bishop of Paris:

Christian piety accepts the Jews who, as a result of their own guilt, are consigned to perpetual servitude because they crucified the Lord, although their own prophets had predicted that he would come in the flesh to redeem Israel. Christian piety permits them to dwell in the Christian midst. Because of their perfidy, even the Saracens who persecute the Catholic faith and do not believe in the Christ whom the Jews crucified cannot tolerate the Jews and have even expelled them from their territory, vehemently rebuking us for tolerating those by whom, as we openly acknowledge, our redeemer was condemned to the suffering of the cross. Thus, the Jews ought not be ungrateful to us and ought not requite Christian favor with contumely and intimacy with contempt. Yet, while they are mercifully admitted into our intimacy, they threaten us with that retribution which they are accustomed to accord to their hosts, in accordance with the common proverb: "Like a mouse in a pocket, like the snake around one's loins, like a fire in one's bosom."[18]

The imagery in this passage is relatively simple, drawing on the traditional portrayal of the Jewish role in the Crucifixion. To this Innocent III adds his strong sense of the Jews of his own day as steeped in animosity toward the Christendom that has—perhaps mistakenly?—offered its hospitality.

A slightly later letter, written in 1208 to the count of Nevers, holder, protector, and partner of a significant number of northern French Jews, offers us more complex imagery and richer insight into Innocent's negative perceptions of Jews.

The Lord made Cain a wanderer and a fugitive over the earth, but set a mark upon him, making his head shake, lest any finding him should slay him. Thus the Jews, against whom the blood of Jesus Christ calls out, although they ought not be killed, lest the Christian people forget the divine law, yet as wanderers ought they remain upon the earth, until their countenance be filled with shame and they seek the name of Jesus Christ, the Lord. That is why blasphemers of the Christian name ought not be aided by Christian princes to oppress the servants of the Lord, but ought rather be forced into the servitude of which they made themselves deserving when they raised sacrilegious hands against him who had come to confer true liberty upon them, thus calling down his blood upon them and upon their children.[19]

This remarkable passage deserves attention because of its parallels to Peter the Venerable's vituperative letter to King Louis VII. The central traditional element in this diatribe is again Jewish guilt for the Crucifixion and the punishment that act demanded. To this traditionally negative image, the pope—like Peter the Venerable—appends a second, that of the murderer Cain. Given my prior tracking of the image of the murderous Jew and my indication that Innocent III himself seems to have accepted this stereotype, invocation of the murderer Cain as a parallel to the Jews is significant.[20] Finally, again along the lines already noted for Peter the Venerable, Innocent III also sees the Jews of his day and age as contemporary enemies of Christianity, reflected in their ongoing blasphemy, and as contemporary enemies of Christians, reflected in their oppression of "the servants of the Lord."

To turn from imagery to church policy under the guidance of Pope Innocent III, it is instructive to note the remarkable attention paid to Jewish issues in the canons of the Fourth Lateran Council, which the pope convened in 1215. Five of the provisions of this celebrated council relate to Jews. Of these five, one deals with converts from Judaism to Christianity and one with technical business arrangements for crusaders. The remaining three all address potentially harmful Jewish actions. Some of the stipulations are highly traditional, for example, prohibition of Jewish office holding and Jewish blasphemy; one addresses an old fear, Jewish influence on Christians, in a new way by instituting distinguishing garb; and one opens up an altogether new area of ecclesiastical concern, the impact of Jewish moneylending. All these stipulations clearly reveal intensifying ecclesiastical anxiety about harm from Jews living in Christian society.

Let us now turn to the church's new disquiet over Jewish moneylending. Inevitably, the movement of Jews into finance aroused ecclesiastical attention, partially because church policy regarding Christian moneylending had contributed to opening this opportunity for the Jews, partly because church policy with respect to moneylending in general had ramifications for Jewish usury, and partly because money-lending is in a broad way a problematic and emotion-laden economic activity. Already in the latter decades of the twelfth century, we have encountered misgivings voiced with respect to Jewish moneylending activity. During the thirteenth century, these anxieties increased mark-edly, with profound implications for the Jews.

Let us look closely at the novel legislation adopted by the Fourth Lateran Council.

The more the Christian religion refrains from the exaction of usury, the more does the Jewish perfidy grow insolent with regard to these matters, so that in a short time they [the Jews] exhaust the financial strength of Christians. There-fore, desiring to protect Christians in this matter, that they should not be ex-cessively oppressed by the Jews, we order by a decree of this synod that hence-forth, if Jews under any pretext extort heavy and immoderate usury from Christians, all relationship with Christians shall be denied them, until they properly make amends for this exorbitant exaction. Christians, if need be, shall be compelled by ecclesiastical punishment without appeal to abstain from rela-tions with them [the said Jews]. We also impose upon the princes that they not be aroused against the Christians because of this, but rather they should re-strain the Jews from such exaction.[21]

In this edict we find a clearcut statement of the traditional doctrine of church responsibility to prevent Jews from bringing harm on Christian society. Immoderate Jewish usury constitutes a burden on the Christian populace. The church is therefore doubly obliged to demand limitation of Jewish usury, in part because of its role as protector of the Christian populace and in part because of its broad responsibility to define Jewish status in Christendom.

While the limitation on rate of interest is the most widely known of the church's initiatives with respect to Jewish moneylending, there were others as well. Church leaders lobbied—generally effectively—for prohibition of distraint of insolvent debtors, for restrictions on the kinds of pledges that might be accepted by Jewish pawnbrokers, for limitations on the range of borrowers who might avail themselves of Jewish loans.[22] The papal letter of 1205 addressed to the king of France offers interesting specifics of Innocent III's own concerns about Jewish usury. Included in the papal letter are three complaints: compounding of interest by Jewish lenders; appropriation of ecclesiastical goods by Jewish lenders; and distraint on Christian property.[23] As we shall see in chapter 7, every one of these papal complaints, along with the demand for limitation of Jewish interest rates, eventuated in enactment of legislative safeguards by the Capetian kings of France. Novel ecclesiastical policies were hardly acted upon overnight. The demand for usury limitation by the Fourth Lateran Council acknowledges overtly that the secular authorities under whose jurisdiction Jews lived might be loathe to support the new church thrust. Church leadership, however, was accustomed to the long view, to policies that might initially be resisted and only slowly accepted. The commitment of church leadership to such long-term policies was real and its success rate impressive. Ecclesiastical anxiety about Jewish usury augured badly for Jewish business activity, particularly in northern Europe, where moneylending had become so central to the Jewish economy.

The anti-usury measures advocated thus far by the church all involve the elimination of abuses associated with Jewish moneylending, again based on the notion that Jews should be prevented from bringing harm on Christian society. Such notions were already in the air in reformist circles of the late twelfth century, as were yet more radical notions challenging the Jewish right to take usury from Christians at all. Some sense of this more radical view is gleaned from a report on the effective preaching of the reforming preacher Fulk of Neuilly across areas of northern France during the closing years of the twelfth century. Fulk's antipathy to Jewish usury is described by Robert of Auxerre: "Since the lord Fulk demanded the complete extirpation of sins and the implanting of virtues and [he] utterly abhorred usurers, he detested the Jews in all ways, because many of us were weakened by infinite and heavy usuries."[24] This description of Fulk's views is not so precise as we might wish—it repeats the contemporary notion of Jewish usury as harmful to the Christian populace—but then Fulk goes on to express such general abhorrence of usurers as to suggest rejection of Jewish usury altogether. Interestingly, the actions that Fulk inspired included elimination of Jewish lending from certain baronies and in some cases expulsion of Jews altogether from given domains. These policies reflect thoroughgoing opposition to Jewish usury, opposition that denies Jews the very right to take interest at all.

Outright rejection of the essential right of Jews to take or pay interest is also evident in a treatise by Robert of Courçon, a leading figure in the circle of late twelfth- and early thirteenth-century northern French reformers which also included Fulk of Neuilly. Robert argued directly that Christians and Jews were not to be viewed as strangers or foreigners with respect to one another and that Jewish taking or giving of usury was prohibited.[25] An interesting late twelfth-century Jewish leader, Rabbi Moses of Paris, living and teaching in precisely the same city in which many of the reformers were found, reflects Jewish awareness of this new thrust.

Perhaps the rebellious [the Christians] contend that they are our brethren, since it is written: "You shall not abhor an Edomite, for he is your brother."[26] Rabbi Moses of Paris replied that the prophet Obadiah removed the status of brotherhood when he said: "When foreigners trooped in by his gates and parceled out Jerusalem by lot, you too were in league with them." There, he [the prophet Obadiah] spoke of Edom, as is written at the beginning of the book: "Thus the Lord has said concerning Edom."[27]

This report reflects Jewish awareness of a new Christian argument and includes an internally directed Jewish riposte, which, however, could have no real impact on Christian thinking. To the extent that this notion of Christian-Jewish brotherhood—or at least non-otherness—gained currency in ecclesiastical thinking, it posed yet further problems for continued Jewish pursuit of moneylending.[28]

Jewish moneylending elicited divergent ecclesiastical views, both theoretical and practical. Many churchmen in late twelfth- and thirteenth-century northern Europe pressed for limitations on what they perceived as harmful aspects of Jewish moneylending seen as essentially permissible; others threw their support behind the more radical notion that Jewish taking of usury was fundamentally illegitimate and thus lobbied for its outright prohibition. The impact of this extreme view of Jewish moneylending was considerable. In France, where the more radical stance won royal backing, the resultant campaign against usury undermined the foundations of what had been a flourishing—and arguably useful—Jewish economic activity.[29]

Our examination of the new mid-twelfth-century image of northern European Jewry has shown that the most radical and most dangerous stereotype of Jews imputed to them a hatred of Christians so profound that it moved them to commit physical violence against their Christian neighbors. Just as the more traditional anti-Jewish accusation of blasphemy found seeming confirmation in the mid-thirteenth-century trial of the Talmud, so too the newer sense of Jewish hatred and violence was ostensibly corroborated through the same public proceedings. One purpose of the investigation of the Talmud was to substantiate the allegation that rabbinic literature condoned, indeed encouraged actions that were profoundly antisocial, including murder of Christian neighbors. The new stereotype of the Jews made the leaders of the church receptive to the allegations of the ex-Jew Nicholas Donin. In the same kind of vicious cycle noted earlier in this chapter, the result of the examination of rabbinic literature was seeming confirmation at the midpoint of the thirteenth century of what had been suspected ever since the middle of the twelfth: Jews were indeed motivated by the deepest imaginable hostility toward their neighbors and used every available opportunity to inflict harm.

In a number of ways the picture is remarkably consistent. The church embarked on an intensive effort to examine accepted principles, to adumbrate their practical implications and applications, and to enforce the programmatic steps this renewed analysis seemed to require. Given the fundamental principle that Jews must be prohibited from inflicting harm on the Christian society that hosted them, the church now sought to scrutinize more carefully than heretofore modes of Jewish behavior that might be considered damaging and to lobby vigorously with the secular authorities for implementation of anti-Jewish policies required by the newly perceived ramifications of the venerable church stance. The new image of Jewish hostility played a considerable role in alerting church leadership to purportedly harmful Jewish practices both traditional and novel. The new programs demanded by the church to contain this alleged hostility and harmfulness added their own impact to the accelerating popular pressures brought to bear on those secular authorities whose support since the late tenth century had been essential to successful Jewish immigration into northern Europe.

7

The Deteriorating Jewish Image and Its Effects: The Temporal Authorities

From the beginning of significant Jewish settlement in northern Europe, the key to successful absorption lay with secular authorities who chose, for a variety of reasons, to support the immigrating Jews. The Jewish newcomers encountered considerable popular resistance. In the face of such resistance, they had two possible allies. The lesser of the two was the leadership of the Roman Catholic church, committed to a balanced program of protection cum limitation. The more potent of the two possible allies was the secular establishment, willing to provide requisite protection in return for diverse advantages to be drawn from the presence of the Jews. Support of the temporal authorities provided the key to the initial successes of the early Ashkenazic Jews. Likewise, the decline in early Ashkenazic fortunes must also be attributed to the temporal authorities, this time to the disappearance or at least diminution of their support. The key question to be posed in this chapter is the impact of the new anti-Jewish imagery on these temporal authorities and on their flagging support for the Jewish clients whom they had earlier encouraged so decisively.[1]

Ongoing Protection

The policies of the temporal authorities, though less articulate than those of the Roman Catholic church, included elements both positive and negative from the Jewish perspective. Secular authorities, in essence, struck a balance between protection and exploitation of the Jews. It is useful to begin by indicating that the government commitment to safeguard Jewish physical well-being and business dealings remained very much in evidence during the later decades of the twelfth century and on into the thirteenth. At this point the rulers of northern Europe were, if anything, more effective and therefore in a better position to afford requisite protections.

In my earlier discussion of the Second Crusade, I emphasized the crucial role of Bernard of Clairvaux in providing safety for the endangered Jews of northern Europe. But this focus on Bernard should not obscure the role played by the secular authorities. Ephraim of Bonn, who highlighted the activities of Bernard, was nonetheless sensitive to the intervention of temporal rulers, in particular the king of England.[2]

A similar pattern of support manifested itself during the Third Crusade as well. Probably the most dangerous moment of this crusade for the Jews took place in 1188 during the famed Court of Christ in Mainz, where the emperor and his leading barons took their crusading vows. We have noted the remarkable Hebrew letter written from Mainz itself (see above, p. 98), giving us unusual firsthand evidence of events at this critical juncture, including the stance of the assembled bishops against violence toward Jews. More striking yet is the staunch protection offered by the emperor and his officials. Our Hebrew letter offers us illuminating insight into the buildup of tensions and into the protective posture of imperial officials. On the Sabbath prior to the formal taking of the cross, the Jewish neighborhood was invaded by crusaders, who were repulsed by resolute imperial officials. According to the Jewish letterwriter, the message conveyed by imperial actions was quickly absorbed by the crusading forces. Prohibition of violence against Jews was formalized a few days later: "On Tuesday [March 29], the emperor extended peace to the Jews, announcing: 'Anyone who harms a Jew and causes an injury, his hand shall be cut off. Anyone who kills a Jew shall be killed.'"[3] Such assertive protection resulted in continued Jewish security through the third and following major crusades. Only in rare instances, such as the few isolated cases in England in the late 1180s and the early 1190s, did the authorities fail in their efforts to provide safeguards for their Jews.[4]

The popular crusading ventures of the thirteenth century occasionally spawned anti-Jewish violence that the authorities were unable to contain immediately. We have noted already the most egregious example of such violence, that associated with the popular crusading of 1236. The papal letter of Pope Gregory IX shows him still very much committed to the safety of the Jews. He addressed an urgent missive to the ecclesiastical authorities of western France and a second letter to the powerful and pious king of France, Louis IX. Royal records indicate that the papal appeal to St. Louis did not go unheeded. Punishment was imposed on purported attackers of Jews, intended both as retribution for past misdeeds and deterrent against future aggression.[5] In sum, despite occasional breakdown, governmental commitment to law and order during the tumult of the crusades, with their potential for heightened anti-Jewish hostility, was firm and effective.

A second spur to violence was the appearance from the mid-twelfth century of a spate of anti-Jewish slanders, including accusations of murder and ritualized crucifixion of Christian youngsters. Here too the secular authorities remained resolute in their protective stance, expressing serious concern for endangered Jews right from the start. In the Norwich incident of 1144, highlighted in my discussion of the new sense of Jewish malevolence (see above, pp. 62–67), the local royal offical, the sheriff of Norfolk, safeguarded the Norwich Jews effectively in the face of hostility triggered by discovery of the body. Subsequent efforts by those convinced of Jewish responsibility for the murder of William to bring the case to the royal court were thwarted by the king's officials. In refusing to countenance claims of Jewish culpability, the English authorities set a precedent in this early incident that became the norm for most of the period under consideration.[6]

The perception that Jews bore an implacable hatred for Christians and Christianity can be seen in the Blois incident of 1171 and its aftermath (see above, pp. 68–69). This particular incident was especially frightening to the Jews because of the combination of weak evidence of Jewish murder (no body was ever discovered), appeal to outdated procedures of trial by ordeal, support of the allegation by a major northern French baron, and heavy loss of Jewish life. All these factors served to strengthen Jewish anxieties and to set in motion concerted efforts to elicit support from leading figures of both church and state, all related in one way or another to the count of Blois himself. Ecclesiastical support came from Count Theobold's brother, who was archbishop of Sens. More important yet was the appeal made by leaders of Paris Jewry to King Louis VII, Theobald's brother-in-law, and the approach to

Count Henry of Champagne, another of Theobald's brothers. The appeals to these two powerful political figures, the king and the count of Champagne, were wholly successful, with both promising to shield their Jews against the new murder allegation. The Boppard incident of 1180 and the Speyer incident of 1196 depicted by Ephraim ben Jacob also illustrate energetic protection of German Jews against the new malicious murder allegation.

Governmental protection of Jews was also strikingly elicited in the wake of the new charge of murder and ritualized Jewish use of Christian blood of the 1230s. We have noted rejection of this innovative charge by Pope Innocent IV. The ecclesiastical response was paralleled by the reaction of the emperor Frederick II. In an important edict the emperor made mention of the accusation of Jewish use of Christian blood raised at Fulda in 1235 and the resultant danger to all the Jews of his empire. Determined to investigate the new allegation seriously, Frederick first convened his ecclesiastical and lay advisers to ponder the matter. The next step was to assemble a panel of experts, former Jews who were assumed to be knowledgeable about Jewish law and practice and unsympathetic to Judaism and Jews. The findings of this panel were for Frederick II decisive and clearcut. On a number of grounds, the conclusion was that it was unthinkable that Jews utilized human blood for any ritual purpose at all, leading the emperor to the following summary declaration:

By this sentence of the princes, we pronounce the Jews of the aforesaid place and the rest of the Jews of Germany completely absolved of this imputed crime. Therefore, we decree by the authority of the present privilege that no one, whether cleric or layman, proud or humble, whether under the pretext of preaching or otherwise, judges, lawyers, citizens, or others, shall attack the aforesaid Jews individually or as a group as a result of the aforesaid charge. Nor shall anyone cause them notoriety or harm in this regard.[7]

Imperial rejection of the new allegations was firm and authoritative.

In general, effective governmental protection of Jewish persons and property continued through the second half of the twelfth century and on into the thirteenth.[8] This conclusion accords well with our broad sense of the period, during which the mechanisms of governance improved markedly as did the government's capacity for providing security for a group like the Jews. There is, at the same time, no reason for suggesting diminution in the authorities' desire to afford Jews safety and security in the face of popular hostility. Any outbreak of popular violence was dangerous to governmental interests, and the authorities were most anxious to ensure order throughout their domains. Thus the new and dangerous popular imagery did not translate directly into a reduction in Jewish safety. While the new stereotypes did not have immediate and direct impact on Jewish fortunes, in the long run they contributed significantly to the loss of governmental support of the Jews.

Exploitation of Jewish Business

The shift of northern European Jews from their concentration in commerce to a new, useful, and profitable but restricted and unpopular specialization in the money trade reinforced the already tight alliance between the Jews and their secular lords. The strengthening of this bond between the Jews and their baronial protectors served to fan popular discontent with the Jews. Yet important as the enhanced bond between the Jews and their lords was in generating popular animosity, more significant by far was the opportunity the relationship afforded the secular authorities to exploit their Jewish clients.

From the outset the barons and monarchs who supported Jewish immigration into northern Europe did so in their own interests. With the move into moneylending, the potential for baronial or royal exploitation of the Jews intensified. The money trade was more lucrative than commerce had been; the dependency of the Jews on the authorities was deeper; these late twelfth- and thirteenth-century lords were more effective and sophisticated than their predecessors had been. The net result was a northern European Jewry more fully at the mercy of its protectors.

From the middle of the twelfth century the Jews of northern Europe were subjected to increasingly intense fiscal manipulation by their temporal lords. Not surprisingly, the most advanced governments of northern Europe led the way in exploiting Jewish resources. The English monarchy, as is almost to be expected, was in the forefront. The English Jewish community was the most deeply enmeshed in its alliance with the authorities, and the English crown was more sophisticated than any other in northern Europe at the time in its bureaucracy and in its capacity for tapping resources available to it.[9]

Evidence for increasingly heavy taxation of Jews in late twelfth- and thirteenth-century England abounds. This tendency had manifested itself already during the reign of Henry II. Two items are of particular interest from the closing years of Henry's long reign. The first involves the Guildford assessment of 1186, intended to raise funds for the king's proposed crusading venture. The Jewish contribution was fixed at one-fourth the value of all property of Jewish taxpayers, considerably higher than the general levy of one-tenth imposed on the Christians. While there is some disagreement as to the actual sum anticipated from the Jews, it does seem clear that the total was expected to be extremely large, particularly in view of the restricted number of Jews in England.[10] The second indicator of exploitation of Jewish resources was royal confiscation of the wealth of Aaron of Lincoln on his death, also, coincidentally, in 1186. The precise sums realized are not identifiable, but there has been no challenge to the overall impression of an enormous windfall for the royal treasury.[11]

The reign of King John introduced unusually heavy financial burdens on the monarchy, both because of the ongoing and eventually disastrous warfare with the Capetians and because of John's problems with both the English barony and the papacy. While the Jews suffered financially all through John's tenure, the most significant developments took place in 1207 and 1210. In 1207 the Jews were subjected to a tallage of 4,000 marks and a levy of one-tenth of the value of their bonds. Given the bureaucracy already developed, royal officials could readily amass information on the bonds held by Jews, or at least by the wealthiest Jews of the kingdom. Income from the tallage of 1207 does not seem to have met royal expectations, suggesting to the king and his officials that in fact the evidence for Jewish bond holding was deficient and that the Jews had somehow succeeded in withholding important information on their assets. In 1210 major Jewish lenders were arrested and their charters were seized and studied, leading to a massive tallage, with extensive confiscation of Jewish property and punishment for Jews accused of withholding information on assets. The result was considerable profit for the royal treasury and extensive damage to the Jewish lending business in England.[12]

The recent research of Robert C. Stacey on English Jewry under Henry III provides us with our fullest sense of regular and special taxation of the Jews during the middle decades of the thirteenth century. According to Stacey, the first quarter century of Henry III's rule shows a pattern "of modest but fairly steady contributions to the king's finances of between 2,000 and 3,000 marks per year."[13] For Stacey the critical point came late in the 1230s with the royal demand that the Jews pay a special tax of one-third of their holdings, including all their unredeemed bonds. Disappointment with the returns of this extraordinary levy led to intensified efforts to tax Jewish resources. In June of 1240 the royal archae, the offices that held Jewish loan instruments, were closed, and full scale investigation of Jewish holdings was undertaken. The Worcester assembly of February 1241 levied on the Jews a one-year tallage of 20,000 marks, to be paid in two installments, with responsibility for collecting the enormous sum laid upon the Jews themselves. This heavy burden was subsequently intensified with the imposition in 1244 of a 60,000-mark tallage, to be paid in annual installments between 1244 and 1250. It is worth citing Stacey's own evaluation of the impact of these fiscal moves of the 1240s:

The double blows of the 20,000-mark tallage of 1241–1242 and the 60,000-mark tallage of 1244–1250 ruined the Jewish magnates of England, and effectively decapitated the class structure of medieval Anglo-Jewry. By so doing, Henry broke the financial backbone of the English Jewish community, and permanently reduced its financial value to the Crown.[14]

Clearly, the key factor at work here was the new possibility for governmental profit that the intensified alliance between monarchy and Jews had created. The alliance was in essence so heavily weighted in favor of the powerful royal partner that there were no safeguards for the weaker partner, the Jews. Over time the temptation to exploit the Jews to the breaking point became almost irresistible.

The French authorities, both royal and baronial, never achieved quite the same level of exploitation of Jewish resources. Evidence does show, however, movement in the same direction. The innovator, as was true in other elements in royal policy as well, was Philip Augustus.[15] The explosive anti-Jewish measures of the very first years of Philip's reign derived in large part from the desperate circumstances in which the young king found himself. The anti-Jewish actions seem to have been intended to buy ecclesiastical and popular backing while at the same time affording the king considerable revenue.[16] The sum total of these activities, whatever their motivation or motivations might have been, was considerable capital for a badly strapped royal purse.

Perhaps not coincidentally the year 1210 that saw extensive despoliation of English Jewry by King John witnessed parallel exploitation of Jewish wealth by King Philip Augustus. While evidence for this set of actions by the French monarch is fragmentary, there seems to have been an investigation of Jewish holdings, an arrest of leading Jews, and heavy imposts levied on these Jews.[17] Where the English-French parallels cease is in the 1240s, when heavy English exactions took place. Because the French monarchy had by that time virtually suspended its support of Jewish moneylending, the Jews of France no longer possessed the resources to make such despoliation profitable.

The relative absence of efforts to exploit Jewish wealth in German lands is a result of the slower development of both business and governance in these areas. Jewish businessmen never followed the route of intense involvement in governmentally sponsored moneylending against land. The failure to develop such lending activity meant a lack of business success of the kind achieved in England and France and a corresponding lack of exploitation that such wealth would almost inevitably have engendered. The curve of German-Jewish economic activity is far flatter than that observed farther westward; it lacks both the rapid rise of the middle decades of the twelfth century and the subsequent decline that the mid-twelfth-century successes spawned.

Ecclesiastical Pressures and Their Impact

Thus far our look at the shifting alliance between the Jews and their temporal lords has not reflected in any meaningful way the new stereotypes that are the focus of this study. What we have seen rather is continuation of the original relationship, involving a combination of protection of Jews balanced by fiscal exploitation, both considerably enhanced by the growing maturation of governmental bureaucracies across most of northern Europe.

Yet the new negative stereotypes of Jews did in fact impinge considerably on governmental policies vis-à-vis the Jews during the latter decades of the twelfth century and on into the thirteenth. The first avenue of impact was through the ecclesiastical authorities, who absorbed the new negative perceptions of Jews and mounted a campaign for limitation of allegedly harmful Jewish behaviors.

The most significant expression of church pressure and eventual governmental response involved Jewish moneylending. We have identified a range of ecclesiastical demands with respect to Jewish usury. By the end of the twelfth century a number of northern French barons had responded to the preaching of the ecclesiastical reformer Fulk of Neuilly during the 1190s (see above, p. 107). Fulk seems to have agitated for repudiation of half the debts owed the Jews and repayment of the remainder. The repudiation of half the debts owed the Jews probably reflects an accusation of excessive usury. The repayment of the other half, ostensibly the principal of the loans extended, indicates a desire to fulfill obligations that were legitimate and deserved to be honored. This was a reformist campaign, not a populist effort toward exploitation of the Jews. Fulk's success lay in his ability to win over both ecclesiastical leaders and secular authorities to his program. Beyond implementation of Fulk's demands with respect to debts owed the Jews, some of the affected barons proceeded to expel the Jews from their domains in 1198. Whether Fulk himself agitated for such an expulsion is not clear, but some of the barons he influenced clearly saw such expulsion as a reasonable ramification of the campaign against usury. The demands of Fulk of Neuilly were extreme, as were the actions undertaken in the wake of his vigorous and effective preaching.

A yet more extreme instance of ecclesiastical pressure and positive response on the part of a major secular authority involved Philip Augustus of France and a little known hermit named Bernard of Vincennes. At the very beginning of his reign (1180–1223) the young monarch took a number of harsh steps against the Jews of the royal domain. One of these actions is described by the royal biographer Rigord of St. Denis, who describes the young king, distressed over the abuses associated with Jewish moneylending, as turning for guidance to a revered holy man:

When the most Christian king Philip heard [of certain Jewish usury practices], moved by Christian piety, he took counsel with a certain hermit, Bernard by name, a holy and pious man, who at that time dwelled in the forest of Vincennes, as to what should be done. By his [Bernard's] advice, he [King Philip] released all Christians of his kingdom from their debts to the Jews, keeping a fifth part of the whole amount for himself.[18]

This early act on the part of Philip Augustus, which preceded his banishment of Jews from the royal domain in 1182, is a precursor of later actions stirred up by the preaching of Fulk of Neuilly. Like Fulk,

Bernard of Vincennes seems to have agitated for repudiation of Jewish usury. In two ways the actions taken by the young monarch were yet harsher than those stirred up by Fulk of Neuilly: The forgiveness of obligations involved fully 80 percent of the amounts owed and the Jews received no part of the sums repaid, the money reimbursed going directly to the royal treasury. As in the case of Fulk, it is unclear whether Bernard himself agitated for the expulsion that succeeded this forgiving of loans. Both these late twelfth-century actions show the secular authorities responding to extreme demands imposed by churchmen. Despite the radical nature of these actions, they serve as a valuable prelude to the slower and more measured thirteenth-century royal campaign against Jewish moneylending in France.[19]

Philip Augustus's precipitous expulsion of the Jews from the royal domain in 1182 was succeeded by their return in 1198, with arrangements undertaken for the renewal of the Jewish lending business. The mature Philip Augustus took the first major steps to restrict in more considered fashion some of the abuses associated with the Jewish lending business. Working in concert with two other major baronial holders of Jews, the king decreed in 1206 a critical limitation on Jewish moneylending. In a move related to the slightly later statement of the Fourth Lateran Council (1215) on Jewish usury, the monarch set a maximum rate of interest of approximately 43 percent per annum to protect Christian debtors. While there was surely some impact on Jewish profits, it is hardly fair to see here the beginning of a severe downturn in Jewish lending. Had this remained the only step taken by the French authorities, Jewish moneylenders would have had little cause for serious complaint.

Rather than the end of a process of limitation, however, Philip Augustus's stipulations represented only the beginning. The next major milestone came in the first year of the reign of Louis VIII.[20] In 1223 the new king, in one of the early acts of his reign, led a number of major northern French barons in swearing to a departure in Capetian usury legislation. Let us note the key stipulations of this enactment.

1. No Jews' debts shall accumulate interest from this November 8 and further. Neither we nor our barons shall henceforth cause to be returned to the Jews usury which accrues from this November 8 and further. . . .

4. The Jews henceforth shall not have seals for sealing their debts.[21]

While there is some ambiguity associated with the opening stipulation of this legislation, on balance the broad meaning of the enactment is clear.[22] The authorities of northern France—the king and the assembled barons—agreed to terminate their support for the Jewish moneylending business as it had heretofore existed. This constitutes a watershed in Capetian policy toward Jewish lending. While the pre-1223 steps indicate responsiveness to ecclesiastical calls for limitation of harmful practices associated with moneylending, the 1223 regulation reflects a new approach: Essentially, the authorities dissociated themselves from Jewish usury. Clerical critics of Jewish moneylending and of governmental support for the practice had long castigated the ruling class for its collusion with the Jews and for the profits that accrued from such collusion. The 1223 regulation reflects sensitivity to these critiques and an effort to remove many of the political authorities of northern France from involvement with Jewish usury and from the attendant moral stain.

From the perspective of the Jewish lenders this edict was epochal in its impact on Jewish business. In effect, the sophisticated Jewish lending that underlay the economic successes of the English and northern French Jews, the lending that required the backing of the authorities, had now been eliminated from France. For all practical purposes, this legislation signaled the end of the Jewish business that had enriched northern French Jewry since the middle of the twelfth century and in the process had augmented royal and baronial coffers as well. For more than seventy years Jews had depended on the willingness of the authorities to back their lending—recall the observation of Ephraim ben Jacob of Bonn that by the period of the Second Crusade "most of the loans extended by the Jews of France are by charter," that is to say, backed by royal or baronial enforcement. That support had now come to a close. While further restrictive actions lay in the offing, deprived of the governmental apparatus that had ensured enforcement of usurious loans, the sophisticated lending business of the French Jews was over. Lending along the lines already noted in Germany remained open to the Jews, but such business had to seem paltry in comparison with the heights achieved by Jewish lenders in northern France prior to 1223.

The final stage in the progressively harsher Capetian measures prohibited the Jews from all forms of usury, ordering that Jews support themselves by their own labor or by nonusurious business dealing. This action (probably from 1253) represents the third and last stage in the royal embrace of ecclesiastical critiques of Jewish lending.[23] The first stage constituted Capetian response to criticisms of alleged abuses associated with Jewish lending; the second involved a commitment to extricate secular authorities from their involvement with Jewish lending; the third took the radical position that Jewish lending was in fact illegitimate, that the Jews themselves did not have the right to lend at interest to Christians. The steps taken between 1206 and 1253 thus reflect increasing opposition to the Jewish lending business. Ecclesiastical hostility to Jewish business activities was slowly but surely absorbed into the legislation of the French monarchy, resulting in total disruption of the business alliance that had been struck between the Jews and their temporal protectors, the kings of France.

A parallel process can be noted with respect to the church's new concern with blasphemy in the corpus of rabbinic literature. Once again, heightened ecclesiastical sensitivity to the purported harmfulness of Jewish behavior resulted in concerted church pressure, which slowly but effectively affected royal and baronial policy. In this indirect way, through the medium of ecclesiastical absorption, the new and negative stereotypes of Jewish malevolence and harmfulness contributed significantly to the decline of early Ashkenazic Jewry.[24]

Direct Absorption of the New Stereotypes: Genuine and Feigned

The new negative Jewish stereotypes generated during the middle decades of the twelfth century affected Jewish fate in two more direct ways. In some instances rulers feigned acceptance of the accusations of harmful Jewish behavior in order to curry favor with their Christian subjects; in other instances, they seem to have genuinely accepted the notion of Jewish malevolence and harmfulness and acted accordingly. To be sure, it is difficult to distinguish between feigned and genuine acceptance of the new stereotypes, and our sources often do not suffice for such distinctions. Nonetheless, we can make some effort at drawing a line between exploitation of the new slanders and genuine conviction.

Perhaps the safest procedure is to begin with a case where the evidence points rather clearly to wholehearted acceptance of the new

sense of implacable Jewish hostility. The figure involved is the renowned King Louis IX of France, subsequently canonized and known
fondly in French history as St. Louis.[25] St. Louis's profound personal
fear and hatred of Jews seems beyond question. While he left us no direct testimony to this fear and hatred, two famous stories recounted
about the great monarch leave little doubt as to the negativity and intensity of his feelings about Jews. William of Chartres, in concluding
his report on the discussion between Louis IX and his advisers with respect to Jewish usury, has the king speaking of Jews as infecting his land
with their poison. The discussion ends with the king telling his advisers: "Let those prelates do what pertains to them concerning those
subject Christians, and I must do what pertains to me concerning the
Jews. Let them abandon usury, or they shall leave my land completely,
in order that it no longer be polluted with their filth."[26] This is unusually strong language, language that in fact foreshadows modern antisemitic rhetoric. While there is no guarantee that these were precisely
the terms in which Louis expressed himself, the correspondence between these observations of William of Chartres and the more famous
story told by Louis's friend John of Joinville suggests that William's
portrait is accurate.

There is less room for doubting the veracity of John of Joinville's report. According to John, the king recounted to him the story of a
knight's physical assault on a group of Jews who had been invited to
the monastery of Cluny to discuss religious issues. While this story is in
many senses breathtaking in its report of willful violence committed on
Jews who had come to the monastery at the invitation—or perhaps
even insistence—of the monastic leadership, the king cited the knight's
action with high approval, concluding: "I agree myself that no one who
is not a very learned clerk should argue with them. A layman, as soon as
he hears the Christian faith maligned, should defend it only by the
sword, with a good thrust in the belly, as far as the sword will go."[27]
Again, this report is shockingly crude. After all, this was the saintly king
of France speaking, the monarch celebrated for his devotion to justice
and the peaceable resolution of disputes. The notion that any discussion of religious issues should be terminated with a sword thrust en-
courages us to accept the veracity of the condemnation of the Jews put
in Louis's mouth by William of Chartres. That many of the harsh royal
and baronial actions of the late twelfth and thirteenth century might
have stemmed from visceral sentiments like those reflected in these two

accounts of St. Louis seems likely. Obviously, the ruling class was not immune to the anxieties and hatreds that afflicted the Christian masses.

Assessment of the motives of St. Louis's grandfather Philip Augustus is far more difficult.[28] All through his lengthy reign, Philip Augustus took numerous steps against his Jews. These ranged from measured actions against usury to annulment of obligations owed to Jews, to a heavy fine assessed on them, to banishment from the royal domain, and to violent assault on the Jewish community of Brie-Comte-Robert in a neighboring seigneurie. Were these moves all of one cloth and can we identify the motivation that lay behind them? Alternatively, were these actions in fact occasioned by a multiplicity of considerations, which are almost impossible to reconstruct?

Philip Augustus's biographer Rigord of St. Denis expresses little doubt in this matter. For him, as we have seen, the king was in all these actions moved by desire to do the will of the church and by profound conviction of Jewish enmity and harmfulness.[29] Rigord was rather uncomfortable with the royal decision to bring the Jews back into the royal domain in 1198, and Rigord's discomfort should give us pause as well. Many of Philip Augustus's actions might well be explained as aimed at revenues from the Jews or at currying favor with anti-Jewish elements within the population he ruled. Yet the fury of his attack on the Jewish community of Brie-Comte-Robert suggests a sentiment closer to the visceral animosity of his grandson. The issue can obviously not be resolved. Perhaps it suffices to allow for a variety of motivations at work simultaneously. For our overall purposes, whether Philip Augustus was moved by genuine belief in the new stereotypes or cynically exploited them, the net result is the same: The new stereotypes surely did grave damage to the Jews of northern France by prompting their lords to anti-Jewish actions, either out of real conviction of Jewish wrongdoing or out of exploitation of the general tendency to see the Jews in this new, negative way.

We can conclude this discussion of the relatively direct impact of the new stereotypes of Jewish malevolence and harmfulness by noting the novel phenomenon of banishment of Jews. This forceful reaction makes its first appearance in northern Europe toward the end of the twelfth century when in 1182 Philip Augustus decided to exile the Jews from the French royal domain. This significant precedent was repeated by a number of northern French barons in the closing years of the century, spurred by the preaching of Fulk of Neuilly. Since no formal edicts of banishment have been preserved from this period, we cannot be sure of the legal justification for these banishments or the thinking of the rulers who enacted them. In all these cases, however, expulsion of the Jews was directly linked to the issue of usury, in all likelihood to the notion of Jewish malfeasance. When we do begin to find formal edicts of expulsion, in the later decades of the thirteenth century, the accusation of malfeasance is regularly the legal rationale. It thus seems highly likely that the banishments of the late twelfth century were grounded in the same conception. Of course, the legal rationale for these expulsions need not correspond to the actual motivation for such actions. For the purposes of this study of the new stereotypes and their impact, however, whether Philip Augustus, Edward I, or Philip IV actually shared the new perceptions or merely reacted to or exploited them is beside the point. The new view of the harmful Jews was crucial to the removal of Jews from the areas into which they had been enticed a few centuries earlier.[30]

Chapter 6 opened with the precipitous decline of early Ashkenazic Jewry and raised the questions of the point at which decline set in and the factors responsible for it. Now it seems reasonable to essay a succinct answer to these questions. My first line of response is to reject any specific incident as decisive. Rather, what we have seen is a process of accelerating anti-Jewish thinking and action which stretched over a number of decades, with diverse factors underlying it. The process began during the middle years of the twelfth century with a combination of change in the circumstances of Jewish existence—the shift in Jewish economic activity into moneylending—and the deteriorating image of the Jews, which was related to but went far beyond the new Jewish economic specialization. Both these developments influenced the leadership of the church, traditionally concerned with potentially unfavorable Jewish impact on Christian society. All these factors eventually undermined the critical alliance between the Jews and the temporal authorities: The new Jewish economic specialization made the Jews an increasingly appealing target for fiscal exploitation; the church's pressure for limitation of harmful Jewish impact was slowly but surely absorbed by the secular authorities; many of the temporal rulers came to share the new negative imagery of the Jews or at least to exploit its prevalence among those whom they ruled. Out of this complex came rapid decline in the fortunes of early Ashkenazic Jewry.

8

Medieval Stereotypes
and Modern Antisemitism

The deteriorating image of medieval Jews in northern Europe set in motion the decline in fortunes of the Ashkenazic community. With the passage of time this young Jewry was banished from the areas of greatest power and highest culture in western Christendom, shunted off to the central and eastern areas of northern Europe, where its subsequent growth and development were deeply affected by its removal from the most vibrant areas of the West.[1] The regrettable impact of the deteriorating Jewish image extended beyond early Ashkenazic Jewry's decline and relocation: The new twelfth-century stereotypes were permanently absorbed into the historic legacy of Christian anti-Jewish thinking. Many of the most damaging motifs in modern antisemitism can be traced to these twelfth- and thirteenth-century perceptions.

Terminology

While it is exceedingly irksome to begin our discussion of the long-range impact of mid-twelfth-century stereotypes with observations on terminology, there is simply no alternative. The terms with which anti-Jewish imagery has been expressed, analyzed, and evaluated are highly problematic. To neglect these problems is to court disaster.

125

The term *antisemitism*, a curious designation in many ways, was popularized in 1879 by Wilhelm Marr and very rapidly gained currency among those sympathetic to it and those opposed. The purpose of coining such a new term was to distinguish a supposedly innovative understanding of the Jewish issue from prior conceptions of the Jews and the dangers they allegedly presented. Antisemites, who bore the new appellation with pride, wished to set themselves apart from others holding older forms of religious hatred of Jews. The name they chose for themselves and their movement was intended to highlight a biological-racial approach to the Jews and the Jewish issue, an approach they believed dispelled the miasma of misunderstanding that had long obscured the "real" Jewish problem.[2]

Whatever the intentions of those who coin new terminology, the terms they create inevitably have a life of their own. The desire of the antisemites to create a new appellation and to highlight thereby a novel insight was thwarted in diverse ways. The successes of the antisemitic movements transformed the specific term they concocted into a generic designation for anti-Jewish animus, in very much the same way—to be banal—that Kleenex has become a generic designation for tissues. Thus, for example, by 1894 Bernard Lazare published a broad survey of anti-Jewish sentiment entitled *L'Antisémitisme: Son histoire et ses causes*, in which he treated anti-Jewish views from antiquity to his own day.[3] Clearly, expansion of the new term was hardly welcome among its coiners. The term antisemitism, however, continues to be used as a designation for all manifestations of anti-Jewish sentiment, stretching from antiquity to the present and ranging from the most serious to the pettiest.

In fact, the tendency to extend use of the term antisemitism has often involved more than simply natural transformation of a specific into a generic. Many observers and analysts of late nineteenth- and twentieth-century antisemitism were determined to negate the claim of innovation, to argue that what was trumpeted as new was simply a modern reworking of older themes. One of the simplest techniques for asserting such continuity was to transform the purportedly new term into a catch-all designation for anti-Jewish sentiment over the ages. To some extent, Lazare adopted such a polemical stance in giving his study the title he did. Perhaps more strikingly the fullest survey of the historic phenomenon of anti-Jewish sentiment—Léon Poliakov's four-volume study—is entitled *L'Histoire de l'antisémitisme*, again reflecting broad negation of the antisemites' claim to innovation.[4]

We are thus faced with two obvious options for use of the term antisemitism, each with its advantages and disadvantages. On the one hand, some prefer to restrict use to modern racial perceptions of the Jews. Such scholars see in the term a reflection of significant innovation, without in any way denying the roots of this new phenomenon in the past. For these researchers, introduction of the term antisemitism into discussions of antiquity or the Middle Ages can only obfuscate. At the same time, others, perhaps in the majority, feel that the advantages conferred by highlighting continuities outweigh all disadvantages and prefer to use the term antisemitism comprehensively, applying it to all periods of the past and into the present.

There is, to be sure, a third option. For many observers the term antisemitism has a special connotation, a sense of unusually intense or even pathological anti-Jewish sentiment. Thus, some scholars seek to avoid the extremes of inclusive or rigorously limited use of the term antisemitism. To cite only the most carefully enunciated version of this option, Gavin I. Langmuir has argued for special use of the term based essentially on considerations of cognitive style and motivation. For Langmuir, "Antisemitism is an irrational reaction to repress rational doubts."[5] Leaving aside for the moment the precise meaning of Langmuir's definition, this view of antisemitism enables him to avoid both the inclusive and exclusive extremes and to establish a framework through which some anti-Jewish perceptions can be identified as antisemitic and others excluded.

In view of my focus on twelfth-century deterioration of the Jewish image in northern Europe, it is worth citing Langmuir's own sense of the onset of antisemitism, as he defines it: "If antisemitism is defined as chimerical beliefs or fantasies about 'Jews,' as irrational beliefs that attribute to all those symbolized as 'Jews' menacing characteristics of conduct that no Jews have been observed to possess or engage in, then antisemitism first appeared in medieval Europe in the twelfth century."[6] Langmuir's criteria for use of the term enable him to exclude all pre-twelfth-century perceptions of Jews as well as many post-twelfth-century views also, his use contrasting with the inclusive use of the term by Lazare and Poliakov; at the same time these criteria enabled him to reject the antisemites' claim of totally new insight and to see the allegedly innovative views of the nineteenth century as a continuation of prior developments. Langmuir is not the only one to seek a middle way between the inclusive and exclusive extremes; I have cited him because he has worked out a definition more painstakingly than any other researcher.[7]

Any discussion of the term antisemitism must take note simultaneously of the related term *anti-Judaism*. As indicated, the coiners of the new designation antisemitism created their terminology in order to distance themselves from prior religious antipathy toward Jews. The antisemitic desire for distinction between its own anti-Jewish understandings and those of its predecessors has been matched by a parallel yearning for distancing on the part of many Christians. The growing focus on traditional Christian images of Jews in the evolution of perceptions that resulted in modern antisemitism narrowly defined has aroused in many quarters the need to distance Christianity from association with a movement and its terminology that, in the wake of World War II, symbolize profound evil.

Most often, the term anti-Judaism has been utilized rather haphazardly, with little care for precision. Put differently, few researchers have been deeply concerned with establishing the point of demarcation between anti-Judaic and antisemitic thinking. The most obvious exception, once again, is Langmuir. For Langmuir, "anti-Judaism [unlike antisemitism] is a nonrational reaction to overcome nonrational doubts."[8] Again leaving aside for the moment the exact meaning of this definition, the sense conveyed by Langmuir's term anti-Judaism is that of normal, albeit lamentable interreligious rivalry. Langmuir emphasizes that historic anti-Judaism could be bloody indeed. He argues, for example, that the crusader assaults of 1096, with their extensive casualties, were anti-Judaic while the ritual murder allegation of the mid-twelfth century, which rarely produced loss of Jewish lives, was antisemitic.[9] Using Langmuir's distinction, it is possible to look back across Jewish history and assign instances of anti-Jewish animus to one of the two available categories. Once again, Langmuir is not the only researcher to seek such a line of demarcation; no one else, however, has attempted the distinction with as much sophistication as has Langmuir.

With respect to these varying uses of the terms antisemitism and anti-Judaism, one often wishes that it were possible to begin anew and create a lexicon that would do justice to the intricacies of anti-Jewish sentiment over the ages. Were such a new beginning possible, I would start with an all-embracing term for anti-Jewish sentiment which might well be the Hebrew *sin'at Yisra'el*, which means literally "hatred of Israel." This term is almost untranslatable, however, because of the ambiguity of *Yisra'el*, which connotes both Judaism and the Jewish people.[10] Such a comprehensive starting point, lacking the complications associated with the term antisemitism, would then permit careful adjectival specification of divergent forms of anti-Jewish (which conveys some sense of being directed both against Judaism and against Jews) hostility.

Clearly, however, creation of new terminology is not a viable option. I have therefore made my own personal choice of terminology along the following lines: (1) I shall restrict the use of the term antisemitism to the modern phenomenon. It is my sense that introduction of this term into the Middle Ages, either in the simple way followed by Poliakov or even the more complex manner proposed by Langmuir can only be misleading. Since this study is aimed at showing lines of influence between the Middle Ages and the more recent centuries, I am hardly laying myself open to charges of insensitivity to historical continuity. (2) I shall eschew use of the term anti-Judaism altogether. In the first place, it is too flaccid a term. More important, it obscures the inevitable continuity that exists between the religious vision of Judaism and the people who espoused that vision. Over the ages those hostile to Jews have tended by and large to efface the modern distinction between religious faith and the folk who embrace it. I find that the term anti-Judaism adds little and obfuscates considerably. (3) I shall regularly use loose terminology like anti-Jewish sentiment, anti-Jewish perceptions, anti-Jewish hostility, although I am acutely conscious of the ambiguity of the Jewish part of anti-Jewish. I shall then attempt to distinguish among these varying anti-Jewish sentiments by specifying the specific target of non-Jewish displeasure and by distinguishing varying degrees of intensity in anti-Jewish perceptions. Clearly, these are the usages that have already marked the earlier segments of this study. All in all, not an exciting procedure, but hopefully one that will ensure maximal clarity.

Anti-Jewish Sentiment and Its Gradations

The issue of terminology reflects a far deeper problem, that of gradations of anti-Jewish sentiment. Many of those who consciously choose to use the term antisemitism indiscriminately for all forms of anti-Jewish feeling do so out of conviction that there ultimately are no greater and lesser instances of anti-Jewish perception and action, that every manifestation of anti-Jewish sentiment bears within it the potential for drastic results. Not surprisingly, those charged with responsibility for safeguarding Jewish interests in the post-World War II world are loathe to assign gradations to manifestations of anti-Jewish feeling or action. Yet the refusal to allow for such gradations in its turn bears unacceptable results. Particularly in a post-Holocaust setting, it seems crucial to maintain some sense of the truly horrific nature of the genocidal efforts of the Nazis. To transform every instance of social tension into an antisemitic event is ultimately to cheapen language that ought to conjure up unimaginable horror.[11]

Almost all students of historic anti-Jewish sentiment have acknowledged gradations in such feelings, with some sense of more normal and less normal intergroup antipathies. Since Léon Poliakov has been cited for the most comprehensive study of anti-Jewish sentiment and for broad use of the term antisemitism, it is worth noting that despite his use of the term antisemitism in the most encompassing possible way, Poliakov clearly perceives distinctions in the history of antisemitism so defined. Indeed, the very organization of Poliakov's massive endeavor bespeaks divergence. Not surprisingly, Poliakov devoted the first of the four volumes of his study to antisemitism in the sphere of Ashkenazic Jewry, which he defines as those Jews "whose history has been confined to Christian territories," while his second volume addresses antisemitism in the sphere of those Jews "who have lived by turns in Christian and in Moslem territories (Sephardic Jews), or exclusively in Moslem territories." For Poliakov the experience of antisemitism in the Christian world was most intense, hence the decision to open his study with that sector of the globe.[12] The first volume of Poliakov's study shows an obvious progression from the early anti-Jewish sentiment of the pagan world to the stronger anti-Jewish thinking in early Christianity to the yet profounder anti-Jewish biases that began to emerge during the period Poliakov designates "the Age of the Crusades." Poliakov surely projects gradations of anti-Jewish sentiment and in fact focuses heavily on the period and area of our concern as the locus of intensifying anti-Jewish stereotypes.[13]

To be sure, Poliakov does not expend significant energy in distinguishing the various levels of anti-Jewish thinking. Once again, the

most protracted effort to establish sophisticated criteria for distinguishing greater and lesser levels of anti-Jewish sentiment has been that of
Gavin I. Langmuir. As noted, Langmuir defines antisemitism, which
clearly represents the greater evil in intergroup perceptions, in terms of
cognitive style and motivation. In view of the sophistication of Langmuir's effort, I feel obliged to explain why I have chosen to diverge.

Let me begin with the issue of cognitive style. For Langmuir, irrationality, which lies at the heart of his definition of antisemitism, involves assertions of truth for "expressions that could be demonstrated
at the time to be empirically false (for example, Jews have horns)."[14]
Let us note first a criticism leveled recently by Robert C. Stacey. In
a lengthy and perceptive review of Langmuir's *History, Religion, and
Antisemitism*, Stacey examines carefully Langmuir's definition of irrationality through consideration of the ritual murder allegation that surfaced in Lincoln in 1255, an incident that Langmuir himself analyzed
meticulously.[15] Stacey suggests that given the evidence amassed, pro-
cessed by the royal court, and duly registered in the official rolls of the
court, it is difficult to maintain that this particular ritual murder allegation against the Jews of Lincoln could have been demonstrated *at the
time* to be empirically false. Stacey's conclusion is that the narrow
Langmuir definition of irrationality is ultimately too confining.[16]

Let us pursue the matter a bit further. The specific assertion that
Langmuir adduces in the passage cited—that Jews have horns—is
hardly a terribly important assertion; Langmuir is ultimately interested
in weightier statements, such as the claim that Jews commit ritualized
murder, which he believes could also be empirically proven false. Now,
if the Langmuir definition of antisemitism is taken seriously, then we
can easily find such irrational (in the strict Langmuir sense) views of
Jews prior to the middle of the twelfth century. Perhaps the most readily accessible of such prior perceptions is the well-known notion that
the Jews of antiquity worshipped an ass's head in their Holy of
Holies.[17] If we range these three statements—Jews have horns, Jews
worship an ass's head, Jews commit ritualized murder—side by side, it
seems clear that the first two have very little meaning for the history of
antisemitism; the third does, not by virtue of its "irrationality" but by
virtue of the image it projects of Jewish cruelty and harmfulness.

Let us examine another set of assertions with respect to the Jews. In
medieval sources we regularly encounter statements that portray the
Jews as steeped in unremitting hostility toward Christianity and Chris-

tians or as allies of the devil. The latter Langmuir would surely classify as nonrational; the former is more problematic but would probably be identified with the nonrational as well. Yet do these three assertions—Jews commit ritual murder, Jews are allied with the devil, Jews are unremittingly hostile to Christianity and Christians—really deserve to be sundered in the manner that Langmuir proposes? In one way or another, they are all reflections of the drastic danger that Jews purportedly pose to their neighbors. As a group, the assertions have much more to do with antisemitism than do the prior assertions about horns or an ass's head.

In forcing his distinction on such statements, Langmuir is ultimately distorting our everyday use of the word "irrational." In ordinary parlance we do not reserve the term for perceptions of beings or behaviors that have never been observed or that can be empirically proven false. Much of what constitutes the domain of the irrational involves exaggerated perceptions of the realities of everyday life. For someone to be considered "irrational" need not involve apprehension that leaving home will result in an encounter with the Loch Ness monster; to be fearful that a normal crowd, which is acknowledged to be real and occasionally to be lethal, will do terrible harm or to fear crossing a street because of the dangers posed by traffic, even though cars are real and occasionally strike pedestrians, warrants the designation "irrational." Similarly, although Jews could on occasion have been proved to harbor hostility, to posit that Jews were unremittingly hostile constitutes in its own right a highly distorted and irrational perception or statement.

Indeed, more is involved here than normal use of terminology. In order to establish the important distinction he seeks, Langmuir is drawn to focus too heavily on the cognitive aspect of anti-Jewish assertions. The statements that interest him (and me) are meant to convey more than empirical information; the claims that Jews have horns or tails, that Jews commit ritualized murder, and that Jews are allied with the devil are all, at another level, metaphorical, aimed at alerting others to the alleged malevolence and inhumanity of the Jews. The implications of these statements for the nature and behavior of the Jews are crucial. Ultimately, it seems to me that gradations of anti-Jewish perception are best established through focus on the projected image of alleged Jewish harmfulness rather than emphasis on the imaginative quality of anti-Jewish assertions.[18]

Langmuir's second criterion for defining antisemitism seems equally problematic. He distinguishes between efforts to repress rational doubts (antisemitism) and efforts to overcome nonrational doubts (anti-Judaism). The initial problem with this distinction is the frailty already noted in Langmuir's definitions of rational, nonrational, and irrational. More important is the difficulty in establishing human motivation. In light of the grave obstacles to an individual's full comprehension of his or her own present-day motivations, the effort to fathom the present-day motivations of others becomes highly questionable and the effort to reconstruct the motivations of human beings no longer directly observable becomes almost unthinkable.

More is involved than simple methodological difficulty in assessing the psychological motivations of past individuals or groups. Ultimately, it seems to me that my analysis of the deteriorating image of early Ashkenazic Jewry suggests that Langmuir focuses too heavily on religious doubt. We have noted, to be sure, that one of the core anti-Jewish perceptions manifest during the earliest stages of Jewish migration into northern Europe was the sense of Jews as religiously different and—inevitably—religiously threatening. But my analysis of increasingly negative Jewish stereotypes concluded that the most damaging change in imagery highlighted alleged Jewish hatred of Christianity and Christians and acts of anti-Christian violence generated by this purported hatred. The imagery of Jews bringing harm on Christendom through their moneylending activities, their blasphemous abuse of Christian symbols, and their murder of Christian neighbors constitutes the heart of the new anti-Jewish stereotypes. Again, I am by no means eliminating religious threat and religious doubt from the complex of anti-Jewish sentiments of either the twelfth century or succeeding epochs; I am urging, however, that religious doubt not be accorded such a central place in the constellation of elements in anti-Jewish thinking.[19] Far more significant than the threat associated with religious doubt was the fear of direct Jewish harmfulness, in any of the modalities just noted.[20]

In the light of these last observations I propose, as an alternative to Langmuir's hierarchy of anti-Jewish sentiments based on cognitive style and motivation, an emphasis on the straightforward or implied content of anti-Jewish stereotypes and on the level of anxiety aroused by these anti-Jewish motifs. The most intense and dangerous anti-Jewish perceptions are precisely those which seem to involve the greatest threat to the perceiver's personal being or to the well-being of the community.

The profounder the sense of threat the deeper the fear, the deeper the fear the more intense the hatred and the more irrational the perceptions.[21] Thus, in place of Langmuir's focus on cognitive style and motivation, I would urge that anti-Jewish stereotypes be ranked in terms of the dangers that Jews are alleged to present. The most pernicious anti-Jewish imagery (antisemitic imagery if one wishes to use that terminology) involves stereotypes alleging mortal threats purportedly posed by Jews.[22]

Anti-Jewish Sentiments Historically Considered: Context versus Legacy

In the effort to understand the thinking that led to modern antisemitism and the Nazi assault on European Jewry, a mini-controversy has arisen between those who emphasize the structural context in which racial antisemitism developed and those who stress the legacy of ideas and perceptions that underlay the thinking of modern antisemites. Hannah Arendt's social science perspective is often cited as an example of the contextual approach and such historians as Léon Poliakov and Jacob Katz are noted for their emphasis on the legacy of ideas and perceptions.[23]

Not surprisingly, neither approach can be sustained unilaterally. Hannah Arendt, to take the one side, was strongly opposed to certain metaphysical views of immutable anti-Jewish hostility. Early in her analysis of antisemitism, Arendt identifies and rejects a number of traditional explanations of the phenomenon, including what she calls the "doctrine of an 'eternal antisemitism' in which Jew-hatred is a normal and natural reaction to which history gives only more or less opportunity."[24] In her opposition to such a doctrine, however, Arendt would be readily joined by Poliakov, Katz, and most other present-day historians. To be sure, Arendt chose to emphasize in her epochal study the contextual constellation that shaped modern antisemitism. Her study of antisemitism was, after all, the first element of a three-part political analysis of totalitarianism. In choosing to highlight the contemporary context of modern antisemitism, Arendt was by no means oblivious to the specific perceptions that constituted the anti-Jewish thinking of the antisemites. That she chose in her broad study of totalitarianism to emphasize the context of modern antisemitism and to deemphasize the legacy of anti-Jewish ideas and perceptions that impinged on this context does not imply negation of this legacy and its impact.

Similarly, Poliakov and Katz, it seems to me, have chosen to highlight the legacy of anti-Jewish thinking without denying the reality and importance of changing contexts. Both accord attention to altered environments, particularly in the shift from the medieval to the modern. Again, however, given the nature of their enterprise—for Poliakov a total history of anti-Jewish sentiments and for Katz a survey of modern anti-Jewish thinking—it is hardly surprising that they emphasize the commonalities of legacy rather than the differences of particular contexts.

I suggest that in fact every new stage in the evolution of anti-Jewish thinking is marked by dialectical interplay between a prior legacy of negative stereotypes and the realities of a new social context. Out of this interplay emerge novel anti-Jewish perceptions, which in turn become part of the historic tradition of anti-Jewish sentiment. In this way, anti-Jewish thought maintains a measure of stability and continuity, while in fact evolving considerably over the ages.

We have in effect seen such a process at work in this study, exemplified in the historical experience of early Ashkenazic Jewry. As Mediterranean Jews pushed northward into areas of Europe heretofore of little interest to them and little interested in them, they inevitably evoked prior Christian images of Jews and Jewish life. This imagery played a considerable role in shaping the circumstances of these immigrants in their new environment. New realities of Jewish life were fashioned by the novel conditions of the twelfth century. Similarly, new perceptions of Jews were shaped by the social and spiritual climate of the middle decades of the twelfth century, imagery dominated by alleged Jewish hostility and suspicion of immediate threat to Christianity and Christians. These new perceptions of the Jews offer a case study of the interaction of context and perceptual legacy, the result of which is a new imagery.

The imagery created by this twelfth-century interaction was by no means confined to that particular time period. The new and destructive stereotypes we have studied were quickly integrated into the complex of Christian perceptions of Jews. As the medieval world gave way to modernity and, somewhat later, as industrialized societies took shape, the new patterns created during the twelfth century played a role in further evolution of the negative Jewish image, fated to intensify and to produce yet greater devastation than did the emergent twelfth-century imagery upon which we have focused.

The Christian Legacy and Its Evolution

When after World War II there commenced a serious effort to plumb the wellsprings of the antisemitic thinking that had wrought such havoc in Europe, much attention focused on the role of Christian thinking in the adumbration of the virulent Nazi imagery of the Jews. While many have contributed to this focus, it seems fair to identify two figures above all others—the Christian cleric James Parkes, whose concern with antisemitism and the Christian role in it much predates the outbreak of the war, and the Jew Jules Isaac, whose personal tragedy during the war years moved him to devote the rest of his life to studying the Christian roots of antisemitism.[25] Both these men did much more than simply study the issue; both were intensely involved in the effort to alter the Christian imagery that they believed underlay much traditional anti-Jewish thinking. Isaac is generally credited with considerable personal influence on Pope John XXIII and the Second Vatican Council.

Let us gain some sense of the relationship of Christianity to antisemitism through a quick look at the views of Jules Isaac, utilizing his 1962 *L'Enseignement du mépris.*[26] In this work, as in his others, Isaac argues for the preponderant role of what he calls Christian antisemitism in the development of modern antisemitism. Isaac acknowledges that anti-Jewish sentiment predated Christianity. He argues, however, that this Greco-Roman anti-Jewish sentiment was limited and exercised little impact in its own time or subsequently. For Isaac Christian anti-Jewish thinking has been incomparably more widespread and influential. He identifies three key Christian teachings that have promoted anti-Jewish thinking: the evaluation of Judaism at the time of Jesus as degenerate; the fixing of guilt on the Jews for the Crucifixion; the conclusion that Jews have been punished for the crime of crucifixion by their dispersion and suffering. (Recall the centrality of the church stand on the blame and punishment for the Crucifixion in the traditionalist teachings of Bernard of Clairvaux and, more broadly, in my foregoing analysis.)

Isaac makes two mitigating observations as to the culpability of Christianity in the development of modern antisemitism. First, he assesses the place of anti-Jewish teachings within the totality of authentic Christian belief and comes to the conclusion that the Christian anti-Jewish teachings he identifies and decries are by no means fundamental to Christianity. Indeed, Isaac's protracted and somewhat successful efforts at altering Christian doctrine with respect to the Jews were of course based on the assumption that anti-Jewish teachings do not lie at the core of Christianity, that a Christianity purged of these teachings would remain authentic.[27]

More important for our purposes is a second mitigating observation made by Isaac, the claim that "all authorities are agreed that anti-Semitism is by definition unchristian, even anti-Christian," a statement buttressed by citation of a wide range of Christian authorities who denounce antisemitism.[28] Herein lies a fundamental problem for Isaac himself and for others who similarly emphasize the centrality of Christian teachings in the emergence of modern antisemitism. How in fact can Christian doctrine lie at the core of an ideology that is unchristian, even anti-Christian? And how can the three central Christian teachings identified by Isaac have influenced modern movements and views that are indifferent, for example, to the Crucifixion, which is so essential to Christian anti-Jewish tradition?

Many scholars have wrestled with this issue of the centrality of Christian teaching to modern antisemitic movements that were ostensibly hostile to Christianity. Let me cite the views of Jacob Katz. Katz notes the problem and makes a number of suggestions. The first is simply that modern antisemites were by no means unanimous in their opposition to the tenets of Christianity. While Nazi doctrine—and that of many other antisemitic movements as well—may have formally rejected traditional Christianity, not all antisemitic groups and leaders did. Moreover, even within those movements that did repudiate Christianity, not all members subscribed to such rejection. Thus, there remained many traditional Christians in the anti-Christian antisemitic movements, traditional Christians for whom the legacy of Christian anti-Jewish thinking remained alive and potent. Katz further argues that even for those who overtly repudiated Christianity, the impact of teachings that had pervaded the European atmosphere for so long could not be readily dissipated. It was therefore possible to break with official Christianity and with most of its doctrines and yet remain under the influence of a portion of the Christian legacy, in this case its anti-Jewish imagery. This is a perfectly reasonable approach. A full-blown break with a prior mindset is rare; traditions tend to be tenacious; revolutionary social movements in fact absorb many of the teachings of the environment against which they rebel.[29] Having said all this, however, my analysis of the development of novel anti-Jewish imagery during the twelfth century offers further clarification of the impact of traditional Christian anti-Jewish thinking on the modern antisemitic, often anti-Christian worldview.

In fact, the imagery of the Crucifixion is by no means central to modern antisemitic thinking. The stereotype that is central projects Jews as powerful, as implacably hostile to Western civilization, as committed to and capable of bringing profound harm to the majority society in which they live. This imagery represents a specific and intermediate stage in the long history of Christian anti-Jewish imagery, a stage that has formed the center of attention in this study. Building on the doctrine of Jewish culpability for the Crucifixion and moved by the realities of Jewish minority life and the anxieties of Christian majority existence, northern European society of the twelfth century spun out an altered set of fantasies about Jews—fantasies of Jewish hatred, Jewish malevolence, Jewish injury to Christianity and to Christians. This view of Jews was hardly doctrinal, although its roots lay firmly in the most significant of the three Christian teachings specified by Isaac, the fastening of responsibility for the Crucifixion on the Jews. Once this popular view of the everyday Jew became fixed in the minds of northern European Christians (and more slowly in the minds of southern European Christians as well), it left the realm of religious teaching and entered the realm of European folklore and folk wisdom.[30] The hostile, puissant, and harmful Jew became a staple of the thinking of the European civilization that had by and large banished real Jews to its peripheries. The imagery absorbed by modern antisemitic movements might ultimately be traceable to Christian teachings, but these fundamental Christian teachings had evolved into a new set of stereotypes that no longer required religious doctrine to support them.

A brief look at Shakespeare's Shylock will serve as telling illustration of this thesis.[31] Shakespeare wrote *The Merchant of Venice* at a point when Jews had long been absent from the English scene. While Shakespeare was surely a Christian of considerable conviction, his Shylock need not be explained as deriving from the traditional doctrine of Jewish guilt for the Crucifixion. Indeed, the leap from this doctrine to the character of Shylock is long. The intermediate step between guilt for the Crucifixion and the wickedness of Shylock is certainly the set of developments we have tracked. Shylock epitomizes the mid-twelfth-century imagery we have analyzed. He represents the new Jewish specialization in moneylending, with all the baggage that image carries with it; he is consumed with hatred for Christianity and Christians; his demand for his pound of flesh represents a remarkably faithful rendition of the malevolence and cruelty that twelfth-century northern European Christians began to attribute to their Jewish neighbors. Shakespeare labored with some success to transform this folkloristic figure into a living, believable, and even somewhat sympathetic villain.[32] Nonetheless, the roots of the Shakespearean portrait lie in the rich European folklore that the twelfth century began to create, and its literary and dramatic effectiveness only served to reinforce the pernicious stereotypes.[33] In other words, Shakespeare's Shylock is unthinkable prior to the mid-twelfth century; after this period, he is almost a commonplace.

Thus, the final argument of this study is that Christian—and by extension Western—anti-Jewish thinking is far from fixed and immutable.[34] Anti-Jewish imagery, arguably central to the classical period in the development of Christian faith, shows considerable historic growth and alteration as one moves from the earliest stratum in Christian teaching down through virulent twentieth-century antisemitism. The evolution of modern antisemitism takes us through a number of related but by no means inevitable phases. One of the most influential of these stages took place in mid-twelfth-century northern Europe. There a rapidly evolving new society attracted energetic immigrant Jews; there new circumstances and a new context of Jewish living were created, both for good and for ill; there the new circumstances of Jewish life, the preexistent legacy of prior Christian anti-Jewish views, and the high level of anxiety spawned in this rapidly developing society combined to create a novel set of damaging anti-Jewish stereotypes. These sinister images were slowly absorbed throughout all sectors of majority society, influencing the leadership of both church and state and eventually contributing to the decline of early Ashkenazic Jewry and the demise of many segments of this immigrant community.

Long after the Jews had left much of northern Europe, the ideational legacy of the mid-twelfth century maintained its hold on the

European imagination. Even when the power of the Christian synthe-sis—including its traditional anti-Jewish component—had waned all across modern Europe, the potent imagery of the hostile and puissant Jew was maintained. The nineteenth and twentieth centuries added new elements to evolving anti-Jewish imagery: Jewish exploitation of modern democracy, Jewish control of the mass media, the racial base of Jewish identity, to cite but a few. All these new elements were, however, absorbed into the broad ideational framework of the hostile and pow-erful Jew that emerged in mid-twelfth-century northern Europe.[35] An area and an era noted for its rich and positive contribution to the mod-ern West left simultaneously a legacy of hate-filled and hateful imagery that has inflicted incalculable harm.

Notes

1. An Immigrant Jewry: Protection, Persecution, Perception

1. Not a great deal has been written about pre-tenth-century northern European Jewry, reflecting both the lack of materials and (I would argue) the lack of importance of the community. For an overview of Jewish fate under the Merovingians and the Carolingians, see Solomon Katz, *The Jews in the Visigothic and Frankish Kingdoms of Spain and Gaul* (Cambridge, Mass., 1937); a number of the essays collected in Cecil Roth, ed., *The Dark Ages: Jews in Christian Europe 711–1096*, The World History of the Jewish People (Tel Aviv, 1966); Bernard S. Bachrach, *Early Medieval Jewish Policy in Western Europe* (Minneapolis, 1977).

2. The remarkable vitalization of northern Europe has been addressed by major twentieth-century historians. Perhaps the most influential statement is Marc Bloch's depiction of what he called "the first feudal age" in his *Feudal Society*, trans. L. A. Manyon (London, 1961), parts 1 and 2. Note the reissue of the French original, *La Société féodale*, in 1989, fifty years after its initial appearance, with an interesting preface by Robert Fossier. For a recent reconsideration of these matters, with the introduction of climatic change into the mix, see Robert Fossier, *Le Moyen Âge*, 3d ed., 3 vols. (Paris, 1990), 2:5–15.

3. We have sources that tell us of the invitation of Jews to settle in the county of Flanders early in the eleventh century, of the invitation to settle in England in the middle of the eleventh century, and of the invitation to settle in the town of Speyer toward the end of that century. In all three cases the initiative of the relevant lord is highlighted.

4. The term *Ashkenaz* remains something of a puzzle. More precisely, the basis for transformation of the biblical designation into an appellation for Germany (more narrowly) or northern Europe (more broadly) is still unclear. See, inter alia, Samuel Kraus, "The Names Ashkenaz and Sepharad" (in Hebrew), *Tarbiẓ* 3 (1931–32): 423–435, and Judah Rosenthal, "Ashkenaz, Sefarad, and Zarfat," *Historia Judaica* 5 (1943): 58–62. The position taken here with respect to early Ashkenazic Jewry as an immigrant community that developed toward the end of the tenth century represents the accepted consensus of present-day historians of the Jews. The one divergent view was expressed by Irving A. Agus, especially in *The Heroic Age of Franco-German Jewry* (New York, 1969). Agus argued that the roots of Ashkenazic Jewry go back into antiquity, that small numbers of northern European Jews survived the disruptions of the fourth-fifth and ninth-tenth centuries, and that the eventual growth of this community took place largely through biological increase. Weighty considerations militate against the Agus view. The first is lack of evidence for considerable Jewish settlement in northern Europe prior to the disruptions of the fourth-fifth centuries or of the ninth-tenth centuries. As noted, there are random indications of transient Jews during this early period and even a few data on Jewish communities. Nothing in this evidence, however, suggests the kind of presence posited by Agus. Second, the current sense of disintegration of urban life during the disorders of the ninth and tenth centuries makes the ongoing presence of these putative Jews even less likely. There is no way urban Jews could have sustained themselves in any significant numbers through a period in which city life and trade virtually disappeared. Finally, it would be strange in the extreme that the tenth- and eleventh-century northern European Jews would have lost all recollection of these heroic ancestors if such had existed. Yet one of the striking features of tenth- and eleventh-century Ashkenazic Jewry is the lack of identifiable forebears to whom appeal could be made for a number of important purposes. Given the inherent unlikeliness of the Agus thesis and the specific problems advanced, we are justified in rejecting this view and accepting the broad consensus that the economic and social progress palpable during the late tenth century eventually made this heretofore backward area an appealing site for establishment of new, small, and dynamic Jewish communities.

5. Recurrently in general observations on medieval European Jewry, scholars facilely contrast the peaceful circumstances for the Jews in the first half of the Middle Ages and the tumultuous conditions of their existence from the late eleventh century onward. Rarely is there adequate recognition of the geography of these altered circumstances. All the eleventh-century tumult and most of the twelfth-century problems were concentrated in the northern sectors of Europe, the area of recent Jewish immigration. Clearly, immigration itself played a role in the new tensions. Southern European Jewry continued to enjoy relatively peaceful circumstances into the thirteenth century. A similar failure to acknowledge properly the importance of geography and immigration vitiates the central argument of Mark R. Cohen's recent study of the comparative fate of medieval Jews in Christendom and in the realms of Islam; see his *Under Cres-*

cent and Cross: The Jews in the Middle Ages (Princeton, 1994). Cohen sets the terms for his contrasts by noting that "for comparative purposes, I have found it fruitful to focus on the Latin West and mainly on the *northern* [Cohen's italics] lands, even though the study takes full cognizance of the fact that the religious and legal foundations of the Christian-Jewish relationship were Mediterranean in origin." The justification for this choice lies in the fact that "the contrasts in the North are simply more vivid and less encumbered than in the South." What this ultimately means is that Cohen contrasts the circumstances of an old and large Islamicate Jewry and a new and small subset of Jewish settlements in Christendom. Do the differences he discerns flow from essential divergence between the worlds of Islam and Christianity or do they simply reflect distinctions between well-settled and newcomer communities?

6. The instability of life in late tenth- and eleventh-century northern Europe is a central motif in the Bloch treatment of the "first feudal age," cited above, this chapter, note 2.

7. See my study of this incident, "1007–1012: Initial Crisis for Northern European Jewry," *Proceedings of the American Academy for Jewish Research* 38–39 (1970–71): 101–117. In a recent essay Richard Landes has added further considerations to the argument I mounted for the relationship of the anti-Jewish activities to incipient heresy. See his "La Vie apostolique en Aquitaine en l'an mil: Paix de Dieu, culte des reliques, et communautés hérétiques," *Annales—Économies, Sociétés, Civilisations* 46 (1991): 573–593, esp. 584–586. To be sure, the evidence is still sparse and the suggested link far from firm.

8. The five sources are the lament of Rabbenu Gershom ben Judah of Mainz, the *Annales Quedlinburgenses*, Adhémar of Chabannes, Raoul Glaber, and the anonymous Hebrew narrative. All these sources are discussed in Chazan, "1007–1012," 102–106. With respect to the anonymous Hebrew narrative, Kenneth R. Stow, in *The "1007 Anonymous" and Papal Sovereignty: Jewish Perceptions of the Papacy and Papal Policy in the High Middle Ages* (Cincinnati, 1984), has argued for a thirteenth-century dating. I disputed his arguments in my review of his book in *Speculum* 62 (1987): 728–731. While the narrative was clearly not composed at the time of the events depicted, I still see no reason for positing a late provenance for this valuable source or for rejecting its usefulness.

9. "The Solomon bar Simson Chronicle," in Adolf Neubauer and Moritz Stern, eds., *Hebräische Berichte über die Judenverfolgungen während der Kreuzzüge* (Berlin, 1892), 3; Abraham Habermann, ed., *Sefer Gezerot Ashkenaz ve-Zarfat* (Jerusalem, 1945), 26.

10. See above, this chapter, note 8.

11. Robert Chazan, *European Jewry and the First Crusade* (Berkeley, 1987). I have recently published a more popularly oriented study of the 1096 events, *In the Year 1096: The First Crusade and the Jews* (Philadelphia, 1996).

12. Alfred Hilgard, ed., *Urkunden zur Geschichte der Stadt Speyer* (Strasbourg, 1885), 11.

13. "The Solomon bar Simson Chronicle," in Neubauer and Stern, *Hebräische Berichte*, 31, and in Habermann, *Sefer Gezerot*, 59–60.

14. "The Solomon bar Simson Chronicle," in Neubauer and Stern, *Hebräische Berichte*, 2 and 14, and in Habermann, *Sefer Gezerot*, 25 and 40.

15. It is increasingly clear that the lengthy narrative attributed to an unknown Solomon bar Simson is in fact a composite work, with a later editor amassing material from a variety of sources available to him, including reports that are highly questionable. Nonetheless, this later editor was obviously not able to find evidence of further assaults on northern European Jewry. To be sure, there are occasional claims in both the Hebrew and Latin sources of wide-ranging massacres of Jews. Until specific evidence is adduced, I have seen these as the kind of unwarranted generalizations that disaster often produces.

16. The Hebrew narratives themselves offer instances in which animosity was evoked, without resulting in extensive destruction. The most striking case was Speyer, described in some detail in the older and shorter of the narratives. There the bishop intervened energetically and effectively on behalf of the Jews.

17. For an overview of Jewish fate during the Second Crusade, see Chazan, *European Jewry and the First Crusade*, 169–179.

18. I have studied the narrative of Ephraim ben Jacob of Bonn in "R. Ephraim of Bonn's *Sefer Zechirah*," *Revue des études juives* 132 (1973): 587–594.

19. R. I. Moore, in his "Anti-Semitism and the Birth of Europe," in *Christianity and Judaism: Papers Read at the 1991 Summer Meeting and the 1992 Winter Meeting of the Ecclesiastical History Society*, ed. Diana Wood (Oxford, 1992), 33–57, discusses extensively the proper meaning of the term *popular*, which he restricts to

that great majority of the population which, being effectively subject to the seigneural ban, enjoyed neither noble nor clerical status, the unfree and the illiterate. Modern historians have no excuse for blurring a distinction which is quite plain, socially, legally, and conceptually, in their sources and in particular no excuse for using "popular" as a synonym for "lay."

I wish to note that I am not using the term *popular* in the technical sense that Moore projects. I am using the term in a loose sense to signify attitudes that were widespread throughout society, cutting across all social groupings.

20. For a strong statement on the embeddedness of the church and churchmen in the affairs of society, see R. W. Southern, *Western Society and the Church in the Middle Ages*, The Pelican History of the Church (Harmondsworth, 1970), chapter 1. For an extended argument for the impact of medieval society on the church, see Adriaan H. Bredero, *Christendom and Christianity in the Middle Ages*, trans. Reinder Bruinsma (Grand Rapids, 1994).

21. Note the interesting evidence provided in the epistle composed by the late tenth-century Jewish community of Le Mans. In this letter there is brief description of the assassination of a prominent Jew by hired killers. As the Jew was assaulted early in the morning, he called out and was assisted by the townspeople of Le Mans, clearly both Jewish and non-Jewish. See "The 992 Le Mans Letter," ed. Abraham Berliner, *Ozar Tov* (1878): 50; Habermann, *Sefer Gezerot*, 12.

22. "The Solomon bar Simson Chronicle," in Neubauer and Stern, *Hebräische Berichte*, 4, and in Habermann, *Sefer Gezerot*, 28.

23. "The Solomon bar Simson Chronicle," in Neubauer and Stern, *Hebräische Berichte*, 15, and in Habermann, *Sefer Gezerot*, 40.

24. See Chazan, *European Jewry and the First Crusade*, 87–88.

25. "The 1007 Account," ed. Abraham Berliner, *Ozar Tov* (1878): 46; Habermann, *Sefer Gezerot*, 19.

26. For observations on the use of this material, see my "The Facticity of Medieval Narrative: A Case Study of the Hebrew First Crusade Narratives," *AJS Review* 16 (1991): 31–56, esp. 44.

27. Hilgard, *Urkunden zur Geschichte der Stadt Speyer*, 11.

28. Ibid.

29. Note the important study of the deicide theme by Jeremy Cohen, "The Jews as Killers of Christ in the Latin Tradition, from Augustine to the Friars," *Traditio* 39 (1983): 3–27.

30. Elaine Pagels, *The Origins of Satan* (New York, 1995).

31. Albert of Aachen, *Historia Hierosolymitana*, in *Recueil des historiens des croisades, Historiens occidentaux*, 5 vols. (Paris, 1844–1895), 4:292.

32. Guibert of Nogent, *Autobiographie*, ed. and trans. Edmond-René Labande, Les Classiques de l'histoire de France au moyen âge (Paris, 1981), 118.

33. Recall my observations in the introduction on the importance of Jewish sources for providing a balanced picture of majority anti-Jewish sentiment.

34. "The Mainz Anonymous," in Neubauer and Stern, *Hebräische Berichte*, 47, and in Habermann, *Sefer Gezerot*, 93.

35. "The Solomon bar Simson Chronicle," in Neubauer and Stern, *Hebräische Berichte*, 1, and in Habermann, *Sefer Gezerot*, 24. Note that in this source, as well as in the following two, the image of the Jewish enemy is compounded by the call for vengeance against the historic foe. On the centrality of vengeance in crusader thinking in general, see Jonathan Riley-Smith, *The First Crusade and the Idea of Crusading* (London, 1986); Riley-Smith emphasized the centrality of the vengeance motif in the 1096 anti-Jewish violence in his "The First Crusade and the Persecution of the Jews," in *Persecution and Toleration: Papers Read at the Twenty-second Summer Meeting and the Twenty-third Winter Meeting of the Ecclesiastical History Society*, ed. W. J. Sheils (Oxford, 1984), 51–72.

36. "The Mainz Anonymous," in Neubauer and Stern, *Hebräische Berichte*, 49, and in Habermann, *Sefer Gezerot*, 96.

37. "The Mainz Anonymous," in Neubauer and Stern, *Hebräische Berichte*, 53, and in Habermann, *Sefer Gezerot*, 99.

38. "The 992 Le Mans Letter," Berliner, *Ozar Tov*, 50–51; Habermann, *Sefer Gezerot*, 13.

39. Adhémar does not make this causal link between alleged Jewish complicity in the destruction of the Church of the Holy Sepulcher and the early eleventh-century pressures brought to bear on northern European Jewry.

40. "The Mainz Anonymous," in Neubauer and Stern, *Hebräische Berichte*, 49, and in Habermann, *Sefer Gezerot*, 95. When this valuable text was first pub-

lished at the end of the nineteenth century, it was occasionally suggested that this well-poisoning motif indicated fourteenth-century provenance. Clearly, such a conclusion is not at all warranted. I have argued in fact for the early provenance of this Hebrew narrative in an essay to appear in a Festschrift in honor of Yosef Haim Yerushalmi.

2. Real Change and Reality-Based Imagery

1. On the innovations in talmudic study, see the synthesizing effort of Ephraim E. Urbach, *Baʿaley ha-Tosafot* [The Tosafists], 5th ed., 2 vols. (Jerusalem, 1986). On the innovations in biblical studies, see the path-breaking studies of Sarah Kamin, including *Rashi: Peshuto shel Mikra u-Midrasho shel Mikra* [Rashi: The Plain Meaning and the Midrashic Meaning of the Bible] (Jerusalem, 1986) and the essays collected in *Jews and Christians Interpret the Bible* (Jerusalem, 1991). On the innovative mystical speculation of the German Pietists, see the recent work of Elliot R. Wolfson, including "Circumcision and the Divine Name: A Study in the Transmission of Esoteric Doctrine," *Jewish Quarterly Review* 78 (1987–88): 77–112; "The Mystical Significance of Torah Study in Haside Ashkenaz," *Jewish Quarterly Review* 84 (1993–94): 43–78; "The Image of Jacob Engraved on the Throne: Further Reflexion on the Esoteric Doctrine of the German Pietists," in E. R. Wolfson, *Along the Path: Studies in Kabbalistic Myth, Symbolism, and Hermeneutics* (Albany, 1995), 1–62, and *Through a Speculum That Shines: Vision and Imagination in Medieval Jewish Mysticism* (Princeton, 1995), 188–269.
2. I have argued extensively against the view that the First Crusade constituted a watershed in early Ashkenazic history in my *European Jewry and the First Crusade* (Berkeley, 1987), 197–210. Independently, Simon Schwarzfuchs came to parallel conclusions—see his "The Place of the Crusades in Jewish History" (in Hebrew), in *Tarbut ve-Ḥevrah be-Toldot Yisra'el bi-Me ha-Benayim,* [Culture and Society in Medieval Jewish History], ed. Menahem Ben-Sasson et al. (Jerusalem, 1989), 251–267.
3. R. W. Southern, *The Making of the Middle Ages* (London, 1953), 12.
4. Peter Spufford, *Money and Its Use in Medieval Europe* (Cambridge, 1988), chaps. 5, 10, and 11.
5. On these reforming circles, see the magisterial study of John W. Baldwin, *Masters, Princes, and Merchants: The Social Views of Peter the Chanter and His Circle*, 2 vols. (Princeton, 1970).
6. Ephraim of Bonn, "The Book of Remembrance," in Adolf Neubauer and Moritz Stern, eds., *Hebräische Berichte über die Judenverfolgungen während der Kreuzzüge* (Berlin, 1892), 64, and in Abraham Habermann, ed., *Sefer Gezerot Ashkenaz ve-Ẓarfat* (Jerusalem, 1945), 121.
7. The papal position at this juncture involved remission of interest to cru-

saders, which is a far cry from annulment of obligations in their totality. On this papal position and its development, see my *European Jewry and the First Crusade*, 179–182.

8. Peter Abelard, *Dialogus inter Philosophum, Iudaeum et Christianum*, ed. Rudolf Thomas (Stuttgart, 1970), 51. The translation is taken from P. J. Payer, *Dialogue of a Philosopher with a Jew and a Christian* (Toronto, 1979), 33.

9. Confiscation and sale of Jewish property after the expulsions of the late twelfth century and the early fourteenth century clearly indicate ongoing Jewish landowning and land working.

10. Note that Abelard does not have the Jew suggest that farming was prohibited, only that it was dangerous and difficult.

11. See below, my chapter 3, for full analysis of this important statement.

12. J. Leclercq and H. M. Rochais, eds., *Sancti Bernardi opera*, 8 vols. (Rome, 1957–1977), 8:316.

13. "The Blois Letters," in Neubauer and Stern, *Hebräische Berichte*, 35, and in Habermann, *Sefer Gezerot*, 146.

14. H. G. Richardson, *The English Jewry under Angevin Kings* (London, 1960); Robert C. Stacey, "Jewish Lending and the Medieval English Economy," in *A Commercialising Economy, England 1086 to c. 1300*, ed. Richard H. Britnell and Bruce M. S. Campbell (Manchester, 1995), 78–101. Both reinforce the reality of a twelfth-century Jewish shift into moneylending.

15. For a recent sketch of Aaron of Lincoln, see Robert C. Stacey, "Aaron of Lincoln," in *The Dictionary of National Biography: Missing Persons*, ed. C. S. Nicholls (Oxford, 1993), 1. On the *Scaccarium Aaronis*, see Richardson, *The English Jewry under Angevin Kings*, 115–120.

16. See my *European Jewry and the First Crusade*, 189–191. On the York massacre, see the excellent study by R. B. Dobson, *The Jews of Medieval York and the Massacre of March 1190* (York, 1974).

17. On this enhanced system of governmental protection and control, see Cecil Roth, *A History of the Jews in England*, 3d ed. (Oxford, 1964), 28–30.

18. Rigord of St. Denis, *Gesta Philippi Augusti*, ed. Henri-François Delaborde, *Oeuvres de Rigord and de Guillaume le Breton, historiens de Philippe Auguste*, 2 vols. (Paris, 1882–1885), 1:14–16 and 24–31.

19. Sara Gillian Lipton, "Jews in the Commentary Text and Illustrations of the Early Thirteenth-Century *Bibles moralisées*" (Ph.D. diss., Yale University, 1991), 43. A revised version of the dissertation is soon to be published by the University of California Press. In a subsequent essay, "The Root of All Evil: Jews, Money, and Metaphor in the *Bible moralisée*," *Medieval Encounters* 1:2 (August 1995): 1–16, Lipton notes that prior to the middle of the twelfth century artworks do not represent usurers as Jews; see p. 3, n. 7.

20. Robert of Auxerre, *Chronologia*, in *Recueil des historiens des Gaules et de la France*, ed. Martin Bouquet et al., 24 vols. (Paris, 1737–1904), 18:263.

21. Henri-François Delaborde, ed., *Recueil des actes de Philippe Auguste, roi de France*, 3 vols. (Paris, 1916–1966), vol. 2, no. 582.

22. See below, my chapter 7.

23. On the well-to-do French-Jewish moneylenders, see Robert Chazan, *Medieval Jewry in Northern France: A Political and Social History* (Baltimore, 1973), 93–95.

24. For Ephraim's account of the York massacre, see Neubauer and Stern, in *Hebräische Berichte*, 70, and in Habermann, *Sefer Gezerot*, 127.

25. *Monumenta Germaniae Historica: Legum sectio IV*, 11 vols. (Hanover, 1893–1992), 1:227–229, no. 163.

26. J. E. Scherer, *Die Rechtsverhältnisse der Juden in den deutsch-österreichischen Ländern* (Leipzig, 1901), 180–181.

27. This is, of course, a crude sort of trickle-down economics, for which I duly apologize.

28. Rigord of St. Denis, *Gesta Philippi Augusti*, 24.

29. A classic study of popular religiosity during the twelfth century and on into the thirteenth is Herbert Grundmann, *Religious Movements in the Middle Ages*, trans. Steven Rowan (Notre Dame, 1995). The German original was published in 1935 and has influenced subsequent work on popular religious sentiment. A number of researchers have continued the investigation of popular religiosity during the twelfth and thirteenth centuries. Among the most important of these scholars is the French historian André Vauchez, one of whose collections of essays is now available in English as *The Laity in the Middle Ages: Religious Beliefs and Devotional Practices*, ed. Daniel E. Bornstein, trans. Margery J. Schneider (Notre Dame, 1993). In a brief essay in this collection, entitled "The Crusades: The Masses Appear on the Scene," Vauchez makes the case for the First Crusade as the initial eruption of mass religious sentiment during the Middle Ages.

30. On the religious enthusiasm exhibited by the Jewish victims of the First Crusade aggression, see my *European Jewry and the First Crusade*, 103–136, and my *In the Year 1096: The First Crusade and the Jews* (Philadelphia, 1996), 79–103. For the broad Jewish religious creativity of the twelfth century, see above in this chapter, note 1.

31. Similarly, there is also overlap in these two reality-grounded images of the Jews and the traditional sense of the Jews as enemies. Again, however, despite the overlap, I find it valuable to treat each of these motifs individually.

32. It seems fair to say that those in the money trade remain somewhat questionable figures in popular culture even today. Note the interesting review by William Chester Jordan of Joseph Shatzmiller's *Shylock Reconsidered: Jews, Moneylending, and Medieval Society* (Berkeley, 1990) in the *Jewish Quarterly Review* 82 (1991–1992): 221–223. Jordan is concerned that Shatzmiller's convincing portrait of a sympathetic Jewish moneylender not obscure the general hostility felt toward moneylenders as a group.

33. Note the dilemma of the thirteenth-century Jews of Narbonne who were quite unwilling to identify the protective archbishop as anything other than a friend. See the discussion in Robert Chazan, "Anti-Usury Efforts in Thirteenth-Century Narbonne and the Jewish Response," *Proceedings of the American Academy for Jewish Research* 41–42 (1971–1972): 45–67, esp. 59–63.

34. Jacques Le Goff, *Your Money or Your Life: Economy and Religion in the Middle Ages*, trans. Patricia Ranum (New York, 1988), 10. See also Lester K. Little, *Religious Poverty and the Profit Economy in Medieval Europe* (Ithaca, 1978).

35. On this aspect of Innocent III, see Achille Luchaire, *Innocent III*, 6 vols. in 3 (Paris, 1903–1908), 1:3–4. As I cite Innocent III frequently, his stay in Paris and absorption of the thinking of its environment should be borne in mind.

36. Shlomo Simonsohn, ed., *The Apostolic See and the Jews: Documents*, 6 vols. (Toronto, 1988–1990), 1:93, no. 88; Solomon Grayzel, ed. and trans., *The Church and the Jews in the Thirteenth Century*, 2 vols. (Philadelphia and New York, 1933–1989), 1:126–127, no. 24. In citing papal documents I shall refer to both the Simonsohn and Grayzel collections. In general, my translations of these materials will be based on Grayzel, with occasional modifications.

37. It seems likely that this demand for further repayment reflects disputed sums of usury.

38. Simonsohn, *The Apostolic See and the Jews*, 1:82, no. 79; Grayzel, *The Church and the Jews*, 1:106–107, no. 14.

39. Again, note the important observations on Jews and the money trade in the Lipton studies cited above, this chapter, note 19.

40. Richardson, *The English Jewry under Angevin Kings*, chapter 5.

3. Intensified Perceptions of Jewish Enmity: Diverse Testimonies

1. On Bernard of Clairvaux, see, inter alia, Jean Leclercq, *Saint Bernard mystique* (Paris, 1948); Watkin Williams, *St. Bernard of Clairvaux* (Westminster, Md., 1952); Jean Leclercq, *Bernard of Clairvaux and the Cistercian Spirit* (Kalamazoo, 1977); G. R. Evans, *The Mind of St. Bernard of Clairvaux* (Oxford, 1983); Jean Leclercq, *A Second Look at Saint Bernard* (Kalamazoo, 1990); Brian Patrick McGuire, *The Difficult Saint: Bernard of Clairvaux and His Tradition* (Kalamazoo, 1991). The fullest study of Bernard's stance or stances toward Judaism and the Jews is that of David Berger, "The Attitude of St. Bernard of Clairvaux toward the Jews," *Proceedings of the American Academy for Jewish Research* 40 (1972): 89–108. On Peter the Venerable, see, among others, Jean Leclercq, *Pierre le Vénérable* (Abbey St. Wandrille, 1946); Giles Constable and James Kritzeck, eds., *Petrus Venerabilis 1156–1956 — Studies and Texts Commemorating the Eighth Centenary of His Death* (Rome, 1956); James Kritzeck, *Peter the Venerable and Islam* (Princeton, 1964); Jean-Pierre Torrell and Denise Bouthillier, *Pierre le Vénérable et sa vision du monde* (Leuven, 1986). Peter the Venerable's stance toward the Jews has been studied extensively. See Yvonne Friedman, "An Anatomy of Anti-Semitism: Peter the

Venerable's Letter to King Louis VII, King of France (1146)," in *Bar-Ilan Studies in History*, ed. Pinhas Artzi (Ramat-Gan, 1978), 87–102; Manfred Kniewasser, "Die antijüdische Polemik des Petrus Alfonsi und des Abtes Petrus Venerabilis von Cluny," *Kairos* 22 (1980): 34–76; Marianne Awerbuch, "Petrus Venerabilis: Ein Wendepunkt im Anti-judaismus des Mittelalters?" in M. Awerbuch, *Christlich-jüdische Begegnung im Zeitalter der Frühscholastik* (Munich, 1980), 177–196; Jean-Pierre Torrell, "Les Juifs dans l'oeuvre de Pierre le Vénérable," *Cahiers de civilisation médiévale* 30 (1987): 331–346; Gavin I. Langmuir, "Peter the Venerable: Defense against Doubt," in his *Toward a Definition of Antisemitism* (Berkeley, 1990), 197–208. At a conference held in October 1993 at the Herzog August Bibliotek in Wolfenbüttel, entitled "Juden und Judentum in der Sicht der christlicher Denker im Mittelalter," a number of the papers addressed Bernard, Peter, and their views of the Jews. Unfortunately, illness kept me from attending the conference and hearing the papers. I have seen only the résumés of these papers and look forward to reading the published versions of these presentations. My own paper for the conference was an earlier version of the present contrast of Bernard of Clairvaux and Peter the Venerable.

2. Ephraim of Bonn, "The Book of Remembrance," in Adolf Neubauer and Moritz Stern, eds., *Hebräische Berichte über die Judenverfolgungen während der Kreuzzüge* (Berlin, 1892), 59, and in Abraham Habermann, ed., *Sefer Gezerot Ashkenaz ve-Zarfat* (Jerusalem, 1945), 116.

3. Berger, "The Attitude of St. Bernard of Clairvaux toward the Jews," 106–108.

4. This important letter can be found in J. Leclercq and H. M. Rochais, eds., *Sancti Bernardi opera*, 8 vols. (Rome, 1957–1977), 8:311–317. On the place of the Jewish issue in the crusading theology of Bernard, see Jeremy Cohen, "'Witnesses of Our Redemption': The Jews in the Crusading Theology of Bernard of Clairvaux," *Medieval Studies in Honour of Avrom Saltman*, ed. Bat-Sheva Albert et al. (Ramat-Gan, 1996), 67–81.

5. It is interesting to note in passing that Ephraim of Bonn, in depicting Bernard's intervention on behalf of the Jews, seems to present—albeit in most cursory fashion—the range of Bernard's argument. Ephraim attributes to Bernard the following speech to the crusaders: "It is fitting that you go forth against the Muslims. But anyone who inflicts injury on a Jew, killing him, is as though he inflicts injury on Jesus himself. Ralph my disciple who urged you to destroy the Jews spoke improperly. For concerning the Jews, it is written in the book of Psalms: 'Do not kill them lest my people be unmindful.'" On the one hand, Ephraim emphasizes the argument from Psalms, with its derogatory implications. On the other, he portrays the far more positive sense on Bernard's part that Jews are especially beloved.

6. Torrell, "Les Juifs dans l'oeuvre de Pierre le Vénérable," and Torrell and Bouthillier, *Pierre le Vénérable et sa vision du monde*.

7. *Petri Venerabilis adversus Iudeorum inveteratam duritiem*, ed. Yvonne Friedman, Corpus Christianorum: Continuatio Medievalis (Turnhout, 1985), 141.

8. *Petri Cluniacensis abbatis de miraculis libri duo*, ed. Denise Bouthillier, Corpus Christianorum: Continuatio Medievalis (Turnhout, 1988), 125.

9. Giles Constable, ed., *The Letters of Peter the Venerable*, 2 vols. (Cambridge, Mass., 1967), 1:328–329.

10. For a general study of the Cain imagery, see Ruth Mellinkoff, *The Mark of Cain* (Berkeley, 1981); the fastening of this imagery on the Jews is treated by Mellinkoff in the closing chapter of her book.

11. These episodes are analyzed in my *Medieval Jewry in Northern France: A Political and Social History* (Baltimore, 1973) and in William Chester Jordan, *The French Monarchy and the Jews: From Philip Augustus to the Last Capetians* (Philadelphia, 1989).

12. For a discussion of Rigord of St. Denis's imagery of Philip Augustus, see John W. Baldwin, "*Persona et Gesta*: The Image and Deeds of the Thirteenth-Century Capetians: The Case of Philip Augustus," *Viator* 19 (1988): 195–207, esp. 196–197.

13. Rigord of St. Denis, *Gesta Philippi Augusti*, in Henri-François Delaborde, ed., *Oeuvres de Rigord et de Guillaume le Breton, historiens de Philippe Auguste*, 2 vols. (Paris, 1882–1885), 1:15. It is of course ironic that Rigord has Philip Augustus refer to the burning of Jews in Blois, while Philip's father King Louis VII had exculpated Jews of the murder accusation in the Blois incident. On the Jewish efforts to secure this royal denunciation of the new charge, see below, chapters 4 and 7.

14. Rigord of St. Denis, *Gesta Philippi Augusti*, 24–31.

15. Ephraim's listing of late twelfth-century anti-Jewish incidents can be found in Neubauer and Stern, *Hebräische Berichte*, 66–75, and Habermann, *Sefer Gezerot*, 124–132. On this important compilation, see my "Ephraim ben Jacob's Compilation of Twelfth-Century Persecutions," *Jewish Quarterly Review* 84 (1994): 397–416.

16. For a full list of the sources available for reconstructing this incident, see Robert Chazan, "The Blois Incident of 1171: A Study in Jewish Intercommunal Organization," *Proceedings of the American Academy for Jewish Research* 36 (1968): 14, n. 3. I have recently treated the historical views reflected in the post-Blois material in "The Timebound and the Timeless: Medieval Jewish Narration of Events," *History and Memory* 6 (1994): 5–34.

17. For a listing of the English chroniclers who depict this incident, see Cecil Roth, *A History of the Jews in England*, 3d ed. (Oxford, 1964), 20, n. 1.

18. For the further sources available for this incident, see R. B. Dobson, *The Jews of Medieval York and the Massacre of March 1190* (York, 1974). Recall that the Christian versions of this incident, noted in chapter 2, page 27, vary considerably from that of Ephraim.

19. While I argued in "The Bray Incident of 1192: Realpolitik and Folk Slander," *Proceedings of the American Academy for Jewish Research* 37 (1969): 1–18, for the town of Bray-sur-Seine (in Champagne) as the locale of this incident, Jordan in *The French Monarchy and the Jews*, 36–37, argued for Brie-Comte-Robert, lying between Champagne and the royal domain. It seems to me that the arguments marshaled by Jordan are compelling and that Brie-

Comte-Robert should be acknowledged as the site of the 1192 incident. Ephraim does not provide us with the date of this incident; the dating emerges clearly, however, from the account of Rigord.

20. For a full listing of the sources, see my "The Bray Incident of 1192," 1, n. 2.

21. Rigord of St. Denis, *Gesta Philippi Augusti*, 118–119.

22. Note the doubling back in time, which I discuss in "Ephraim ben Jacob's Compilation of Twelfth-Century Persecutions."

23. For a full study of the decisive stand of the emperor, with identification of further sources, see Robert Chazan, "Emperor Frederick I, the Third Crusade, and the Jews," *Viator* 8 (1977): 83–93.

4. Intensified Perceptions of Jewish Enmity: Principal Themes

1. Gavin I. Langmuir, "The Faith of Christians and Hostility to Jews," in *Christianity and Judaism: Papers Read at the 1991 Summer Meeting and the 1992 Winter Meeting of the Ecclesiastical History Society*, ed. Diana Wood (Oxford, 1992), 77–92, makes an eloquent case for the coexistence of core doctrine with considerable variability in Christian teaching vis-à-vis the Jews. For a more general case for the interaction of core Christian belief and the changing circumstances of medieval social life, see Adriaan H. Bredero, *Christendom and Christianity in the Middle Ages*, trans. Reinder Bruinsma (Grand Rapids, 1994).

2. In his recent *Antichrist* (New York, 1994), Bernard McGinn argues that the Christian view of Antichrist was similarly shaped by the core doctrine of Jesus as both divine and human.

3. Note from the Christian side the attacks on synagogues and Torah scrolls and from the Jewish side the excoriation of the central figures and symbols of Christianity.

4. For a discussion of this particular style of martyrdom, see my *European Jewry and the First Crusade* (Berkeley, 1987), 108–109.

5. On the terms in which Christianity is portrayed by the subsequent Jewish narrators, see Anna Sapir Abulafia, "Invectives against Christianity in the Hebrew Chronicles of the First Crusade," in *Crusade and Settlement*, ed. P. W. Edbury (Cardiff, 1985), 66–72.

6. Israel J. Yuval has proposed that the Jewish behaviors of 1096 had considerable impact on the thinking of twelfth-century Christians with respect to Jews. For discussion of the Yuval thesis, see below, my chapter 5, pp. 75–77.

7. *Annales Herbipolenses*, in *Monumenta Germaniae Historica: Scriptores*, 34 vols. (Hanover, 1826–1980), 16:3–4. Note the interesting parallel between popular threat to the clergy of Wurzburg as a result of their pro-Jewish stance and similar dangers encountered by the bishop of Trier in 1096.

8. Thomas of Monmouth's text was published by Augustus Jessopp and Montague Rhodes James, eds. and trans., *The Life and Miracles of St. William of Norwich* (Cambridge, 1896). Thomas's concoction of the ritual murder allegation has been analyzed brilliantly by Gavin I. Langmuir, "Thomas of Monmouth: Detector of Ritual Murder," *Speculum* 59 (1984): 822–846, reprinted in Langmuir's *Toward a Definition of Antisemitism* (Berkeley, 1990), 209–236. See further the careful analysis of both the Norwich incident and the spread of the crucifixion allegation in Friedrich Lotter, "Innocens Virgo et Martyr: Thomas von Monmouth und die Verbreitung der Ritualmordlegende im Hochmittelalter," in *Die Legende vom Ritualmord: Zur Geschichte der Blutbeschuldigungen gegen Juden*, ed. Rainer Erb (Berlin, 1993), 25–72.

9. Note the careful study of the flaws in Thomas's presentation in Langmuir, "Thomas of Monmouth."

10. Thomas of Monmouth, *The Life and Miracles of St. William of Norwich*, 27–30. The only way to understand this puzzling incident is to suggest that Aelward Ded assumed that the human body he felt was the corpse of a deceased Jew. It is unthinkable that he could have suspected a Christian corpse in Jewish hands and let the matter pass.

11. Ibid., 32–34.

12. Ibid., 35. I have used the Jessopp and James translation, with occasional minor modifications.

13. Ibid., 36.

14. Ibid., 43–44.

15. I owe my awareness of the significance of the ecclesiastical venue to a comment by Robert C. Stacey, for which I am grateful.

16. Thomas of Monmouth, *The Life and Miracles of St. William of Norwich*, 20–21.

17. These earlier charges of venting animosity through magic or through the poisoning of wells are noted above, in my chapter 1.

18. Thomas of Monmouth, *The Life and Miracles of St. William of Norwich*, 40–41. Psychoanalytic interpretation of this incident would probably be most interesting.

19. Ibid., 93–94.

20. See my study "The Blois Incident of 1171: A Study in Jewish Intercommunal Organization," *Proceedings of the American Academy for Jewish Research* 36 (1968): 13–31, for a full analysis of this extensive diplomatic effort.

21. "The Blois Letters," in Adolf Neubauer and Moritz Stern, eds., *Hebräische Berichte über die Judenverfolgungen während der Kreuzzüge* (Berlin, 1892), 34, and in Abraham Habermann, ed., *Sefer Gezerot Ashkenaz ve-Zarfat* (Jerusalem, 1945), 145. Recall Rigord's suggestion, noted above in my chapter 3, that Louis VII's son Philip Augustus saw the Blois burning of Jews as proof of the truth of the murder allegation.

22. "The Blois Letters," in Neubauer and Stern, *Hebräische Berichte*, 35, and in Habermann, *Sefer Gezerot*, 146.

23. Ephraim of Bonn, "The Book of Remembrance," in Neubauer and Stern, *Hebräische Berichte*, 62, and in Habermann, *Sefer Gezerot*, 119.

24. "The Blois Letters," in Neubauer and Stern, *Hebräische Berichte*, 34, and in Habermann, *Sefer Gezerot*, 145.

25. Shlomo Simonsohn, *The Apostolic See and the Jews: Documents*, 6 vols. (Toronto, 1991), 1:82, no. 79; Solomon Grayzel, ed. and trans., *The Church and the Jews in the Thirteenth Century*, 2 vols. (Philadelphia and New York, 1933–1989), 1:108–109, no. 14. Again, recall Pope Innocent's connections with northern France and northern French attitudes (see above, chapter 2, n. 33).

26. Recall the 992 incident discussed above in chapter 1, where the malevolent Seḥok ben Esther, in claiming that the Jews of Le Mans were attempting to magically harm the count of Maine, articulated the connection between the alleged actions of these contemporary Jews and what their ancestors in Jerusalem had done slightly more than a thousand years earlier.

27. See Gavin I. Langmuir's listing of crucifixion allegations in "The Knight's Tale of Young Hugh of Lincoln," *Speculum* 47 (1972): 462–463, reprinted in his *Toward a Definition of Antisemitism*, 240–242. In his essay on Thomas of Monmouth Langmuir argues for the enormous significance of the slander concocted by Thomas. Indeed, as we shall see in my closing chapter, Langmuir sees in this concoction the beginnings of antisemitism as he carefully defines it. To be sure, in a 1985 essay, "Historiographic Crucifixion," *Les Juifs au miroir de l'histoire: Mélanges en l'honneur de Bernhard Blumenkranz*, ed. Gilbert Dahan (Paris, 1985), 109–127, reprinted in Langmuir, *Toward a Definition of Antisemitism*, 282–298, Langmuir notes in passing (pp. 111 and 282) that the crucifixion slander was in fact overshadowed by the charge of murder. For a full discussion of these issues, see below, my chapter 8.

28. During the crusader assaults on the Jewish communities of Worms, Mainz, and Cologne, Jewish martyrs regularly invoked the imagery of re-creating the Temple sacrificial system.

29. Recall that Thomas of Monmouth connected the murder of the lad William with the Jewish celebration of Passover, without specifying the precise nature of the connection. The theme of reenactment of the ancient Jewish sacrificial rites lends itself to both Easter and Passover.

30. For recent essays on the blood libel and a considerable bibliography, see Alan Dundes, ed., *The Blood Libel Legend: A Casebook in Anti-Semitic Folklore* (Madison, 1991), and Rainer Erb, ed., *Die Legende vom Ritualmord: Zur Geschichte der Blutbeschuldigung gegen Juden* (Berlin, 1993). Note that not all the essays in each of these collections refer specifically to the blood libel. Note also the important essay by Gavin I. Langmuir, "Ritual Cannibalism," in his *Toward a Definition of Antisemitism*, 263–281. On the efforts to protect Jews from this potent new slander, see below, my chapters 6 and 7.

31. On the Jewish opposition to the doctrine of the Incarnation, see the important observations of David Berger, *The Jewish-Christian Debate in the High Middle Ages* (Philadelphia, 1979), 350–354.

32. On development of the host accusation, see the recent essay of Miri Rubin, "Desecration of the Host: The Birth of an Accusation," *Christianity and Judaism: Papers Read at the 1991 Summer Meeting and the 1992 Winter*

Meeting of the Ecclesiastical History Society, ed. Diana Wood (Oxford, 1992), 169–185, which should be read against the background of Rubin, *Corpus Christi: The Eucharist in Late Medieval Culture* (Cambridge, 1991). See also the important essay of Gavin I. Langmuir, "The Tortures of the Body of Christ," in *Christendom and Its Discontents*, ed. Scott L. Waugh and Peter D. Diehl (Cambridge, 1996), 287–309. In this essay Langmuir highlights the violent impact that the host accusation had in late thirteenth- and early fourteenth-century Germany.

5. The Deteriorating Jewish Image and Its Causes

1. A briefer and earlier version of parts of this chapter was read at a conference held at the University of California, Los Angeles, in early 1991; that paper has recently appeared as "The Deteriorating Image of the Jews—Twelfth and Thirteenth Centuries" in the valuable collection edited by Scott L. Waugh and Peter D. Diehl, *Christendom and Its Discontents* (Cambridge, 1996), 220–233.

2. Israel Yuval, "Vengeance and Damnation, Blood and Defamation: From Jewish Martyrdom to Blood Libel Accusations," *Zion* 58 (1993): 33–90. The Yuval thesis created a stir in Israeli academic circles. An entire fascicle of the following year's *Zion* was devoted to the Yuval essay, with most of the reactions strongly negative.

3. For the complex belief system that underlay the Jewish martyrdom of 1096, see my *European Jewry and the First Crusade* (Berkeley, 1987), 114–131. In a general way I believe that the role of millenarian yearnings and convictions as a causative factor in human behavior is often exaggerated in modern historiography. This is especially true among some twentieth-century historians writing from a Zionist perspective. It seems to me that Bernard McGinn's approach in *Antichrist* (New York, 1994), which treats millenarian thinking largely as an interesting projection of human longings and hatreds, is more accurate and fruitful. Treating Christian millenarian expectations in this way—as a gauge of deepening anti-Jewish sensitivities—would add an interesting dimension to the present analysis, but such an effort will not be undertaken.

4. In an essay in the 1994 fascicle of *Zion* devoted to the Yuval essay, Mary Minty took up the issue of Christian awareness of the Jewish martyrdoms of 1096: "*Kiddush ha-Shem* in German Christian Eyes in the Middle Ages," *Zion* 59 (1994): 209–266. While Minty brings a variety of sources from the twelfth through the sixteenth centuries which show awareness of Jewish martyrdom, the critical period for my purposes (and in fact for Yuval's purposes as well) is the first half of the twelfth century, the period between the martyrdoms of 1096 and the first surfacing of the stereotype of the Jew as murderer. For that period Minty cites only the three sources already noted by Yuval: Albert of

Aachen, the *Gesta Treverorum*, and Bernold of Constance. Given the volume of Latin material depicting aspects of the First Crusade, these three rather brief references hardly suggest widespread Christian awareness of the Jewish behaviors of 1096 prior to the mid-twelfth century. Moreover, it is noteworthy that none of the sources depicting the murder allegation or its more imaginative offshoots, the charges of crucifixion or Jewish sacrifice, mention Jewish martyrdoms. That a writer like Thomas of Monmouth, so detailed in his depiction of Jewish cruelty, might have been influenced by knowledge of Jews killing their own children without introducing such stories into his lavish narrative strains credulity.

5. For a valuable review of post-World War II social science treatment of prejudice, see Gavin I. Langmuir, "Toward a Definition of Antisemitism," in *The Persisting Question: Sociological Perspectives and Social Contexts of Modern Antisemitism*, ed. Helen Fein (New York, 1987), 86–127, reprinted as the title essay in Langmuir's *Toward a Definition of Antisemitism* (Berkeley, 1990). The works reviewed by Langmuir focus on the majority, as does Langmuir's own theorizing. For Langmuir's views and their emphasis on majority needs, see below, my chapter 8.

6. It is interesting that the editors of *Christendom and Its Discontents*, in their introductory observations to the volume, chose to highlight the work of Boswell and Moore, as have I.

7. John Boswell, *Christianity, Social Tolerance, and Homosexuality: Gay People in Western Europe from the Beginning of the Christian Era to the Fourteenth Century* (Chicago, 1980).

8. Ibid., 269–270. Note the extensive argument for this distinction between the open eleventh and twelfth centuries and the closed thirteenth and fourteenth by Friedrich Heer, *The Medieval World*, trans. Janet Sondheimer (Cleveland, 1962). Heer devotes chapter 13 of his study to Jews and women.

9. R. I. Moore, *The Formation of a Persecuting Society* (Oxford, 1987). In his subsequent essay, "Anti-Semitism and the Birth of Europe" (in *Christianity and Judaism*, ed. Diana Wood [Oxford, 1992]), Moore reinforces his earlier case by again arguing that the anti-Jewish perceptions and actions of the period we are studying must be treated as central to this epoch. After indicating alternative views that see the Jews and their maltreatment as incidental phenomena, Moore asserts: "The burden of this argument has been, on the contrary, that the persecution of the Jews, and the growth not only of anti-Judaism but of anti-Semitism, were quite central to the developments which taken together I choose to describe, without the faintest tincture of originality, as the birth of Europe" (p. 53).

10. Moore, *The Formation of a Persecuting Society*, vii.

11. Ibid., 5.

12. Ibid., 65.

13. Ibid., 67.

14. Boswell, *Christianity, Social Tolerance, and Homosexuality*, 37.

15. Moore, *The Formation of a Persecuting Society*, 110.

16. Ibid., 123.

17. Moore has not been totally consistent in his insistence on the interchangeability of the Jews with other outgroups. In *The Formation of a Persecuting Society* Moore suggests that one special group in medieval society—other than the ruling class—was particularly influential in the formation of the tendency toward persecution of the Jews, and that was the newly literate group that had achieved its power through its monopolization of literacy. According to Moore, this group was especially negative to Jews, whom it feared as competitors:

It is hard to evade the conclusion that the urgent and compelling reason for the persecution of the Jews at this time—a persecution, as we have seen, which reversed the previous and well-established tendency to integration between the two cultures—was that they offered a real alternative, and therefore a real challenge, to Christian *literati* as the advisers of princes and the agents and beneficiaries of bureaucratic power (p. 150).

This view is doubly problematic. In the first place, there is no real evidence of the Jews playing a role as advisers and agents of the authorities in northern Europe, as they of course did in the south. Moreover, this suggestion effectively undermines Moore's argument of interchangeability. In his recent essay "Anti-Semitism and the Birth of Europe," Moore again seems to diverge from his assertion of the interchangeability of outgroups and the related notion of elites creating the patterns of intolerance and persecution. This essay begins by noting the high level of Jewish culture in medieval Europe and then portrays the growing intolerance of Jews as rooted in the need to diminish the status of Jews. This assertion of course means that Jews were not interchangeable with the other outgroups and that persecution of Jews (and others as well) was rooted in some measure in the realities of Jewish (and other outgroup) life.

18. Recall the literature cited above, in chapter 2, note 29, which highlights the increasingly active role of the masses in western Christendom, beginning with the First Crusade.

19. Moore, *The Formation of a Persecuting Society*, 106–107.

20. Boswell, *Christianity, Social Tolerance, and Homosexuality*, 38.

21. Charles Homer Haskins, *The Renaissance of the Twelfth Century* (Cambridge, Mass., 1927). A major conference took place on the fiftieth anniversary of the publication of the Haskins book, with the conference papers published by Robert L. Benson and Giles Constable, eds., *Renaissance and Renewal in the Twelfth Century* (Cambridge, Mass., 1982). The recent book by Giles Constable, *Three Studies in Medieval Religious and Social Thought* (Cambridge, 1995), which will be cited shortly, makes reference to a forthcoming work by Constable entitled *The Reformation of the Twelfth Century*. On the appearance of this important new study, our understanding of the twelfth century will undoubtedly be much advanced.

22. Peter the Venerable was in the forefront of the effort to acquire new knowledge about Jewish and Islamic tradition, but his new knowledge merely served as grist for his mill of vituperative denunciation. The travel literature

of the twelfth century would be interesting to investigate in this regard. For general orientation to this literature, see Mary B. Campbell, *The Witness and the Other World* (Cornell, 1988). For a fascinating discussion of the famous fourteenth-century travel diary attributed to Sir John Mandeville and its decidedly anti-Jewish bent, see Benjamin Braude, "*Mandeville's* Jews among Others," in *Pilgrims and Travelers*, ed. Bryan F. Le Beau and Menachem Mor (Omaha, 1995), 141–168.

23. Amos Funkenstein, "Changes in the Patterns of Christian Anti-Jewish Polemic in the Twelfth Century" (in Hebrew), *Zion* 33 (1968): 125–144, constituted a trail-blazing effort in examining the changes produced in the image of the Jews by the altered cultural environment of the twelfth century. This effort has been pursued further by Anna Sapir Abulafia in her numerous studies, culminating in her *Christians and Jews in the Twelfth-Century Renaissance* (London, 1995). Although her book reached me only in the very last stages of revision of this study, I am pleased to have had the opportunity to read it and include reference to it. The central thesis of the Abulafia book is the twelfth-century commitment to reason and the twelfth-century assumption that the findings of reason would be consistent with Christian truth. Let me cite briefly her clear formulation (p. 6):

> My book will argue that what developed was a universalistic construct of humanity based on reason which was deemed to coincide with universal Christendom. The inherent inclusiveness of this construct (everyone has reason, so everyone can be a Christian and the Church is open to all true believers) was, in fact, decidedly exclusive to anyone or any group who could not conform to the agreed philosophical and religious formulae. Thus a sideline of the intellectual endeavours of the twelfth-century renaissance was the marginalization of Jews.

For a broad overview of medieval Christian thinking on the Jews, see the synthesis of Gilbert Dahan, *Les Intellectuels chrétiens et les Juifs au moyen âge* (Paris, 1990), especially parts 3 and 4.

24. Funkenstein, "Changes in the Patterns of Christian Anti-Jewish Polemic," 129–133. See also Abulafia, *Christians and Jews in the Twelfth-Century Renaissance*, chapter 6.

25. Pioneering work in this area was done by Beryl Smalley, *The Study of the Bible in the Middle Ages*, 3d ed. (Oxford, 1983). For a more recent overview of accelerating Christian knowledge of Hebrew, see Dahan, *Les Intellectuels chrétiens et les Juifs au moyen âge*, 239–270.

26. Abulafia, *Christians and Jews in the Twelfth-Century Renaissance*, chap. 7.

27. Funkenstein, "Changes in the Patterns of Christian Anti-Jewish Polemic," 137–142. During the thirteenth century Christian attention shifted away from the purported ludicrousness of rabbinic teachings to their blasphemies and antisocial tendencies.

28. A classic statement of this humanization can be found in R. W. Southern, *The Making of the Middle Ages* (London, 1953). See the rich recent treatment by Constable, *Three Studies*, 169–217. Note also the citation in note 33,

this chapter, from Jeffrey Burton Russell, *Witchcraft in the Middle Ages* (Ithaca, 1972). In her *Christians and Jews in the Twelfth-Century Renaissance* Abulafia notes the impact of the growing humanization of Jesus on the image of the Jews; see her chapter 8.

29. Waugh and Diehl, in their introductory comments to *Christendom and Its Discontents*, note that the humanization of Jesus also had positive implications for other groups, for example women.

30. Jeremy Cohen, "The Jews as the Killers of Christ in the Latin Tradition from Augustine to the Friars," *Traditio* 39 (1983): 3–27.

31. Note especially the important study by Giles Constable, "The Second Crusade as Seen by Contemporaries," *Traditio* 9 (1953): 213–281.

32. For conflation of Jews and heretics, see Sara G. Lipton, "Jews in the Commentary Text and Illustrations of the Early Thirteenth-Century *Bibles moralisées*" (Ph.D. diss., Yale Univ., 1991), chapter 5, and Lipton, "Jews, Heretics, and the Sign of the Cat in the *Bible moralisée*," *Word and Image* 8 (1992): 362–377. Jeremy Cohen proposed in *The Friars and the Jews: The Evolution of Medieval Anti-Judaism* (Ithaca, 1982) that the church in the thirteenth century came to see the Jews as heretical deviants. For discussion of this thesis, see below, my chapter 6, note 1. For the intertwining of the themes of Jews and moneylending, see Lipton, "Jews in the Commentary Text and Illustrations," chapter 3, and Lipton, "The Root of All Evil: Jews, Money, and Metaphor in the *Bible moralisée*," *Medieval Encounters* 1:2 (August 1995): 1–16. For conflation of heretics and lepers, see R. I. Moore, "Heresy and Disease," in *The Concept of Heresy in the Middle Ages*, ed. W. Lourdaux and D. Verhelst (Leuven, 1976), 1–11.

33. In 1096 it does seem that the call to arms against the Muslim world touched off sensitivity to the Jews; during the twelfth century the sentiment against outgroups was broader and no causative impact can be discerned.

34. Lipton, "Jews in the Commentary Text and Illustrations," "Jews, Heretics, and the Sign of the Cat," and "The Root of All Evil," argues convincingly for recurrent manipulation of iconographic imagery in the *Bibles moralisées*.

35. Jeffrey Burton Russell, *Witchcraft in the Middle Ages* (Ithaca, 1972), 102. I have opted against treating the intensified focus on the devil as a causative factor in the deteriorating image of the Jews. Robert Bonfil, "The Devil and the Jews in Christian Consciousness of the Middle Ages," in *Antisemitism through the Ages*, ed. Shmuel Almog, trans. Nathan H. Reisner (Oxford, 1988), 91–98, makes a convincing case for augmented perceptions of a Jew-devil connection during the twelfth and thirteenth centuries. I have chosen to see growing awareness of the devil in general as evidence of heightened insecurity and specific claims of a Jew-devil alliance as reflective of the increasingly potent anti-Jewish perceptions I have been analyzing.

36. I wish to acknowledge that my case for heightened anxiety in majority society is largely inferential, based on the evidence provided by hostility to outgroups. Further research aimed at establishing or negating majority disequilibrium would of course be welcome.

6. The Deteriorating Jewish Image
and Its Effects: Ecclesiastical Policies

1. The stance of the church toward Judaism and the Jews has been the object of considerable analysis over the past few decades. Note, Jeremy Cohen, *The Friars and the Jews: The Evolution of Medieval Anti-Judaism* (Ithaca, 1982); Kenneth R. Stow, "Hatred of the Jews or Love of the Church: Papal Policy toward the Jews in the Middle Ages," in *Antisemitism through the Ages*, ed. Shmuel Almog, trans. Nathan H. Reisner (Oxford, 1988), 71–89; Shlomo Simonsohn, *The Apostolic See and the Jews: History* (Toronto, 1991). The most striking view of this relationship is that of Cohen. In choosing to analyze changes in the church position vis-à-vis the Jews as a traditional combination of recognition of the Jewish right to existence within Christian society tempered by prohibition of Jewish behaviors deemed harmful, I am implicitly rejecting the alternative of a new ecclesiastical ideology proposed by Cohen, and I believe that this rejection requires some justification. It is certainly clear that the notion of Judaism as inherently illegitimate, indeed heretical, is expressed during the late twelfth and thirteenth century. Reference has already been made to the Lipton study, "Jews, Heretics, and the Sign of the Cat," which analyzes elements of conflation of the two groups. But I do not think this conflation reached the status of a new ecclesiastical ideology. Cohen's evidence for such a new ideology is drawn from three sources: the church's campaign against the Talmud, the church's missionizing campaign, and statements by individual churchmen. In *Daggers of Faith* (Berkeley, 1989) I argued that Cohen's use of the fourth agenda item from the Barcelona disputation constitutes a misreading of that item—it has nothing to do with Jewish veneration of rabbinic texts; it is simply an assertion that with the coming of the Messiah Jewish law had lost its authority. In my "The Condemnation of the Talmud Reconsidered (1239–1248)," *Proceedings of the American Academy for Jewish Research* 45 (1988): 11–30, I argued that while the charge that the Talmud represented an unwarranted deviation from the Bible was surely raised by the ex-Jew Nicholas Donin and was casually repeated in papal rhetoric, the actual condemnation of the Talmud rested on other grounds, such as blasphemy and exhortation to anti-Christian behavior, both of which were prohibited in prior church policy. Thus the proofs afforded by the two thirteenth-century campaigns seem to me to evaporate. I agree that there are individual expressions of the illegitimacy of talmudic Judaism, but I find it strange that the major thinkers of this period, during which the church was focused on codifying doctrine, show no formal recognition of this purportedly new view. Had such a doctrine been evolving at this juncture, we would surely expect theologians like Alexander of Hales or Thomas Aquinas, both at the center of innovative ecclesiastical thinking, to provide a full formulation, which they do not. A new and comprehensive study of Aquinas on the Jews, written by John Y. B. Hood, *Aquinas and the Jews* (Philadelphia, 1995), examines the views of St. Thomas

carefully in relation to the Cohen thesis and concludes that St. Thomas's thinking on the Jews is highly traditional and shows no sign of the innovative ideology asserted by Cohen. For these reasons, I see the claim of a new ideology as unwarranted and I have chosen to depict the church's stance in more traditional terms. Important comments by Hood in his study of Aquinas parallel my sense of a traditional church stance on Judaism and the Jews which allowed for considerable latitude in interpretation. After rejecting Cohen's sense of a theological revolution, Hood continues:

The mainstream Christian theological view of Jews and their place in history was substantially the same in 1400 as it had been in 1200. The persecutions and expulsions of the intervening two hundred years did not reflect fundamental theological changes; rather, they proved that the medieval attitude toward Jews was ambiguous enough to justify relatively oppressive as well as relatively tolerant social policies. All that was required was a shift in emphasis.

In this chapter I will argue that the new popular perception of the malevolent Jew was enough to provide such a shift in emphasis.

2. On the *Constitutio pro Judeis*, see the classic study by Solomon Grayzel, "The Papal Bull Sicut Judeis," in *Studies and Essays in Honor of Abraham A. Neuman*, ed. Meir Ben-Horin et al. (Leiden, 1962), 243–280.

3. Elazar ben Judah, "Recollections," in Adolf Neubauer and Moritz Stern, *Hebräische Berichte über die Judenverfolgungen während der Kreuzzüge* (Berlin, 1892), 78, and in Abraham Habermann, ed., *Sefer Gezerot Ashkenaz ve-Zarfat* (Jerusalem, 1945), 164. For a full discussion of these matters, see Robert Chazan, "Emperor Frederick I, The Third Crusade, and the Jews, *Viator* 8 (1977): 83–93.

4. Shlomo Simonsohn, ed., *The Apostolic See and the Jews: Documents*, 6 vols. (Toronto, 1988–1990), 1:163–164, no. 154, and 165, no. 155; Solomon Grayzel, ed. and trans., *The Church and the Jews in the Thirteenth Century*, 2 vols. (Philadelphia and New York, 1933–1989), 1:226–229, no. 87, and 228–231, no. 88.

5. "The Blois Letters," in Neubauer and Stern, *Hebräische Berichte*, 34–35, and in Habermann, *Sefer Gezerot*, 145–146.

6. Simonsohn, *The Apostolic See and the Jews*, 1:194, no. 185; Grayzel, *The Church and the Jews*, 1:268–271, no. 116.

7. Simonsohn, *The Apostolic See and the Jews*, 1:192, no. 183; Grayzel, *The Church and the Jews*, 1:274–275, no. 118.

8. Grayzel, *The Church and the Jews*, 1:296–297, no. I.

9. Simonsohn, *The Apostolic See and the Jews*, 1:82, no. 79; Grayzel, *The Church and the Jews*, 1:106–107, no. 14.

10. Grayzel, *The Church and the Jews*, 1:308–309, no. X.

11. Simonsohn, *The Apostolic See and the Jews*, 1:83, no. 79; Grayzel, *The Church and the Jews*, 1:106–109, no. 14.

12. Easter week and Passover often coincide. The papal complaint raised here may reflect the simple reality of coincidental Jewish celebration of Passover.

13. Grayzel, *The Church and the Jews*, 1:308–309, no. X.

14. There is a considerable literature on the new church concern with the Talmud. See, inter alia, Isidore Loeb, "La Controvèrse de 1240 sur le Talmud," *Revue des études juives* 1 (1880): 247–261, 2 (1881): 248–269, 3 (1881): 39–57; Judah Rosenthal, "The Talmud on Trial," *Jewish Quarterly Review* 47 (1956–1957): 58–76 and 145–169; Chen Merchavia, *Ha-Talmud be-Re'i ha-Naẓrut* [The Talmud in the View of Christianity] (Jerusalem, 1970); Joel Rembaum, "The Talmud and the Popes: Reflections on the Talmud Trials of the 1240s," *Viator* 13 (1982): 203–223; Cohen, *The Friars and the Jews*, 60–76; Chazan, "The Condemnation of the Talmud Reconsidered (1239–1248)," *Proceedings of the American Academy for Jewish Research* 45 (1988: 11–30. For the claims that the Talmud includes encouragement of antisocial behaviors, see below, pp. 108–109.

15. For discussion of the moderate versus radical anti-Talmud positions, see Chazan, "The Condemnation of the Talmud Reconsidered."

16. The importance of Innocent III is reflected in the ongoing focus on his pontificate. While the groundwork for assessment of his papacy was laid in the multivolume opus by Achille Luchaire, a number of recent studies of this pope and his papacy have appeared. Note particularly Helene Tillman, *Pope Innocent III*, trans. Walter Sax (Amsterdam, 1980), and Jane Sayers, *Innocent III: Leader of Europe 1198–1216* (London, 1994). The centrality of the pontificate of Innocent III is likewise reflected in the attention accorded it in recent surveys of the history of the medieval church, such as Colin Morris, *The Papal Monarchy: The Western Church from 1050 to 1250*, Oxford History of the Christian Church (Oxford, 1989).

17. Simonsohn, *The Apostolic See and the Jews*, 1:75, no. 71; Grayzel, *The Church and the Jews*, 1:94–95, no. 5.

18. Simonsohn, *The Apostolic See and the Jews*, 1:86–87, no. 82; Grayzel, *The Church and the Jews*, 1:114–115, no. 18. Sara Lipton informs me that in the *Bibles moralisées* there is a depiction of Synagoga with mice nestling in her lap and another with a snake wrapped around her head.

19. Simonsohn, *The Apostolic See and the Jews*, 1:92–93, no. 88; Grayzel, *The Church and the Jews*, 1:126–127, no. 24.

20. For Peter the Venerable's use of the Cain imagery, see above, my chapter 3; for Innocent III's acceptance of the murder allegation, see above, my chapter 4.

21. Grayzel, *The Church and the Jews*, 1:307, no. IX.

22. For institution of some of these demands, see below, chapter 7.

23. Simonsohn, *The Apostolic See and the Jews*, 1:82–83, no. 79; Grayzel, *The Church and the Jews*, 1:126–131, no. 24.

24. Robert of Auxerre, *Chronologia*, in *Recueil des historiens des Gaules et de la France*, ed. Martin Bouquet et al., 24 vols. (Paris, 1737–1904), 18:263. For an exhaustive study of the reforming circles of which Fulk was a part, see again John W. Baldwin, *Masters, Princes, and Merchants: The Social Views of Peter the Chanter and His Circle*, 2 vols. (Princeton, 1970).

25. Robert of Courçon, *Le Traité "De Usura" de Robert de Courçon*, ed. Georges Lefèvre (Lille, 1902), 7.

26. Deut. 23:8. Given the traditional Jewish identification of Edomites and Christians, the conclusion would seem to be that Jews and Christians are in fact brethren, which would result in the prohibition of the taking of usury one from the other.

27. *Sefer Yosef ha-Mekane* [The Book of Joseph the Zealot], ed. Judah Rosenthal (Jerusalem, 1970), 61. The combination of verses from Obadiah, verses 11 and 1, suggests to the Jewish interpreter that Edom, that is, Christendom, had acted in league with Israel's enemies and thus forfeited any prior links it might have had with the Jewish people.

28. Again note the difficult bind in which the Jews of Narbonne found themselves, as discussed in my "Anti-Usury Efforts in Thirteenth Century Narbonne" and the Jewish Response," *Proceedings of the American Academy for Jewish Research* 41–42 (1971–1972): 45–67.

29. On the anti-usury program in France and its impact, see my chapter 7.

7. The Deteriorating Jewish Image and Its Effects: The Temporal Authorities

1. One of the special features of William Chester Jordan's *The French Monarchy and the Jews: From Philip Augustus to the Last Capetians* (Philadelphia, 1989) is his insistence on setting royal policy against the backdrop of broader popular sentiment.

2. See Ephraim's comments in Adolf Neubauer and Moritz Stern, *Hebräische Berichte über die Judenverfolgungen während der Kreuzzüge* (Berlin, 1892), 64, and in Abraham Habermann, ed., *Sefer Gezerot Ashkenaz ve-Zarfat*, (Jerusalem, 1945), 121.

3. Elazar ben Judah, "Recollections," in Neubauer and Stern, *Hebräische Berichte*, 78, and in Habermann, *Sefer Gezerot*, 164.

4. On these English incidents, see Cecil Roth, *A History of the Jews in England*, 3d ed. (Oxford, 1964), 18–26, and Chazan, *European Jewry and the First Crusade* (Berkeley, 1987), 189–191. On York in particular, see R. B. Dobson, *The Jews of Medieval York and the Massacre of March 1190* (York, 1974).

5. Chazan, *Medieval Jewry in Northern France: A Political and Social History* (Baltimore, 1973), 137.

6. Thomas of Monmouth, *The Life and Miracles of William of Norwich*, ed. and trans. Augustus Jessopp and Montague Rhodes James (Cambridge, 1896), 29–30, 36–37, 46–49, 107–112.

7. *Monumenta Germaniae Historica: Legum Sectio IV*, 11 vols. (Hanover, 1893–1992), 2:275, no. 204.

8. There was clear deterioration of Jewish security during the second half of the thirteenth century, including attacks on Jews in England during the chaotic years of the 1260s, the loss of Jewish life in England as a result of the coin-clipping episode of the late 1270s, and the disastrous outbreaks of violence in

Germany at the end of the thirteenth and the beginning of the fourteenth century. Since our focus is on the period of transition, all this lies beyond the scope of the present analysis.

9. Nicholas C. Vincent, "Jews, Poitevins, and the Bishop of Winchester, 1231–1234," in *Christianity and Judaism: Papers Read at the 1991 Summer Meeting and the 1992 Winter Meeting of the Ecclesiastical History Society*, ed. Diana Wood (Oxford, 1992), 119–132, analyzes the heavy revenues extracted from the Jews in England during the 1230s. In the course of this analysis, Vincent argues for the influence of some of the king's French advisers and indeed of French policies. To be sure, most of the evidence he adduces has to do with the imposition of ecclesiastical demands. With respect to financial exploitation, Vincent himself noted that "the Plantagenets appear to have been more successful and more precocious in their exploitation of Jewish finance."

10. See H. G. Richardson, *The English Jewry under Angevin Kings* (London, 1960), 161–163.

11. See above, chapter 2, note 15.

12. See Richardson, *The English Jewry under Angevin Kings*, 166–172.

13. Robert C. Stacey, *Politics, Policy, and Finance under Henry III, 1216–1245* (Oxford, 1987), 143. See also Stacey, "Royal Taxation and the Social Structure of Medieval Anglo-Jewry: The Tallages of 1239–42," *Hebrew Union College Annual* 56 (1985): 175–249, and "1240–60: A Watershed in Anglo-Jewish Relations?" *Historical Research* 61 (1988): 135–150. In the last of these, Stacey pays tribute to R. B. Dobson's "The Decline and Expulsion of the Medieval Jews of York," *Transactions of the Jewish Historical Society of England* 26 (1979): 34–52.

14. Stacey, *Politics, Policy, and Finance under Henry III*, 154.

15. For a strong sense of the reign of Philip Augustus as a point of significant change in medieval French—and indeed European—history, see John W. Baldwin, *The Government of Philip Augustus* (Berkeley, 1986), xvii. For broad corroboration, see also Robert-Henri Bautier, "La Place du règne de Philippe Auguste dan l'histoire de la France médiévale," in *La France de Philippe Auguste: Le Temps de mutations*, ed. Bautier (Paris, 1982), 11–27.

16. See Chazan, *Medieval Jewry in Northern France*, 63–68, and Jordan, *The French Monarchy and the Jews*, chapter 2.

17. Baldwin, *The Government of Philip Augustus*, 52–55. See, more generally, Jordan, *The French Monarchy and the Jews*, chapter 4.

18. Rigord of St. Denis, *Gesta Philippi Augusti*, in Henri-François Delaborde, ed., *Oeuvres de Rigord et de Guillaume le Breton, historiens de Philippe Auguste*, 2 vols. (Paris, 1882–1885), 1:25.

19. This summary of the French campaign against usury is based on my own work in *Medieval Jewry in Northern France* and on Jordan, *The French Monarchy and the Jews*. The Jordan analysis is fuller than mine.

20. For some of the royal actions on Jewish usury in the years between 1206 and 1223, see Jordan, *The French Monarchy and the Jews*, chapter 5.

21. Alexandre Teulet et al., eds., *Layettes du Trésor des Chartes*, 5 vols. (Paris, 1863–1909), 2:12, no. 1610.

22. Jordan argues that the first clause relates only to current Jewish loans, not to future Jewish loans. He acknowledges, however, that the withdrawal of the special seals for Jewish loans was a watershed:

Despite misgivings about the system, these methods of authentication under the aegis of the crown, especially the sealing of bonds by local government officials, were continuous features of royal supervision of the Jews from 1198 until 1223. In a terse sentence, Louis VIII's *stabilimentum* withdrew the seal: "Henceforth Jews will not have seals for the sealing of their debts." An entire structure was collapsing.

See *The French Monarchy and the Jews*, 96.

23. It has traditionally been argued that this new policy was first enunciated in 1235. Jordan suggests, however, that this conclusion has been based on defective textual evidence, that the best version of the 1235 document simply depicts the Jews as living by their own labor or by nonusurious business, and that the decree stipulating that Jews *must* abandon usury was enacted only in 1253. See *The French Monarchy and the Jews*, 296, n. 38.

24. For important reflections on the impact of ecclesiastical pressures on the English monarchy during the thirteenth century, see J. A. Watt, "The English Episcopate, the State and the Jews: The Evidence of the Thirteenth-Century Conciliar Decrees," in *Thirteenth Century England II: Proceedings of the Newcastle upon Tyne Conference 1987*, ed. P. R. Coss and S. D. Lloyd (Woodbridge, 1988), 137–147.

25. Many biographies of King Louis IX have been written, and all highlight his noble character. The most interesting observations have been advanced by William Chester Jordan. In his *Louis IX and the Challenge of the Crusade* (Princeton, 1979), Jordan devoted chapter 7 to a discussion of the king's personality seen from the perspective of his commitment to charity and devotion, to Christian warfare, and to the reform of the royal coinage. In a subsequent study, "*Persona et Gesta*: The Image and Deeds of the Thirteenth-Century Capetians: The Case of Saint Louis," *Viator* 19 (1988): 209–217, Jordan suggested that "there was a significant level of tension or a significant number of contradictions between Louis IX's mature notions of the ideal behavior of a king and other accepted ideals of the appropriate 'public image' of a monarch"; he then explored a few of these contradictions. Some of Louis's extreme views of the Jews seem to serve as instances of the tension suggested by Jordan.

26. William of Chartres, *De vita et actibus regis Francorum Ludovici*, in *Recueil des historiens des Gaules et de la France*, ed. Martin Bouquet et al., 24 vols. (Paris, 1737–1904), 20:34.

27. Jean de Joinville, *Histoire de Saint Louis*, ed. M. Natalis de Wailly (Paris, 1868), 30. I have used the translation of René Hague, *The Life of St. Louis* (New York, 1955), 36. The account of the encounter at Cluny is extremely vague. It is hard to imagine that Jews were invited for a simple exchange of views. It seems far likelier that this encounter was part of the new missionary activities that began during the middle decades of the thirteenth century, involving forced Jewish attendance at missionizing sermons and "debates." If this is in fact the case, then the behavior of the knight in attacking the Jews was

even more outrageous and the recommendation of the king yet more startling. Recall the Jordan suggestion cited above, this chapter, note 25.

28. The personality and image of Philip Augustus have been widely studied of late. Note Robert-Henri Bautier, "Philippe Auguste: La Personnalité du roi," in *La France de Philippe Auguste: Le Temps des mutations*, 32–57, in which Bautier discerns a combination of impulsiveness, craftiness, and piety, and Raymonde Foreville, "L'Image de Philippe Auguste dans les sources contemporaines," in *LaFrance de Philippe Auguste*, 115–132. In his studies of Philip Augustus John W. Baldwin has attempted to juxtapose the royal image to the realities that can be reconstructed from the documentary evidence—see *The Government of Philip Augustus*, 355–359, and *"Persona et Gesta*: The Image and Deeds of the Thirteenth-Century Capetians: The Case of Philip Augustus," *Viator* 19 (1988): 195–207.

29. Recall Baldwin's treatment of Rigord, cited above, chapter 3, note 12.

30. The fullest treatment of the 1306 expulsion from France is that of Jordan, *The French Monarchy and the Jews*. At the 1992 annual conference of the Association for Jewish Studies, Jordan presented a paper on the expulsion of 1306, arguing that the expulsion was immediately related to Philip IV's efforts to assert royal authority. The 1290 expulsion from England has been treated by a number of scholars. Robert C. Stacey, "The Conversion of Jews to Christianity in Thirteenth-Century England," *Speculum* 67 (1992): 263–283, notes briefly that "the expulsion was the unpremeditated outcome of a four-month-long parliamentary negotiation in which the financially indebted Edward sought permission to raise a tax from his Christian subjects without being able to claim any ongoing military necessities which would have justified one." This thesis is developed more fully in Stacey, "Thirteenth-Century Anglo-Jewry and the Problem of the Expulsion" (in Hebrew), in *Gerush ve-Shivah: Yehudey Angeliyah be-Ḥilufey ha-Zemanim* [Expulsion and Return: The Jews of England in Changing Epochs], ed. David S. Katz and Yosef Kaplan (Jerusalem, 1993), 9–25. Like the enhanced violence of the second half of the thirteenth century, the expulsions lie beyond the purview of this study, which focuses on the period and dynamics of transition. It seems to me fair to say, however, that whatever the precise immediate circumstances, the foundations for both expulsions lay in the interlocking popular, ecclesiastical, and governmental changes that have been the subject of this analysis.

8. Medieval Stereotypes and Modern Antisemitism

1. For fullest treatment of the early development of Polish Jewry out of the earlier Ashkenazic matrix, see Bernard Weinryb, *The Jews of Poland* (Philadelphia, 1973).

2. The introduction of the term *antisemitism* has been subjected to careful reconstruction. Reinhard Rurup, *Emancipation und Antisemitismus: Studien zur "Judenfrage" der bürgerlichen Gesellschaft* (Göttingen, 1975), meticulously tracked the prehistory of the term and its first use in 1879 in its widely accepted usage. Moshe Zimmermann, *Wilhelm Marr: The Patriarch of Antisemitism* (New York, 1986), 89–95, closely studied Marr's avoidance of the term, earliest use of it, and eventual popularization of the designation.

3. Bernard Lazare, *L'Antisémitisme: Son histoire et ses causes* (Paris, 1894). The work was quickly translated into English, appearing as *Antisemitism: Its History and Causes* (New York, 1903); the English translation has been reissued periodically, most recently with a useful introduction by Robert S. Wistrich (Lincoln, 1995).

4. Léon Poliakov, *Histoire de l'antisémitisme*, 4 vols. (Paris, 1955–1977), available in English as *The History of Anti-Semitism*, 4 vols., trans. Richard Howard et al. (New York, 1965–1985). Note the recent overviews of the history of antisemitism provided in the collaborative Shmuel Almog, ed., *Antisemitism through the Ages*, trans. Nathan H. Reisner (Oxford, 1988); in Robert S. Wistrich, *Antisemitism: The Longest Hatred* (London, 1991); and in William Nicholls, *Christian Antisemitism: A History of Hate* (Northvale, N.J., 1993); all three define their subject in an all-inclusive way. For a fairly full review of various theories of antisemitism, see Yves Chevalier, *L'Antisémitisme: Le Juif comme bouc émissaire* (Paris, 1988), 21–97.

5. Gavin I. Langmuir, *History, Religion, and Antisemitism* (Berkeley, 1990), 276. *History, Religion, and Antisemitism* represents an encompassing statement by Langmuir of work he has pursued since the 1960s on antisemitism. Most of Langmuir's prior essays were published, with a valuable introduction, as *Toward a Definition of Antisemitism* (Berkeley, 1990).

6. Langmuir, *History, Religion, and Antisemitism*, 297.

7. An interesting effort in this same direction is that of Joel Carmichael, *The Satanizing of the Jews: Origins and Development of Mystical Anti-Semitism* (New York, 1992). Carmichael's notion of mystical antisemitism offers interesting possibilities not fully realized in his study.

8. Langmuir, *History, Religion, and Antisemitism*, 297.

9. See ibid., chapter 14.

10. A valuable collection of Hebrew essays, edited by Shmuel Almog, appeared in 1987 under the Hebrew title *Sin'at Yisra'el le-Doroteha* (meaning the phenomenon of *sin'at Yisra'el* [hatred of Israel] through the ages). The translator, Nathan H. Reisner, had little choice but to make the English title *Antisemitism through the Ages*, although the English loses the valuable ambiguity of the Hebrew.

11. Maintaining a distinction between common hatreds and the horrific has clearly been a central intellectual and moral priority for Langmuir.

12. Poliakov, *The History of Anti-Semitism*, 1:vi. Poliakov's organizational pattern is in fact somewhat strange. After beginning with a brief chapter entitled "Anti-Semitism in Pagan Antiquity," he devotes the rest of volume 1 to early Christianity, the Middle Ages in northern Europe, and the early modern

period in northern Europe. Only in volume 2 does he return to the Mediterranean world, from whence the anti-Jewish materials from pagan antiquity stem. This rather skewed organizational scheme reflects, I suggest, Poliakov's sense of the preponderant role played by medieval northern European society in the overall history of anti-Jewish thinking, a sense that this study in general and this chapter in particular has tried to argue. Like so many others, Poliakov shows insufficient sensitivity to the newness of early Ashkenazic Jewry.

13. Note Poliakov's extensive treatment of the eleventh through sixteenth centuries.

14. Langmuir, *History, Religion, and Antisemitism*, 265.

15. Langmuir, "The Knight's Tale of Young Hugh of Lincoln," *Speculum* 47 (1972): 459–482; also reprinted in Langmuir, *Toward a Definition of Anti-semitism* (Berkeley, 1990), 237–262.

16. Robert C. Stacey, "History, Religion, and Medieval Antisemitism: A Reply to Gavin Langmuir," *Religious Studies Review* 20 (1994): 95–101.

17. For the ass's head allegation, see the authors cited in Menahem Stern, *Greek and Latin Authors on Jews and Judaism*, 3 vols. (Jerusalem, 1974–1984), specifically Mnaseas of Patara (1:97–101), Diodorus (1:181–185), Apion (1:409–410 and 412–413), Damocritus (1:530–531, where the worship of an ass's head is juxtaposed to the allegation of human sacrifice), and the famous Tacitus passage (2:18–25).

18. For another criticism of Langmuir's emphasis on the empirical nature of twelfth-century anti-Jewish statements, see Anna Sapir Abulafia, *Christians and Jews in the Twelfth-Century Renaissance* (London, 1995), 5–7.

19. Langmuir's emphasis on doubt in the development of intense anti-Jewish sentiment can be seen in his already noted treatment of Peter the Venerable. By contrast I have argued that even for Peter doubt is a lesser theme and that fear of harmful Jewish actions is the greater concern. Writing from a different perspective, Abulafia, *Christians and Jews in the Twelfth-Century Renaissance*, 5–7, expresses her own reservations about Langmuir's emphasis on Christian doubt as the central factor in the development of twelfth-century anti-Jewish stereotypes. Working in a later period James Shapiro, *Shakespeare and the Jews* (New York, 1996), 107–111, similarly insists on proceeding beyond religious doubt as explanation for the tenacity of the murder allegation in England.

20. Recall Langmuir's own acknowledgment that the murder allegation was more significant than the crucifixion slander. See above, my chapter 4, note 27.

21. The entire thrust of the analysis in my chapters 3 and 4 has been toward identification of ways in which northern European Christians during the middle decades of the twelfth century began to feel themselves deeply threatened by their Jewish neighbors.

22. Imagery of profound Jewish harmfulness pervades the most potent works of nineteenth- and twentieth-century antisemitism, such as *The Protocols of the Elders of Zion* and Hitler's *Mein Kampf*.

23. Hannah Arendt's classic study appeared as the first part of her *The Origins of Totalitarianism*, 2d ed. (New York, 1958); Poliakov, *The History of Anti-Semitism*; Jacob Katz, *From Prejudice to Destruction: Anti-Semitism, 1700–1933* (Cambridge, Mass., 1980).

24. Arendt, *The Origins of Totalitarianism*, 7.

25. On James Parkes, see Robert Andrew Everett, *Christianity without Antisemitism: James Parkes and the Jewish-Christian Encounter* (Oxford, 1993). On Jules Isaac, see the brief biographical sketch by Claire Huchet Bishop that introduces the English translation of his *L'Enseignement du mépris* (Paris, 1962), which appeared as *The Teaching of Contempt*, trans. Helen Weaver (New York, 1964), 3–15. Other major authors who have focused on the Christian roots of antisemitism include Rosemary Reuther, *Faith and Fratricide* (New York, 1974); John G. Gager, *The Origins of Anti-Semitism* (New York, 1983); William Nicholls, *Christian Antisemitism*; and John Crossan, *Who Killed Jesus?* (New York, 1995). For Crossan the role of traditional Christian teaching in the evocation of antisemitism necessitates the closest and most accurate reconstruction of the Crucifixion.

26. Isaac, *The Teaching of Contempt*.

27. This mitigating observation by Isaac, so central to his practical mission, has occasioned considerable debate within Christian circles. In his assessment Isaac certainly agreed with Parkes, who likewise believed that anti-Jewish teachings lay outside the core of Christian doctrine and could be altered without affecting the essential beliefs of the Christian faith. Some successors of Parkes and Isaac have gone further, however, arguing that Christianity is to an extent rooted in these anti-Jewish teachings and that fundamental change in Christian doctrine is required. The major protagonist of this view has been Rosemary Reuther, whose *Faith and Fratricide* was yet another milestone in the examination of Christian culpability for centuries of anti-Jewish hostility in general and for much of the thinking of modern antisemitism as well. The disagreement between such observers as Parkes and Isaac and the newer and more damning indictment by Reuther is poignantly captured in the proceedings of a remarkable colloquium arranged to examine (by and large sympathetically) the thesis of Rosemary Reuther. As an act of homage, this colloquium was dedicated to the pioneering work of James Parkes, whose opening address is reprinted as an introduction to the volume of proceedings. This opening statement, however, is critical of the work of Reuther; see the published proceedings, *Antisemitism and the Foundations of Christianity*, ed. Alan Davies (New York, 1979). All this serves to alert us to the sensitivity of the issue within the Christian community. In a certain measure, allegations of the role of Christian teaching in the history of anti-Jewish sentiment have become a touchstone of internal self-perception and self-criticism within Christian circles.

28. Isaac, *The Teaching of Contempt*, 21.

29. Katz, *From Prejudice to Destruction*, 318–321.

30. Shapiro, *Shakespeare and the Jews*, 89–91, provides fascinating information on the everyday inculcation of folkloric anti-Jewish views, drawn from the early nineteenth-century novel *Harrington*. Shapiro also indicates (pp. 103–106) some of the channels through which these anti-Jewish views survived over the centuries in England.

31. See the valuable study of John Gross, *Shylock: A Legend and Its Legacy* (London, 1992). Note also the illuminating review of the Gross book by Robert Alter, "Who Is Shylock," *Commentary* 96:1 (July 1993): 29–34. Over

the past year two important books have treated the Jewish image in Elizabethan England, with considerable focus on Shakespeare and Shylock. See Frank Felsenstein, *Anti-Semitic Stereotypes: A Paradigm of Otherness in English Popular Culture, 1600–1830* (Baltimore, 1995), especially chapter 7, and Shapiro, *Shakespeare and the Jews*, especially chapters 3 and 4.

32. Shakespeare's skill in crafting a complex Shylock figure is central to the Gross book and the Alter review.

33. For a striking example of the deleterious impact of *The Merchant of Venice*, see Shapiro, *Shakespeare and the Jews*, 9–10. Shapiro notes that for the nineteenth-century explorer-scholar Richard Burton, proof of an alleged Jewish "spirit of vengeance" is amply provided by the Shylock figure. According to Burton, "Shakespeare may not have drawn Shylock from a real character, but his genius has embodied in the most lifelike form the Jew's vengefulness and the causes that nourished it." Shapiro cites Burton's quotation of the famous "Hath not a Jew eyes" speech; he notes ironically, however, that Burton closes his citation with the line "and if you wrong us, shall we not revenge?" thus omitting Shakespeare's complicating "if we are like you in the rest, we will resemble you in that." As noted, both Gross and Alter highlight the artistic ambiguity in the Shakespearian portrait; precisely such ambiguity opened the way for observers like Burton to draw the most negative conclusions from the Shylock figure. Gross, *Shylock*, 312, suggests that "we can argue forever about whether Shakespeare was expressing anti-Semitic sentiments, or merely describing them. But when it comes to the question of influence, there can be no serious dispute: Shylock has a prominent place in anti-Semitic mythology."

34. Recall Gavin I. Langmuir, "The Faith of Christians and Hostility to Jews," in *Christianity and Judaism: Papers Read at the 1991 Summer Meeting and the 1992 Winter Meeting of the Ecclesiastical History Society*, ed. Diana Wood (Oxford, 1992), 77–92, who makes a strong argument for the variability of religious sentiment, as does John Boswell throughout *Christianity, Social Tolerance, and Homosexuality: Gay People in Western Europe from the Beginning of the Christian Era to the Fourteenth Century* (Chicago, 1980). Recall also Adriaan H. Bredero, *Christendom and Christianity in the Middle Ages*, trans. Reinder Bruinsma (Grand Rapids, 1994).

35. It seems to me reasonable to argue that the period of the Reformation represents yet another formative juncture when Western anti-Jewish imagery — including the accretions developed during the period analyzed in this study — underwent further evolution. On this latter period and its anti-Jewish thinking, see the overview provided by Heiko A. Obermann, *The Roots of Anti-Semitism in the Age of Renaissance and Reformation*, trans. James I. Porter (Philadelphia, 1984). Shapiro, *Shakespeare and the Jews*, 1, makes the following observation early in his introduction: "From our own perspective their [Shakespeare and his contemporaries] interest in Jews provides unusual insight into the cultural anxieties felt by English men and women at a time when their nation was experiencing extraordinary social, religious, and political turbulence." This view of late sixteenth- and early seventeenth-century England closely parallels the sense I have attempted to convey of mid- and late twelfth-century northern Europe.

Obviously, the industrialization of Western societies during the nineteenth century constituted yet another such point of development for anti-Jewish imagery. I would argue, nonetheless, that neither of these two important later periods introduced stereotypes as novel and as destructive as those tracked in this study.

Bibliography

Primary Sources

Adhémar of Chabannes. *Chronique.* Ed. Jules Chavanon. Collection de textes pour servir à l'étude et à l'enseignement de l'histoire. Paris, 1897.

Albert of Aachen. *Historia Hierosolymitana.* In *Recueil des historiens des croisades, historiens occidentaux,* 4:265–713.

Anonymous. *Annales Herbipolenses.* In *Monumenta Germaniae Historica: Scriptores,* 16:1–12.

Anonymous. "The 992 Le Mans Letter" [a communal letter depicting endangered Le Mans Jewry in 992]. Ed. Abraham Berliner, *Ozar Tov* 1878: 49–52. Ed. Abraham Habermann, *Sefer Gezerot,* 11–15.

Anonymous. "The 1007 Account" [a report on persecution in early eleventh-century northern France]. Ed. Abraham Berliner, *Ozar Tov* 1878: 46–48. Ed. Abraham Habermann, *Sefer Gezerot,* 19–21.

Anonymous. "The Blois Letters" [a set of four letters written after the Blois disaster of 1171]. Ed. Adolf Neubauer and Moritz Stern, *Hebräische Berichte,* 31–35. Ed. Abraham Habermann, *Sefer Gezerot,* 142–145.

Anonymous. "The Mainz Anonymous" [the oldest of the Hebrew narratives of the First Crusade, focused on the Jewish communities of Speyer, Worms, and Mainz]. Ed. Adolf Neubauer and Moritz Stern, *Hebräische Berichte,* 47–57. Ed. Abraham Habermann, *Sefer Gezerot,* 93–104.

Anonymous. *Sefer Yosef ha-Mekane* [The Book of Joseph the Zealot, a polemical treatise organized according to biblical verses]. Ed. Judah Rosenthal. Jerusalem, 1970.

Anonymous. "The Solomon bar Simson Chronicle" [a composite account of the events of 1096 incorrectly attributed to an unknown Solomon bar Simson]. Ed. Adolf Neubauer and Moritz Stern, *Hebräische Berichte*, 1–31. Ed. Abraham Habermann, *Sefer Gezerot*, 24–60.

Bernard of Clairvaux. *Sancti Bernardi opera*. Ed. J. Leclercq and H. M. Rochais. 8 vols. Rome, 1957–1977.

Delaborde, Henri-François, ed. *Oeuvres de Rigord et de Guillaume le Breton, historiens de Philippe Auguste*. 2 vols. Paris, 1882–1885.

———. *Recueil des actes de Philippe Auguste, roi de France*. 3 vols. Paris, 1916–1966.

Elazar ben Judah. "Recollections" [a brief report on events associated with the Third Crusade, including a letter composed by Elazar's brother-in-law Moses ben Eliezer *ha-cohen* in Mainz]. Ed. Adolf Neubauer and Moritz Stern, *Hebräische Berichte*, 76–78. Ed. Abraham Habermann, *Sefer Gezerot*, 161–164.

Ephraim ben Jacob. "Compendium of Persecutions" [a listing of anti-Jewish incidents from 1171 through 1196]. Ed. Adolf Neubauer and Moritz Stern, *Hebräische Berichte*, 66–75. Ed. Abraham Habermann, *Sefer Gezerot*, 124–132.

———. "The Book of Remembrance" [an account of events associated with the Second Crusade]. Ed. Adolf Neubauer and Moritz Stern, *Hebräische Berichte*, 58–66. Ed. Abraham Habermann, *Sefer Gezerot*, 115–123.

Grayzel, Solomon, ed. and trans. *The Church and the Jews in the Thirteenth Century*. 2 vols. 2d vol. ed. and arranged by Kenneth R. Stow. Philadelphia and New York, 1933–1989.

Guibert of Nogent. *Autobiographie*. Ed. and trans. Edmond-René Labande. Les Classiques de l'histoire de France au moyen âge. Paris, 1981.

Habermann, Abraham, ed. *Sefer Gezerot Ashkenaz ve-Ẓarfat* [The Persecutions of Germany and France]. Jerusalem, 1945.

Hilgard, Alfred, ed. *Urkunden zur Geschichte der Stadt Speyer*. Strasbourg, 1885.

Jean de Joinville. *Histoire de Saint Louis*. Ed. M. Natalis de Wailly. Paris, 1868.

———. *The Life of St. Louis*. Trans. René Hague. New York, 1955.

Monumenta Germaniae Historica: Legum sectio IV. 11 vols. Hanover, 1893–1992.

Monumenta Germaniae Historica: Scriptores. 34 vols. Hanover, 1826–1980.

Adolf Neubauer and Moritz Stern, eds. *Hebräische Berichte über die Judenverfolgungen während der Kreuzzüge*. Berlin, 1892.

Peter Abelard. *Dialogus inter Philosophum, Iudaeum et Christianum*. Ed. Rudolf Thomas. Stuttgart, 1970.

———. *Dialogue of a Philosopher with a Jew and a Christian*. Trans. P. J. Payer. Toronto, 1979.

Peter the Venerable. *The Letters of Peter the Venerable*. Ed. Giles Constable. 2 vols. Cambridge, Mass., 1967.

———. *Petri Cluniacensis abbatis de miraculis libri duo*. Ed. Denise Bouthillier. Corpus Christianorum: Continuatio Medievalis. Turnhout, 1988.

————. *Petri Venerabilis adversus Iudeorum inveteratam duritiem.* Ed. Yvonne Friedman. Corpus Christianorum: Continuatio Medievalis. Turnhout, 1985.

Recueil des historiens des croisades, historiens occidentaux. 5 vols. Paris, 1844–1895.

Recueil des historiens des Gaules et de la France. Ed. Martin Bouguet et al. 24 vols. Paris, 1737–1904.

Rigord of St. Denis. *Gesta Philippi Augusti.* In Henri-François Delaborde, ed., *Oeuvres de Rigord et de Guillaume le Breton, historiens de Philippe Auguste,* 1:1–167. 2 vols. Paris, 1882–1885.

Robert of Auxerre. *Chronologia.* In *Recueil des historiens des Gaules et de la France,* 18:248–290.

Robert of Courcon. *Le Traité "De Usura" de Robert de Courçon.* Ed. Georges Lefèvre. Lille, 1902.

Rodulfus Glaber. *Historiarum libri quinque.* Ed. John France. Oxford Medieval Texts. Oxford, 1989.

Simonsohn, Shlomo, ed. *The Apostolic See and the Jews: Documents.* 6 vols. Toronto, 1988–1990.

Stern, Menahem, ed. *Greek and Latin Authors on Jews and Judaism.* 3 vols. Jerusalem, 1974–1984.

Teulet, Alexandre et al., eds. *Layettes du Trésor des Chartes.* 5 vols. Paris, 1863–1909.

Thomas of Monmouth. *The Life and Miracles of St. William of Norwich.* Ed. and trans. Augustus Jessopp and Montague Rhodes James. Cambridge, 1896.

William of Chartres. *De vita et actibus regis Francorum Ludovici.* In *Recueil des historiens des Gaules et de la France,* 20:27–41.

Secondary Literature

Abulafia, Anna Sapir. *Christians and Jews in the Twelfth-Century Renaissance.* London, 1995.

————. "Invectives against Christianity in the Hebrew Chronicles of the First Crusade." In *Crusade and Settlement,* ed. P. W. Edbury, 66–72. Cardiff, 1985.

Agus, Irving A. *The Heroic Age of Franco-German Jewry.* New York, 1969.

Alter, Robert. "Who Is Shylock." *Commentary* 96:1 (July 1993): 29–34.

Arendt, Hannah. *The Origins of Totalitarianism.* 2d ed. New York, 1958.

Awerbuch, Marianne. "Petrus Venerabilis: Ein Wendepunkt im Anti-judaismus des Mittelalters?" In M. Awerbuch, *Christlich-jüdische Begegnung im Zeitalter der Frühscholastik,* 177–196. Munich, 1980.

Bachrach, Bernard S. *Early Medieval Jewish Policy in Western Europe.* Minneapolis, 1977.

Baldwin, John W. *The Government of Philip Augustus.* Berkeley, 1986.

————. *Masters, Princes, and Merchants: The Social Views of Peter the Chanter and His Circle.* 2 vols. Princeton, 1970.

————. "*Persona et Gesta*: The Image and Deeds of the Thirteenth-Century Capetians: The Case of Philip Augustus." *Viator* 19 (1988): 195–207.

Bautier, Robert-Henri. "Philippe Auguste: La personnalité du roi." In *La France de Philippe Auguste: Le Temps des mutations*, ed. R.-H. Bautier, 32–57. Paris, 1982.

————. "La Place du règne de Philippe Auguste dan l'histoire de la France médiévale." In *La France de Philippe Auguste: Le Temps de mutations*, ed. R.-H. Bautier, 11–27. Paris, 1982.

Benson, Robert L., and Constable, Giles, eds. *Renaissance and Renewal in the Twelfth Century.* Cambridge, Mass., 1982.

Berger, David. "The Attitude of St. Bernard of Clairvaux toward the Jews." *Proceedings of the American Academy for Jewish Research* 40 (1972): 89–108.

————. *The Jewish-Christian Debate in the High Middle Ages.* Philadelphia, 1979.

Bishop, Claire Huchet. "Jules Isaac: A Biographical Introduction." In Jules Isaac, *The Teaching of Contempt*, trans. Helen Weaver, 3–15. New York, 1964.

Bloch, Marc. *Feudal Society.* Trans. L. A. Manyon. London, 1961.

Bonfil, Robert. "The Devil and the Jews in Christian Consciousness of the Middle Ages." In *Antisemitism through the Ages*, ed. Shmuel Almog, trans. Nathan H. Reisner, 91–98. Oxford, 1988.

Boswell, John. *Christianity, Social Tolerance, and Homosexuality: Gay People in Western Europe from the Beginning of the Christian Era to the Fourteenth Century.* Chicago, 1980.

Braude, Benjamin. "*Mandeville's* Jews among Others." In *Pilgrims and Travelers*, ed. Bryan F. Le Beau and Menachem Mor, 141–168. Omaha, 1995.

Bredero, Adriaan H. *Christendom and Christianity in the Middle Ages.* Trans. Reinder Bruinsma. Grand Rapids, 1994.

Campbell, Mary B. *The Witness and the Other World.* Ithaca, 1988.

Carmichael, Joel. *The Satanizing of the Jews: Origins and Development of Mystical Anti-Semitism.* New York, 1992.

Chazan, Robert. "Anti-Usury Efforts in Thirteenth-Century Narbonne and the Jewish Response." *Proceedings of the American Academy for Jewish Research* 41–42 (1971–1972): 45–67.

————. "The Blois Incident of 1171: A Study in Jewish Intercommunal Organization." *Proceedings of the American Academy for Jewish Research* 36 (1968): 13–31.

————. "The Bray Incident of 1192: Realpolitik and Folk Slander." *Proceedings of the American Academy for Jewish Research* 37 (1969): 1–18.

————. "The Condemnation of the Talmud Reconsidered (1239–1248)." *Proceedings of the American Academy for Jewish Research* 45 (1988): 11–30.

————. *Daggers of Faith.* Berkeley, 1989.

————. "The Deteriorating Image of the Jews—Twelfth and Thirteenth Centuries." In *Christendom and Its Discontents*, ed. Scott L. Waugh and Peter D. Diehl, 220–233. Cambridge, 1996.

————. "Emperor Frederick I, the Third Crusade, and the Jews." *Viator* 8 (1977): 83–93.

————. "Ephraim ben Jacob's Compilation of Twelfth-Century Persecutions." *Jewish Quarterly Review* 84 (1994): 397–416.

————. *European Jewry and the First Crusade*. Berkeley, 1987.

————. "The Facticity of Medieval Narrative: A Case Study of the Hebrew First-Crusade Narratives." *AJS Review* 16 (1991): 31–56.

————. *In the Year 1096: The First Crusade and the Jews*. Philadelphia, 1996.

————. *Medieval Jewry in Northern France: A Political and Social History*. Baltimore, 1973.

————. "R. Ephraim of Bonn's *Sefer Zechirah*." *Revue des études juives* 132 (1973): 587–594.

————. "Review of Stow, *The '1007 Anonymous' and Papal Sovereignty*." *Speculum* 62 (1987): 728–731.

————. "1007–1012: Initial Crisis for Northern-European Jewry." *Proceedings of the American Academy for Jewish Research* 38–39 (1970–1971): 101–117.

————. "The Timebound and the Timeless: Medieval Jewish Narration of Events." *History and Memory* 6 (1994): 5–34.

Chevalier, Yves. *L'Antisémitisme: Le Juif comme bouc émissaire*. Paris, 1988.

Cohen, Jeremy. *The Friars and the Jews: The Evolution of Medieval Anti-Judaism*. Ithaca, 1982.

————. "The Jews as Killers of Christ in the Latin Tradition, from Augustine to the Friars." *Traditio* 39 (1983): 3–27.

————. "'Witnesses of Our Redemption': The Jews in the Crusading Theology of Bernard of Clairvaux." In *Medieval Studies in Honour of Avrom Saltman*, ed. Bat-Sheva Albert et al., 67–81. Ramat-Gan, 1996.

Cohen, Mark R. *Under Crescent and Cross: The Jews in the Middle Ages*. Princeton, 1994.

Constable, Giles. "The Second Crusade as Seen by Contemporaries." *Traditio* 9 (1953): 213–281.

————. *Three Studies in Medieval Religious and Social Thought*. Cambridge, 1995.

————, and Kritzeck, James, eds. *Petrus Venerabilis—1156–1956—Studies and Texts Commemorating the Eighth Centenary of His Death*. Rome, 1956.

Crossan, John. *Who Killed Jesus?* New York, 1995.

Dahan, Gilbert. *Les Intellectuels chrétiens et les Juifs au moyen âge*. Paris, 1990.

Davies, Alan, ed. *Antisemitism and the Foundations of Christianity*. New York, 1979.

Dobson, R. B. "The Decline and Expulsion of the Medieval Jews of York." *Transactions of the Jewish Historical Society of England* 26 (1979): 34–52.

————. *The Jews of Medieval York and the Massacre of March 1190*. York, 1974.

Dundes, Alan, ed. *The Blood Libel Legend: A Casebook in Anti-Semitic Folklore.* Madison, 1991.

Erb, Rainer, ed. *Die Legende vom Ritualmord: Zur Geschichte der Blutbeschuldigungen gegen Juden.* Berlin, 1993.

Evans, G. R. *The Mind of St. Bernard of Clairvaux.* Oxford, 1983.

Everett, Robert Andrew. *Christianity without Antisemitism: James Parkes and the Jewish-Christian Encounter.* Oxford, 1993.

Felsenstein, Frank. *Anti-Semitic Stereotypes: A Paradigm of Otherness in English Popular Culture, 1600–1830.* Baltimore, 1995.

Foreville, Raymonde. "L'Image de Philippe Auguste dans les sources contemporaines." In *La France de Philippe Auguste: Le Temps de mutations,* ed. Robert-Henri Bautier, 115–132. Paris, 1982.

Fossier, Robert. *Le Moyen Âge.* 3d ed. 3 vols. Paris, 1990.

Friedman, Yvonne. "An Anatomy of Anti-Semitism: Peter the Venerable's Letter to King Louis VII, King of France (1146)." In *Bar-Ilan Studies in History,* ed. Pinhas Artzi, 87–102. Ramat-Gan, 1978.

Funkenstein, Amos. "Changes in the Patterns of Christian Anti-Jewish Polemic in the Twelfth Century" (in Hebrew). *Zion* 33 (1968): 125–144.

Gager, John G. *The Origins of Anti-Semitism.* New York, 1983.

Grayzel, Solomon. "The Papal Bull Sicut Judeis." In *Studies and Essays in Honor of Abraham A. Neuman,* ed. Meir Ben-Horin et al., 243–280. Leiden, 1962.

Gross, John. *Shylock: A Legend and Its Legacy.* London, 1992.

Grundmann, Herbert. *Religious Movements in the Middle Ages.* Trans. Steven Rowan. Notre Dame, 1995.

Haskins, Charles Homer. *The Renaissance of the Twelfth Century.* Cambridge, Mass., 1927.

Heer, Friedrich. *The Medieval World.* Trans. Janet Sondheimer. Cleveland, 1962.

Hood, John Y. B. *Aquinas and the Jews.* Philadelphia, 1995.

Isaac, Jules. *L'Enseignement du mépris.* Paris, 1962.

———. *The Teaching of Contempt.* Trans. Helen Weaver. New York, 1964.

Jordan, William Chester. *The French Monarchy and the Jews: From Philip Augustus to the Last Capetians.* Philadelphia, 1989.

———. *Louis IX and the Challenge of the Crusade.* Princeton, 1979.

———. "*Persona et Gesta*: The Image and Deeds of the Thirteenth-Century Capetians: The Case of Saint Louis." *Viator* 19 (1988): 209–217.

———. "Review of Shatzmiller's *Shylock Reconsidered: Jews, Moneylending, and Medieval Society.*" *Jewish Quarterly Review* 82 (1991–1992): 221–223.

Kamin, Sara. *Jews and Christians Interpret the Bible.* Jerusalem, 1991.

———. *Rashi: Peshuto shel Mikra u-Midrasho shel Mikra* [Rashi: The Plain Meaning and the Midrashic Meaning of the Bible]. Jerusalem, 1986.

Katz, Jacob. *From Prejudice to Destruction: Anti-Semitism, 1700–1933.* Cambridge, Mass., 1980.

Katz, Solomon. *The Jews in the Visigothic and Frankish Kingdoms of Spain and Gaul.* Cambridge, Mass., 1937.

Kniewasser, Manfred. "Die antijüdische Polemik des Petrus Alfonsi und des Abtes Petrus Venerabilis von Cluny." *Kairos* 22 (1980): 34–76.

Kraus, Samuel. "The Names Ashkenaz and Sepharad" (in Hebrew). *Tarbiz* 3 (1931–1932): 423–435.

Kritzeck, James. *Peter the Venerable and Islam.* Princeton, 1964.

Landes, Richard. "La Vie apostolique en Aquitaine en l'an mil: Paix de Dieu, culte des reliques, et communautés hérétiques." *Annales—Économies, Sociétés, Civilisations* 46 (1991): 573–593.

Langmuir, Gavin I. "The Faith of Christians and Hostility to Jews." In *Christianity and Judaism: Papers Read at the 1991 Summer Meeting and the 1992 Winter Meeting of the Ecclesiastical History Society,* ed. Diana Wood, 77–92. Oxford, 1992.

———. "Historiographic Crucifixion." In *Les Juifs au miroir de l'histoire: Mélanges en l'honneur de Bernhard Blumenkranz,* ed. Gilbert Dahan, 109–127. Paris, 1985. Reprinted in G. I. Langmuir, *Toward a Definition of Antisemitism,* 282–298. Berkeley, 1990.

———. *History, Religion, and Antisemitism.* Berkeley, 1990.

———. "The Knight's Tale of Young Hugh of Lincoln." *Speculum* 47 (1972): 459–482. Reprinted in G. I. Langmuir, *Toward a Definition of Antisemitism,* 237–262. Berkeley, 1990.

———. "Peter the Venerable: Defense against Doubt." In G. I. Langmuir, *Toward a Definition of Antisemitism,* 197–208. Berkeley, 1990.

———. "Ritual Cannibalism." In G. I. Langmuir, *Toward a Definition of Antisemitism,* 263–281. Berkeley, 1990.

———. "Thomas of Monmouth: Detector of Ritual Murder." *Speculum* 59 (1984): 822–846. Reprinted in G. I. Langmuir, *Toward a Definition of Antisemitism,* 209–236. Berkeley, 1990.

———. "The Tortures of the Body of Christ." In *Christendom and Its Discontents,* ed. Scott L. Waugh and Peter D. Diehl, 287–309. Cambridge, 1996.

———. *Toward a Definition of Antisemitism.* Berkeley, 1990.

———. "Toward a Definition of Antisemitism." In *The Persisting Question: Sociological Perspectives and Social Contexts of Modern Antisemitism,* ed. Helen Fein, 86–127. New York, 1987. Reprinted as the title essay in G. I. Langmuir, *Toward a Definition of Antisemitism,* 311–352. Berkeley, 1990.

Lazare, Bernard. *L'Antisémitisme: Son histoire et ses causes.* Paris, 1894.

———. *Antisemitism: Its History and Causes.* Introduction by Robert S. Wistrich. Lincoln, 1995.

Leclercq, Jean. *Bernard of Clairvaux and the Cistercian Spirit.* Kalamazoo, 1977.

———. *Pierre le Vénérable.* Abbey St. Wandrille, 1946.

———. *Saint Bernard mystique.* Paris, 1948.

———. *A Second Look at Saint Bernard.* Kalamazoo, 1990.

Le Goff, Jacques. *Your Money or Your Life: Economy and Religion in the Middle Ages.* Trans. Patricia Ranum. New York, 1988.

Lipton, Sara Gillian. "Jews, Heretics, and the Sign of the Cat in the *Bible moralisée*." *Word and Image* 8 (1992): 362–377.

———. "Jews in the Commentary Text and Illustrations of the Early Thirteenth-Century *Bibles moralisées*." Ph.D. dissertation, Yale University, 1991.

———. "The Root of All Evil: Jews, Money, and Metaphor in the *Bible moralisée*." *Medieval Encounters* 1:2 (August 1995): 1–16.

Little, Lester K. *Religious Poverty and the Profit Economy in Medieval Europe*. Ithaca, 1978.

Loeb, Isidore. "La Controvèrsc de 1240 sur le Talmud." *Revue des études juives* 1 (1880): 247–261, 2 (1881): 248–269, 3 (1881): 39–57.

Lotter, Friedrich. "Innocens Virgo et Martyr: Thomas von Monmouth und die Verbreitung der Ritualmordlegende im Hochmittelalter." In *Die Legende vom Ritualmord: Zur Geschichte der Blutbeschuldigungen gegen Juden*, ed. Rainer Erb, 25–72. Berlin, 1993.

Luchaire, Achille. *Innocent III*. 6 vols. in 3. Paris, 1903–1908.

McGinn, Bernard. *Antichrist*. New York, 1994.

McGuire, Brian Patrick. *The Difficult Saint: Bernard of Clairvaux and His Tradition*. Kalamazoo, 1991.

Mellinkoff, Ruth. *The Mark of Cain*. Berkeley, 1981.

Merchavia, Chen. *Ha-Talmud be-Re'i ha-Nazrut* [The Talmud in the View of Christianity]. Jerusalem, 1970.

Minty, Mary. "*Kiddush ha-Shem* in German Christian Eyes in the Middle Ages." *Zion* 59 (1994): 209–266.

Moore, R. I. "Anti-Semitism and the Birth of Europe." In *Christianity and Judaism: Papers Read at the 1991 Summer Meeting and the 1992 Winter Meeting of the Ecclesiastical History Society*, ed. Diana Wood, 33–57. Oxford, 1992.

———. *The Formation of a Persecuting Society*. Oxford, 1987.

———. "Heresy and Disease." In *The Concept of Heresy in the Middle Ages*, ed. W. Lourdaux and D. Verhelst, 1–11. Leuven, 1976.

Morris, Colin. *The Papal Monarchy: The Western Church from 1050 to 1250*. Oxford History of the Christian Church. Oxford, 1989.

Nicholls, William. *Christian Antisemitism: A History of Hate*. Northvale, N.J., 1993.

Obermann, Heiko A. *The Roots of Anti-Semitism in the Age of Renaissance and Reformation*. Trans. James I. Porter. Philadelphia, 1984.

Pagels, Elaine. *The Origins of Satan*. New York, 1995.

Poliakov, Léon. *Histoire de l'antisémitisme*. 4 vols. Paris, 1955–1977.

———. *The History of Anti-Semitism*. Trans. Richard Howard et al. 4 vols. New York, 1965–1985.

Rembaum, Joel. "The Talmud and the Popes: Reflections on the Talmud Trials of the 1240s." *Viator* 13 (1982): 203–223.

Reuther, Rosemary. *Faith and Fratricide*. New York, 1974.

Richardson, H. G. *The English Jewry under Angevin Kings*. London, 1960.

Riley-Smith, Jonathan. *The First Crusade and the Idea of Crusading*. London, 1986.

———. "The First Crusade and the Persecution of the Jews." In *Persecution and Toleration: Papers Read at the Twenty-second Summer Meeting and the Twenty-third Winter Meeting of the Ecclesiastical History Society*, ed. W. J. Sheils, 51–72. Oxford, 1984.

Rosenthal, Judah. "Ashkenaz, Sefarad, and Zarfat." *Historia Judaica* 5 (1943): 58–62.

———. "The Talmud on Trial." *Jewish Quarterly Review* 47 (1956–1957): 58–76 and 145–169.

Roth, Cecil, ed. *The Dark Ages: Jews in Christian Europe 711–1096*. The World History of the Jewish People. Tel Aviv, 1966.

———. *A History of the Jews in England*. 3d ed. Oxford, 1964.

Rubin, Miri. *Corpus Christi: The Eucharist in Late Medieval Culture*. Cambridge, 1991.

———. "Desecration of the Host: The Birth of an Accusation." *Christianity and Judaism: Papers Read at the 1991 Summer Meeting and the 1992 Winter Meeting of the Ecclesiastical History Society*, ed. Diana Wood, 169–185. Oxford, 1992.

Rurup, Reinhard. *Emancipation und Antisemitismus: Studien zur "Judenfrage" der bürgerlichen Gesellschaft*. Göttingen, 1975.

Russell, Jeffrey Burton. *Witchcraft in the Middle Ages*. Ithaca, 1972.

Sayers, Jane. *Innocent III: Leader of Europe 1198–1216*. London, 1994.

Scherer, J. E. *Die Rechtsverhältnisse der Juden in den deutschen-österreichischen Ländern*. Leipzig, 1901.

Schwarzfuchs, Simon. "The Place of the Crusades in Jewish History" (in Hebrew). In *Tarbut ve-Hevrah be-Toldot Yisra'el bi-Me ha-Benayim* [Culture and Society in Medieval Jewish History], ed. Menahem Ben-Sasson et al., 251–267. Jerusalem, 1989.

Shapiro, James. *Shakespeare and the Jews*. New York, 1996.

Shatzmiller, Joseph. *Shylock Reconsidered: Jews, Moneylending, and Medieval Society*. Berkeley, 1990.

Simonsohn, Shlomo. *The Apostolic See and the Jews: History*. Toronto, 1991.

Smalley, Beryl. *The Study of the Bible in the Middle Ages*. 3d ed. Oxford, 1983.

Southern, R. W. *The Making of the Middle Ages*. London, 1953.

———. *Western Society and the Church in the Middle Ages*. The Pelican History of the Church. Harmondsworth, 1970.

Spufford, Peter. *Money and Its Use in Medieval Europe*. Cambridge, 1988.

Stacey, Robert C. "Aaron of Lincoln." In *The Dictionary of National Biography: Missing Persons*, ed. C. S. Nicholls, 1. Oxford, 1993.

———. "The Conversion of Jews to Christianity in Thirteenth-Century England." *Speculum* 67 (1992): 263–283.

———. "History, Religion, and Medieval Antisemitism: A Reply to Gavin Langmuir." *Religious Studies Review* 20 (1994): 95–101.

———. "Jewish Lending and the Medieval English Economy." In *A Commer-*

cialising Economy, England 1086 to c. 1300, ed. Richard H. Britnell and Bruce M. S. Campbell, 78–101. Manchester, 1995.

———. *Politics, Policy, and Finance under Henry III, 1216–1245*. Oxford, 1987.

———. "Royal Taxation and the Social Structure of Medieval Anglo-Jewry: The Tallages of 1239–42." *Hebrew Union College Annual* 56 (1985): 175–249.

———. "Thirteenth-Century Anglo-Jewry and the Problem of the Expulsion" (in Hebrew). In *Gerush ve-Shivah: Yehudey Angeliyah be-Ḥilufe ha-zemanim* [Expulsion and Return: The Jews of England in Changing Epochs], ed. David S. Katz and Yosef Kaplan, 9–25. Jerusalem, 1993.

———. "1240–60: A Watershed in Anglo-Jewish Relations?" *Historical Research* 61 (1988): 135–150.

Stow, Kenneth R. "Hatred of the Jews or Love of the Church: Papal Policy toward the Jews in the Middle Ages." In *Antisemitism through the Ages*, ed. Shmuel Almog, trans. Nathan H. Reisner, 71–89. Oxford, 1988.

———. *The "1007 Anonymous" and Papal Sovereignty: Jewish Perceptions of the Papacy and Papal Policy in the High Middle Ages*. Cincinnati, 1984.

Tillman, Helene. *Pope Innocent III*. Trans. Walter Sax. Amsterdam, 1980.

Torrell, Jean-Pierre. "Les Juifs dans l'oeuvre de Pierre le Vénérable." *Cahiers de civilisation médiévale* 30 (1987): 331–346.

———, and Bouthillier, Denise. *Pierre le Vénérable et sa vision du monde*. Leuven, 1986.

Urbach, Ephraim E. *Baʿaley ha-Tosafot* [The Tosafists]. 5th ed. 2 vols. Jerusalem, 1986.

Vauchez, André. *The Laity in the Middle Ages: Religious Beliefs and Devotional Practices*. Ed. Daniel E. Bornstein. Trans. Margery J. Schneider. Notre Dame, 1993.

Vincent, Nicholas C. "Jews, Poitevins, and the Bishop of Winchester, 1231–1234." In *Christianity and Judaism: Papers Read at the 1991 Summer Meeting and the 1992 Winter Meeting of the Ecclesiastical History Society*, ed. Diana Wood, 119–132. Oxford, 1992.

Watt, J. A. "The English Episcopate, the State and the Jews: The Evidence of the Thirteenth-Century Conciliar Decrees." In *Thirteenth Century England II: Proceedings of the Newcastle upon Tyne Conference 1987*, ed. P. R. Coss and S. D. Lloyd, 137–147. Woodbridge, 1988.

Waugh, Scott L., and Diehl, Peter D., eds. *Christendom and Its Discontents*. Cambridge, 1996.

Weinryb, Bernard. *The Jews of Poland*. Philadelphia, 1973.

Williams, Watkin. *St. Bernard of Clairvaux*. Westminster, Md., 1952.

Wistrich, Robert S. *Antisemitism: The Longest Hatred*. London, 1991.

Wolfson, Elliot R. "Circumcision and the Divine Name: A Study in the Transmission of Esoteric Doctrine." *Jewish Quarterly Review* 78 (1987–1988): 77–112.

———. "The Image of Jacob Engraved on the Throne: Further Reflexion on the Esoteric Doctrine of the German Pietists." In E. R. Wolfson, *Along the*

Path: Studies in Kabbalistic Myth, Symbolism, and Hermeneutics, 1–62. Albany, 1995.

———. "The Mystical Significance of Torah Study in Haside Ashkenaz." *Jewish Quarterly Review* 84 (1993–1994): 43–78.

———. *Through a Speculum That Shines: Vision and Imagination in Medieval Jewish Mysticism.* Princeton, 1995.

Yuval, Israel. "Vengeance and Damnation, Blood and Defamation: From Jewish Martyrdom to Blood Libel Accusations" (Hebrew). *Zion,* 58:33–90.

Zimmermann, Moshe. *Wilhelm Marr: The Patriarch of Antisemitism.* New York, 1986.

Index

Designer:	U.C. Press Staff
Compositor:	G & S Typesetters
Text:	10/13 Galliard
Display:	Galliard
Printer & Binder:	Thomson-Shore